FLYING FISH
IN THE GREAT
WHITE NORTH

FLYING FISH IN THE GREAT WHITE NORTH

The Autonomous Migration of Black Barbadians

Christopher Stuart Taylor

FERNWOOD PUBLISHING
HALIFAX & WINNIPEG

Editing: Mark Ambrose Harris
Cover design: John van der Woude
Printed and bound in Canada

Published by Fernwood Publishing
32 Oceanvista Lane, Black Point, Nova Scotia, B0J 1B0
and 748 Broadway Avenue, Winnipeg, Manitoba, R3G 0X3

www.fernwoodpublishing.ca

Christopher Stuart Taylor would like to thank the Federation for
the Humanities and Social Sciences and their Awards to Scholarly
Publications Program which aided in the publishing of this book.

Fernwood Publishing Company Limited gratefully acknowledges the financial support of
the Government of Canada through the Canada Book Fund, the Manitoba Department
of Culture, Heritage and Tourism under the Manitoba Publishers Marketing Assistance
Program and the Province of Manitoba, through the Book Publishing Tax Credit, for
our publishing program. We are pleased to work in partnership with the Province of
Nova Scotia to develop and promote our creative industries for the benefit of all Nova
Scotians. We acknowledge the support of the Canada Council for the Arts, which last
year invested $153 million to bring the arts to Canadians throughout the country.

Library and Archives Canada Cataloguing in Publication

Taylor, Christopher Stuart, author
Flying fish in the great white north: the autonomous migration of Black
Barbadians / Christopher Stuart Taylor.

Includes bibliographical references and index.
Issued in print and electronic formats.
ISBN 978-1-55266-894-8 (paperback).—ISBN 978-1-55266-914-3 (kindle).—
ISBN 978-1-55266-913-6 (epub)

1. Barbadians—Canada—History. 2. Immigrants—Canada—History.
3. Racism—Canada—History. 4. Discrimination—Canada—History.
5. Canada—Ethnic relations—History. 6. Canada—Emigration and
immigration—Government policy—History. I. Title.

FC106.C27T39 2016   971'.00496972981
C2016-904991-4   C2016-904992-2

CONTENTS

INTRODUCTION

These first generation migrants had used the name and concept of Barbados as home not only as a mantra, but as a beacon in the dark. (Burrowes 2009: 138)

Their understanding of being Barbadian gave them solace and meaning within the space/s of their exile. (Burrowes 2009: 138)

In plenty and in time of need
When this fair land was young
Our brave forefathers sowed the seed
From which our pride is sprung
A pride that makes no wanton boast
Of what it has withstood
That binds our hearts from coast to coast
The pride of nationhood
We loyal sons and daughters all
Do hereby make it known
These fields and hills beyond recall
Are now our very own
We write our names on history's page
With expectations great
Strict guardians of our heritage
Firm craftsmen of our fate.
(Burgie "The National Anthem of Barbados")

Under the yoke of slavery, colonial domination, poverty and racism, the pride and industry of a nation was born. The epitome of human capitalist greed and disregard for human life — the Transatlantic Slave Trade and the institution of slavery — laid the foundation for the creation of the Black Barbadian beginning in the seventeenth century. Europeans perfected a system of ideological genocide; they destroyed the Self, the being and the existence of the African and created his new being as property. It was a legalized system needed, not for the survival and welfare of European societies, but to provide a luxury for those ignorant to its origins and amass wealth for the few, shielded a continent away from the brutality they created. The Slave Trade was designed to exploit and to profit. It was not a symbiotic relationship; Africans, now slaves in the Americas, did not enter into a binding employment contract with paid wages and benefits. Phenotypic terrorists broke, castrated and raped their bodies, and destroyed their existence. The institution of slavery was a calculated act of terrorism against humanity and human dignity. Seventeenth-, eighteenth-, and early nineteenth-century Barbados and the West Indies were not the tourist paradises that they are now, but a theatre of war, where the enemy disguised itself under a cloak of lies, violence and greed. Men engaged in the trafficking of human flesh as the insidious ideology of race was created to justify the unjustifiable. To be of a darker skin tone meant enslavement; however, the masters perverted the binary colour stratification once the derivatives of sexual terror compelled them to enslave their own. Fathers raped mothers and whipped daughters. Husbands were emasculated as wives were raped and brutalized. Mothers cried as their sons died slow painful deaths. Welcome to Barbados. This is where the story begins.

The loyal sons and daughters of the Rock on the easternmost reaches of the Caribbean Sea fought hard and struggled to sow the seeds that created what Barbados is today. Industrious perseverance is a Barbadian characteristic. Barbadian ancestors survived the Middle Passage; they overcame the brutality of chattel slavery; they recreated and retained their identity in the face of a well-calculated and deliberate ideological genocide; and they carved out a prosperous existence in the face of colonial domination. Despite generations of insurmountable odds, Black Barbadians did not suffer defeat, nor did they accept the negative codification of their ideological Blackness. Black Barbadians pursued excellence and upward mobility as means to overcome the debilitating nature of poverty and the incendiary goals of racial discrimination as slaves, Free Blacks, British colonial subjects and finally as proud and independent Barbadian citizens. Hundreds of years of subjugation forged the yeomen characteristics that defined the early twentieth-century Barbadian. Whether coerced or voluntary, hard work lies at the foundation of Barbadian attitudes towards life. Tens of thousands of Barbadian emigrants have embodied this spirit of dedication to self-improvement and the collective uplifting of the Barbadian nation-state and a prosperous Diaspora abroad. I refer to them as Emigrant Ambassadors.

I have coined both the terms "Emigrant Ambassador" and "Autonomous Bajan," which are at the heart of *Flying Fish in the Great White North*. The Autonomous Bajan ("Bajan" is the colloquial term for "Barbadian") embodies the independent nature and agency of all Barbadian emigrants as they navigated the racialized and oppressive structures of the international migration system. The Emigrant Ambassador builds on the concept of the Autonomous Bajan but refers specifically to the Black Barbadian and Black West Indian women that spearheaded and challenged Canada's discriminatory immigration policy during the 1950s and 1960s. Aided by the concepts of the Autonomous Bajan and the Emigrant Ambassador, this book attempts to capture, as accurately as possible, the spirit of the nurses, the domestics, the teachers, the bus conductors and all of the young Barbadian emigrants. They left the sunny tropical paradise of Barbados for the cold abyss of the unknown, in search of a better life for themselves, their unborn children and the Island. The terms need to be adopted to clearly identify and emphasize the role that the individual, female emigrants in particular, played in the history of international migration.

Flying Fish in the Great White North assesses the political, economic and social characteristics and implications of Barbadian emigration, using historical documents and archival evidence. To some, this book may seem to sit on the disciplinary "fence" — or tensions — between history and sociology. Some historians may argue that this book is not "historical enough," and some sociologists may argue it is not "sociological enough." This tension is deliberate. The disciplinary purpose of this study is to show the influence of social theories on history. For example, how did the theoretical intersectionality of race, class and gender co-exist with the historical migration of Barbadians whose Black identity was sociologically and historically constructed? How and why did sociological interpretations of race and gender impede — and at times facilitate — the migration of Black Barbadian women and men during the mid-twentieth century? This study is a reflection of the historical migration of Black Barbadians up to 1967; however, once I use the racialized qualifier of "Black," it is impossible not to engage with a debate on the sociological and theoretical influences of race and international migration history. Canada rejected and accepted potential immigrants based on "ideas" of Whiteness, Canadianness and nation-building. Thus, in order for me to have a complete examination of Black Barbadian individuals within this paradigm, I must utilize social theories while I create a historical narrative. History is not, and should not, be relegated to simply the interpretations of government documents and archival sources: the "common" individual's story must be written.

While British, Barbadian and Canadian governments facilitated the means and flow for movement, the individual's autonomy and personal choice precipitated and dictated transnational migration. Everyday Barbadians — or the Autonomous Bajan — defined the roles and boundaries of migratory social mobility. Respective governments created legislation which both restricted and expedited the emigration and immigration of Barbadians due to social demographics and race; however, the Autonomous Bajan did sit amongst the autocratic and bureaucratic policy-making elite. The struggle to survive by any means necessary conditioned the Barbadian to achieve more. Hardship, colonialism and racism influenced the Barbadian's character. It simultaneously indoctrinated a sense of pride and perseverance that defined the Autonomous Bajan's transnational *habitus*. Black Barbadians worked within an inherently discriminatory and racist colonial system, one characterized by epistemic violence (Spivak 1988: 24–25). The hegemonic power of epistemic violence marginalized the Black Barbadian's self-worth and identity. It created a system in which his subaltern existence reflected the institutionalized racism of colonial Western society. They lived in a system designed for their assigned marginality and degradation; an ideologically reified class of inferiority encapsulated by the mechanisms of colonialism and racism. Individual Barbadians suffered under the yoke of oppression. However, these extraordinary individuals triumphed and succeeded. Every day was a struggle for survival as they fought to procure the necessary educational, cultural and social capital to emigrate and integrate and subsequently contribute as loyal Commonwealth brethren and naturalized Canadians in a hostile new environment.

The purpose of this book is to engage in the human side of the story. Each statistic is a person: a mother, a father, a son or a daughter. Embedded in the pages of this study is the story of one man's trials and tribulations as a Barbadian emigrant in the United Kingdom and Canada. He was a Barbadian-Canadian in every sense of the contentious hyphenated moniker. This book is dedicated to the life of my father, Reginald Eric Taylor.

My father was not an extraordinary man, but a man who accomplished extraordinary feats. I am telling his story precisely because he is my father and I am his son. He and my mother, whose (her)story is equally important to the narrative of this book, gave me the tools to be in a position to write this book. Without them, this story does not exist. This is a true story — an ongoing family history — defined by perseverance and facilitated by education. Our history in the Americas in the seventeenth century began as property in a world where horses retained more value. For two centuries we worked on plantations, sentenced to death without having committed a crime; convicted for the colour of our skin. We were raped, mutilated, castrated and killed while the world "developed" on the backs of our labour — a world that has yet to pay for their brutal past. In the nineteenth century, we fought to remove the shackles of physical and mental slavery, to be recognized as the human beings we always were. In the twentieth century, my father began his personal fight and that for his children. His life story begins with his struggles as a child stricken by the ubiquitous poverty of pre-Second World War Barbados. His educational possibilities and limitations are examples of what many young Barbadians faced as they were forced to leave school as young adolescents. The narrative of his life within the pages of this book continues with his employment opportunities as a trade apprentice, his personal desire to emigrate and the unique recruitment process in Barbados. His life moved with the tide of the Atlantic and the course of history as he faced the challenges of living and working in postwar England. Finally, Taylor brought peace to the ghosts of his deracinated ancestors as he rooted himself in Canada in pursuit of educational and professional upward mobility as part of the Barbadian and African Diasporas. This book is defined by the narrative of his international migration.

Canadians love to hear an immigrant success story, typically how one down-trodden individual climbed his or her way out of poverty and persecution "back home," overcame insurmountable odds and came to this land of opportunity. Canadians emphasize the socio-economic immigrant "pull" factors that accentuate benevolence. However, the emigrant "push" factors are oftentimes neglected. The promoted positive nature of the "pull" was greater than the supposed all-encompassing negativity of the "push." Why else would someone leave the Caribbean island of the Flying Fish for the cold unknown of the Great White North? Why would Taylor, a young man without secondary education, leave Barbados on the eve of its independence in 1966? The strong winds of independence blew across the Island following the Second World War, so why did thousands of the best and brightest Barbadians emigrate knowing they had a chance to contribute to the newly independent nation-state that needed them? Taylor is an example of Barbadian agency; he chose to emigrate and he chose to pursue educational opportunities abroad that he could not obtain on the Island.

The keyword is "choice." Barbadians did not live within a vacuum of domestic and international policy-makers, devoid of any and all autonomy; they were equal participants and actors of their own fate, and not simply acted upon. Despite institutional barriers (racist immigration policies), Barbadians chose to migrate, and their government leaders were vocal in promoting change to Canadian immigration policy. This book focuses on the emigration push factors of Black Barbadians from Emancipation in 1834 up to the beginning of the Canadian Points System in 1967. Similar to the protagonist of the story, Barbadians chose to emigrate due to personal, geographical and career motivations. Moreover, the Barbadian Government facilitated and supported the deconstruction of slavery's legislated ignorance and how it perpetuated the nihilistic marginalization of Black people and society. Due to overpopulation, and equipped with their educational capital and the desire for upward social mobility abroad, the mid-twentieth-century Autonomous Bajan left their homes for unknown futures. As agents of their government's deliberate policy of emigration, Black Barbadians challenged the denigrating forces of a history of racism, sexism and discrimination. They were conscious of the future they were making and the past they were correcting.

This book represents the agency of the Emigrant Ambassador and the Autonomous Bajan and refutes the claim that Barbadians remained docile migratory bodies of labour at the mercy of governmental and cultural forces. I also challenge Alan B. Simmons and Jean-Pierre Guengant's assessment of a Caribbean "exodus" and "Caribbean culture-of-migration" in their work, "Caribbean Exodus and the World System." The authors argue that "such a culture emerged from the uprooted history of the Caribbean population, first as slaves or indentured labourers from abroad" (Simmons and Guengant 1992: 103). This book challenges Simmons and Guengant's argument and contends that Black Barbadians chose to migrate for a variety of individual, economic and social reasons. I am deconstructing Simmons and Guengant's definition of "culture-of-migration" in the Barbadian historical context and disaggregating what they believed constituted as historically conditioned involuntary migration as opposed to deliberate and conscious decisions made by the individual and facilitated by the Barbadian Government. One of the main issues in their definition is the ambiguity around the term "culture" and the subsequent essentialized and generalized reduction of all Caribbean peoples as one homogenized group with a shared history. The idea of the Caribbean as a monolith negates Barbados' unique position in the British West Indies as the only island to implement government-sponsored emigration schemes in the late nineteenth century. Simmons and Guengant's concept cannot be applied equally to all Caribbean and West Indian islands. The "Caribbean culture-of-migration" argument stereotypes Black Barbadian emigration as an innate cultural phenomenon, and negates the individual and her personal autonomy, as well as economic, social and political conditions. Overpopulation and unemployment in the Island; government-sponsored emigration and employment schemes; the natural movement of a highly skilled and educated populace with little opportunity for upward social and economic movement due to the Island's literal and figurative diminutive size and finite growth; and an individual's want and desire for social mobility abroad and for those back home, facilitated mass Barbadian emigration. A loosely based and ideological "culture-of-migration" was not the push for emigration.

Neglecting the Barbadians' migratory autonomy perpetuates the historical, political and scholarly marginalization of Blacks and Black historiography, specifically in Canada. The "culture-of-migration" conclusion negates the need for further explanatory discourse with regards to why Blacks from the West Indies chose to migrate. Cultural factors may have contributed to the desire to emigrate;

however, the generalization restricts avenues for further research and scholarship of late nineteenth- to mid-twentieth-century Black West Indian migration. The historiography will continue to represent Blacks in Canada as powerless clients of an unjust system, as topics within the framework of Black Canadian history are routinely marginalized on the periphery of accepted and mainstream scholarship. James W. St. G. Walker (1997: 171) argued, "*History as it is understood* (author's emphasis) enters a political discourse, it becomes a participant in a power dialectic and it influences power relationships ... the writing of history is a political act." As a political act, the writing of Canadian history, specifically the history of immigration of Black Barbadians and those of the Black Diaspora, must be viewed critically and within a theoretically racialized paradigm. Theories of race and racial discrimination contextualize the historiographical and social objectification of Black Barbadians in the immigration process. This framework must be understood as a defining characteristic of Canadian immigration policy and domestic hostility towards Black Barbadians in Canada. According to John Price, Canada is reluctant to admit the "role of racism" in its national history and race has been "formative, even while being marginalized," in the historiography (Webster et al. 2012: 2, 19).

Racism is a fundamental part of Canadian history and the Canadian narrative must reflect its prominence and historical influence. There must be a great deal more written on Black immigrants and ethnic groups and race to add to Canadian historical and contemporary scholarship. Black Canadian historiography has made considerable strides since Robin Winks' seminal and much criticized book, *The Blacks in Canada: A History*, in 1971. However, more needs to be done, specifically in the twenty-first century, and this book will serve as a critical step in the production of Black Canadian history. Black ethnic and immigrant history in Canada, and Black Canadian history as a whole, is a relatively new study; for all of the strides it has made in the past forty years, the field is still marginalized. The historiography lacks a large breadth of studies concerned specifically with Black West Indian emigration to Canada during the early to mid-twentieth century. Most scholarship with respect to Barbadian emigration in the mid-twentieth century to Canada has focused on the Domestic Scheme or the Nurses Program and was published during the 1990s. Such scholarly discussions include Agnes Calliste's "Canada's Immigration Policy and Domestics from the Caribbean: The Second Domestic Scheme" in *Race, Class, Gender: Bonds and Barriers. Socialist Studies: A Canadian Annual* and "Women of 'Exceptional Merit': Immigration of Caribbean Nurses to Canada" in *Canadian Journal of Women and the Law* 6 (1993); Linda Carty's "African Canadian Women and the State: 'Labor Only, Please'" in "*We're Rooted Here and They Can't Pull Us Up*": *Essays in African Canadian Women's History*; and Audrey Macklin's "Foreign Domestic Workers: Surrogate Housewife or Mail Order Servant?" in the *McGill Law Journal*. Despite the limited research of Black Barbadian immigrant history in Canada, notable scholars in the field, including Winks and Walker, have laid the foundation for Black Canadian history, Black immigration history and racial discrimination in Canada. The historiography is recognized by its scholarship regarding late eighteenth-, nineteenth- and early twentieth-century Black emigration from the United States, slavery and the Underground Railroad, human rights and racial discrimination in Canada.

With the increase of Black ethnic diversity, specifically the large-scale migrations of the heterogeneous Caribbean Blacks during the 1960s onwards, several scholars noted the relationship between immigrant status, race and Blackness in Canadian society. Walker's *The West Indians in Canada* argued that since the implementation of the Points System in 1967, "West Indians as a group come closest to the desired immigrant to Canada," and that "West Indians are doing a great deal to destroy the old stereotypes and to break the barriers which have restricted Black Canadians" (Walker 1984: 22–24). Furthermore, in *A History of Blacks in Canada*, Walker explicitly addressed and admonished the erasure of Blacks in Canadian historiography and their subsequent marginalization in Canada society. Walker (1980: 3, 6) stated that "to overlook black history is, therefore, to distort our image of ourselves as Canadians and the historical forces that have made us what we are," and "Canadian history as presently understood is not true, and that by including black history (along with others) we can get closer to the truth and closer to the 'historical forces' which are operating in Canadian society." What is most profound in the previous statements is how Walker relates the marginalization of Black history to how Black people are treated in Canadian society. Frances Henry's *The Caribbean Diaspora in Toronto: Learning to Live with Racism* reiterates Walker's sentiment of Canadian anti-Black racism with respect to Black Caribbean peoples in the Greater Toronto Area (Henry 1994). Henry argued that racism was, and is, a real barrier to successful integration and inclusion, and that it "shapes and forms much of [Black West Indian] life in Canada" (Henry 1994: x). Racism, as this work argues, dictated British, American and Canadian immigration policy in the early to mid-twentieth century. The racist White British creation and codification of Blackness in Barbadian society must be highlighted to understand the foundation for ideological exclusion of Black people through Canada's immigration policy. It was the perpetuation of the belief of Black inferiority throughout the Western world and rooted in Barbados during slavery by British ideologues that formed the fundamental basis for exclusionary immigration policy; the "White Canada" ideology was supported by the belief of White superiority and Black inferiority.

Canada, as a member of the British Empire, articulated the same racist characteristics of British slave societies in Barbados and the West Indies. However, unlike Whites in the Caribbean region, Canadians did not have to act on their fear of the Black West Indian "Other" until faced with the prospect of a substantial Black

Barbadian and West Indian immigrant population in the early to mid-twentieth century. What must be emphasized, particularly as an underlying theme of this book, is the arbitrary nature of Canadian immigrant selection prior to the Points System in 1967; no laws racially "codified white supremacy," and the "constant presence and power of illiberal views of racial difference meant that the law in Canada did support racial discrimination in Canada — but passively so — upholding the individual's right to discriminatory treatment against minorities" (Henry 1994: 83). Canadian attitudes towards Blacks and Blackness dictated their immigration policy for West Indian applicants. One particular book that engages with this topic is Barrington Walker's *The African Canadian Legal Odyssey: Historical Essays.* He argued that immigration policy prior to its de-racialization in 1962 "was a major vector of state power through which Jim Crowism (anti-Black racism and social segregation) was institutionalized in Canada," and he provided examples of the 1906 and 1910 *Immigration Acts* that excluded Black migrant settlement through invasive and unnecessary medical examinations (Walker 2012). These exclusionary measures limited the size of the Black population in Canada, and between the late nineteenth to the mid-twentieth century, most Black Canadians were native born (Walker 2012). Black West Indians thus found it nearly impossible to gain admittance through sponsorship initiatives associated with postwar immigration policy reforms since the Black immigrant population was deliberately restricted to maintain the White "character" of Canada since the late nineteenth century.

Throughout the book, the reader will notice that at times I use "Black West Indian" and "Black Barbadian" interchangeably. I must clarify my use of data on West Indian emigrants to supplement the limited available data on Barbadian migrants to Canada prior to 1967. Barbados gained its independence from Britain on November 30, 1966, and before that date the Island was a British colony in the West Indies. This is important to note since most of the evidence used for the period of this study dates back to when Barbados was a British colony and most of the Canadian immigration statistics recognized the region as one homogenous "West Indian" group. Between 1946 and 1960 a total of 4,311 "Negroes" emigrated from the British West Indies out of total of 11,588 West Indian emigrants to Canada. The term "Negro" and the "racial" identifications were further problematized as "many of those claiming 'British' or 'other' ethnic origin were in fact of mixed race. Some of them were of white origin in the paternal line, while others who appeared to be otherwise suitable immigrants were given the benefit of the doubt when their applications were reviewed."[1] It was difficult to define who or what was "Black" or "Negro." Furthermore, Statistics Canada and the Canada Year Books between 1910 and 1967 did not indicate Barbados under "Birthplaces of immigrant arrivals," "Origins of immigrant arrivals," "Citizenship of immigrant arrivals" or "Nationalities." Black Barbadians were not explicitly identified and were ostensibly grouped under the "West Indian (Not British)" nationality, "West Indies" as their birthplace, "Britain and colonies" as their citizenship, and the overarching and sub-jective "Negro" racial category as their origin.[2] Besides confirmed statistics of 560 (327 sponsored and 233 unsponsored) Barbadian emigrants settling in Canada in 1965, there were very little Canadian immigration statistics of Barbadians prior to 1967.[3] Thus it was necessary to use West Indian statistics from Canadian sources as a supplement to Barbadian emigration data when analyzing Barbadian emigration to Canada during this period.

I capitalize the "B" as a proper noun when I refer to Black Barbadians, West Indians or Black people. There is absolutely no difference when describing a Jewish man, an Italian boy, an African-American girl or a Black woman as human beings. If "black" was simply an innocuous colour descriptor and adjective similar to blue eyes or brunette hair, a lowercase "b" would be acceptable. However, that is not the case, and "Black" must be widely accepted as the norm when referring to the racialized group in the 2010s. I do not put "race" in quotation marks, but it is under-stood that race is a social construction. In keeping with historical terminology and archival documents, at times I use the term "Coloured" when referring to mixed race (Black and White) people. However, some historical texts refer to "coloured" as individuals who are "non-White" and I adjust my analysis accordingly. I also use the same principles of capitalization of "Black" when referring to Coloured or Coloured people as proper nouns. "People of Colour" is also an outdated term, but at times I will use it to maintain historical accuracy. I use the contemporary term "racialized" when referring to what was known as "People of Colour," "non-White'" or "Visible Minority." Throughout my research in the Barbados National Archives, many of the official documents I came across capitalized the "G" when they referred to the Barbados Government. I have adopted the same practice here when referring to the Barbados Government and the Canadian Government. I have also capitalized the "I" in island when I write "the Island" as a synonym for Barbados as a proper noun and country.

Flying Fish in the Great White North is a living historical narrative of a generation of young Blacks that shaped the course of Canadian, Barbadian and world history. They were, and are, historical actors as integral to the founding of this country as the greatest politicians and explorers that define our (misrepresented) Canadian cultural narrative. They are Black. And their Lives Matter.

There is a reason that few books on this subject exist: there has been a deliberate marginalization of Blacks in Canada. This phenomenon is rooted in the ideologi-cal, physical and historical denigration of their identity. Chapter One examines the creation of the Black Barbadian and the ideology of colour, race and Blackness within the Western world, generally, and Barbadian slave society, specifically. The chapter argues that the creation of Black Barbadian identity during slavery, and indoctrinated during the colonial period, contributed to the creation of a Canadian society defined by White privilege and White supremacy. I argue that these reified beliefs of White superiority — the Canadian perceptions of what constituted a "rightful" or "authentic" British subject — were challenged by highly educated and socially mobile Black Barbadians. Chapter Two begins with an introduction to the political history of the Barbadian Government during the 1930s to 1960s. This is the period where most reforms and initiatives were implemented that facilitated the emigration of Black Barbadians. This chapter examines the history of formal education in Barbados and provides the historical framework to support the book's argument that a highly educated and overpopulated British colony sought opportunities for upward mobility outside of the Island. This chapter provides the basis of the narrative that challenges the historical and present-day White supremacist view that Blacks were, and are, uneducated and indolent drains on Canadian society. By providing a historical narrative, this chapter effectively dispels a number of insidious myths regarding Black educational capacity, cultural capital and *habitus*.

Chapter Three provides a thorough examination of the waves of Barbadian emigration following the emancipation from slavery in the mid- to late nineteenth century and government initiatives of sponsored emigration and settlement colonies to abate the ominous threat of overpopulation and unemployment. This chapter argues that despite the structures of colonial and racial oppression, Black Barbadian identity and history is defined by their agency and resilience. Historical narratives concerning racialized emigration to Canada, specifically Black migration, tend to place Blacks as subjects of White benevolence. I argue that this thought is misguided and driven by a White saviour complex designed to continue to marginalize the autonomy of the Black historical experience. This case study on Black Barbadian emigration seeks to put Blacks as autonomous actors at the forefront of their history. Chapter Four first discusses the history of West Indian–Canadian relations, followed by Barbadian-Canadian relations. The chapter underscores the political and economic relationships between Canada and the West Indies, including the establishment of Canadian financial institutions and trade agreements in the region in the late nineteenth and early twentieth century. As Emigrant Ambassadors of their Island, race and gender, I argue that Black Barbadian and West Indian women overcame misogyny and racism, challenged Canadian perceptions of "Blackness," and facilitated the emigration of an entire generation of Black men, women and children. This and the following chapter argue that the Barbadian and West Indian female migrant overcame the gendered, sexist and class-based structures of a migration system designed to facilitate the movement of male labour. Black women, not men, were at the forefront of the liberalization of Canadian immigration policy. Chapter Five, and this book, argues that Black Barbadian and West Indian women must be recognized for the sacrifices they made and continue to make for their respective home and host countries. They were codified as pawns in a world system designed to destroy their race and their gender. Nevertheless, education and the pursuit of education were constant themes in their struggle. This chapter provides individual stories that support the book's argument that education facilitated migration. It also pays homage to the many Black female and male educators who, despite the oppressive racism and discrimination they faced in Canada, have contributed to the betterment of generations of young Canadians and Canadian society. They will no longer be silenced; their stories must be told, and their voices will be heard. I argue that they were Emigrant Ambassadors that helped alter the course of Canadian history and made the country what it is today.

The collective misrepresentation of the Underground Railroad and African-American history during Black History Month in Canada has become one of the few outlets for the dissemination of Black Canadian history to public, elementary, secondary and even tertiary levels of education. Canadian historiography has reverted to the idea of the Black Achiever — the one who has "made it" in Canadian society (Walker 1997: 155–177). The ideologies of multiculturalism and de-racialized immigration policies have obfuscated the reified presence of ethnic and immigrant silos in Canadian society. Whether it is the Black immigrant success story or overcoming racism and discrimination, Blacks are marginalized objects on the periphery of Canadian society and historiography.

The way in which Black Canadian history is made and disseminated must be addressed and improved. It must reflect Canadian society and its diversity. The framework must be reinvented to include the presence of distinct Black immigrant ethnic groups and remove the idealist notion of common primordial bonds between all peoples of the same, or similar, phenotypes. This study of Black Barbadian immigrants in Canada must facilitate future comparative research of other Black West Indians, South Americans, Europeans, Africans and those belonging to the Black Diaspora worldwide. The monograph will serve as a potential framework for comparative and interdisciplinary research. Black ethnic history must capitalize on the same paradigm as Walker's five orientations to the study of Black history in Canada in "Allegories and Orientations in African-Canadian Historiography: The Spirit of Africville." His theoretical framework of the Black community, while incorporating elements of the objectification and racialization of Blacks as clients, victims and survivors; the altruistic but de-negrifying nature of the Black Achiever; and the passionate and emotional catharsis of traumatic rage is paramount to the survival and sustainability of Black Canadian historiography (Walker 1997: 155–177). The field must evolve with the evolution of Canada's multicultural society and its immigration policy. The historiography must reflect the changing demographics of Black Canada, while remaining true to historical documents and research methods. White Canadians, as much as immigrant and ethnic Blacks, must be able to relate to African-Canadian and Black Canadian history.

With the emergence of a large community of Black ethnic groups, including Black Barbadians and the progeny of those immigrants who came in the 1960s, the unified paradigm of the Black community will, and must, change. Immigrant and second-generation Black Canadians will not read, nor will they create, history that represents Blacks as a homogenous community. The historiography may continue in its geographical and temporal framework, or it may be usurped by an emphasis on Black ethnic communities. Walker believed the Black community is "the key" in understanding Black Canadian history, and a "powerful political impulse" (Walker 1997: 172). The reality of what the Black community is presently in Canadian society will reinvent the way that the historiography is read and made. Black ethnicity, as created through historical immigration policies and as a historical and a theoretical framework, will be at the forefront of future Black Canadian scholarship. *Flying Fish in the Great White North* continues in this direction.

Notes

1   Library and Archives Canada (hereafter LAC), RG 76, vol. 830, file 552-1-644, pt. 2, Immigration from the British West Indies since the Second World War.

2   "Canada Year Book Collection" <www66.statcan.gc.ca/acyb_000-eng.htm> [accessed May 14, 2013]; "Immigration and emigration" <www65.statcan.gc.ca/acyb01/acyb01_0009-eng.htm> [accessed May 14, 2013].

3   LAC, RG 76, vol. 820, file 552-1-533, Commonwealth Caribbean-Canada Conference, Ottawa, July 6–8, 1966, June 1, 1966; LAC, RG 76, vol. 830, file 552-1-644, Memorandum to A/Chief of Operations. From Head, Administration Section, February 28, 1963.

Chapter One

BLACK FACE FOR BLACK PEOPLE
Ideas of "Black" and "Blackness" in Barbadian History

As colour is the most obvious outward manifestation of race it has been made the criterion by which men are judged, irrespective of their social or educational attainments. The light-skinned races have come to despise all those of a darker colour, and the dark-skinned peoples will no longer accept without protest the inferior position to which they have been relegated. (Fanon 1967: 118)

I was responsible at the same time for my body, for my race, for my ancestors. I subjected myself to an objective examination, I discovered my blackness, my ethnic characteristics; and I was battered down by tom-toms, cannibalism, intellectual deficiency, fetishism, racial defects, slave-ships, and above all else, above all; "Sho' good eatin." (Fanon 1967: 112)

The idea of Blackness and Black identity influenced White British colonial perceptions of Blacks in the West Indies and Canada; it subsequently provided the exclusionary framework for Canada's anti-Black and anti-Black Barbadian immigration policy. One may argue that Barbados and Canada, both products of British imperialism in the Americas, were driven by Anglo-Saxon ideals of race and White superiority throughout their respective histories. White hegemonic rule over the "native savages" defined the European destruction and subjugation of Indigenous peoples, while the same parallel can be drawn for the Barbadian slavocracy of Africans in the Americas. The enslaved Other may have differed; however, Whites' belief in White "goodness" and Black or Coloured inferiority dictated how Whites in both Canada and Barbados saw themselves versus those of a darker phenotype. In relation to this chapter and book, this diachronic White creation and perception of Black inferiority provided the foundation for the exclusion of Barbadians and Black people as a whole in Canada's immigration history. Contrary to popular belief, Canada did not adopt the insidious anti-Black racism from the United States; the Canadian discrimination against Blacks was a product of British ideals and a "liberal racial order" (Walker 2009: 81). The diachronic and geographical transfer of racialized ideas and anti-Black sentiment from the seventeenth-century British West Indian slave codes to early twentieth-century Canadian immigration policy was not entirely a linear historical process, but an ideology that existed throughout the Black Atlantic and Western political thought since the Biblical "fact" of the Curse of Ham. The sons of Ham were (mis)interpreted to be Sub-Saharan, or Black, Africans. From Genesis 9: 18–27:

> And the sons of Noah, that went forth from the ark, were Shem, and Ham, and Japheth; and Ham is the father of Canaan.
>
> And [Noah] drank of the wine, and was drunken; and he was uncovered within his tent.
>
> And Ham, the father of Canaan, saw the nakedness of his father, and told his two brethren without.
>
> And Noah awoke from his wine, and knew what his youngest son had done unto him.
>
> And he said: Cursed be Canaan; a servant of servants shall he be unto his brethren.
>
> And he said: Blessed be the LORD, the God of Shem; and let Canaan be their servant.

The creation of the idea of Blackness and Black identity must be thoroughly discussed. One must also contextualize the relationship between liberalism and a liberal racial order that normalized White privilege and anti-Black racism in Canada prior to the twentieth century. Anti-Black racial attitudes were decidedly British — and subsequently Canadian — in nature and not simply adopted from the United States or transferred from the West Indies.

Black Barbadian colonial identity, specifically during the early to mid-twentieth century, contextualizes Canada's anti-Black sentiment. Black Barbadians adopted — and were forced to adopt — a British colonial identity, an identity that should have allowed them the right to gain admittance to Canada during the mid-twentieth century under its immigration policy that allowed the entry and settlement of British subjects. Canadian racial attitudes and specifically an anti-Black immigration philosophy characterized Canadian immigration policy. Barbadians' Blackness, consolidated during the Transatlantic Slave Trade and slavery, superseded their British character. The Black Barbadian's socially constructed race and Black identity influenced Canadian immigration policy.

Canada's acceptance of racial hierarchies, specifically the racialization of Black Barbadians, paralleled the British social construction and debasement of Blacks throughout the history of slavery in the West Indies. Geographical boundaries did not prohibit the dissemination of ideas. Canada and the West Indies established trading and socio-economic relationships during slavery as members of the British imperialist empire in the Americas. Despite the northern neighbour's lack of a true slavocracy, the British consolidated anti-Black West Indian and Barbadian racism in the eighteenth and early nineteenth centuries that remained relatively dormant until Canada was faced with the prospect of mass migration during the twentieth century.

The malicious and detrimental creation of African and Black identities during the Transatlantic Slave Trade and the institution of slavery in Barbados and the British West Indies are significant contributing factors to anti-Black racism. The misappropriation of African identity, and the subsequent arbitrary and ignorant classification of African ethnicity, precipitated the perpetual debasement of Black identity in the West Indies. This process began during the Slave Trade and is highlighted by the seminal work and comprehensive collection of slave embarkation and disembarkation ports by David Eltis, Stephen D. Behrendt, David Richardson and Herbert S. Klein (Eltis et al. 1999). Eltis et al.'s collection is used to contextualize and provide a framework to understand White perceptions of Black people and their Blackness in Barbados and the West Indies during slavery. This will be complemented by firsthand accounts including Scottish Abolitionist William Dickson's *Letters on Slavery*. His work highlights the arbitrary and socially constructed binary racial categories in late eighteenth-century Barbados. Dickson challenged reified ideological views of White superiority supported by Black inferiority. I have theorized the creation of Black identity in Barbados by grounding sociological interpretations in historical and archival evidence. I have also situated the historical creation of the "Black" Barbadian and explored the White British social construction of race in Barbadian society. Race, and specifically Canada's prejudice against Black West Indians and Barbadians, was a systemic and ideological barrier to their immigration; Canadian beliefs of White superiority and a "White Canada" philosophy dictated their immigration policy prior to its official de-racialization in 1962. The British fabrication of a binary White-Black racial dichotomy is the foundation of the historical social construction of the virtues of Whiteness in Canadian society and the pejorative nature of Blackness in Barbados. One must understand the historical roots of the ascription of Blackness in Barbadian society — and what it means to be deemed "Black" — to contextualize Canada's exclusionary and anti-Black immigration policy. The paucity of works on Black Canadian immigration presents the White antipathy and fear of Blacks as a diachronic historical fact. It does not take into account how Canada, a settler and colonial state, deliberately created racial and ethnic hierarchies to promote and maintain Anglo-Saxon hegemonic power. Furthermore, with this line of argumentation, I begin to deconstruct the historical reductionist essentialization of Black Barbadians that parallels Alan B. Simmons and Jean-Pierre Guengant's "culture-of-migration" theory. Due to the Black Barbadian and West Indian's negative and arbitrary subaltern classification throughout history, scholarship subsequently perpetuated their cultural misrepresentation as an accepted and unchallenged norm. Their racialization negated causal factors for who they were and why they chose to migrate.

The limited discussion of the ideology of Blackness in Canadian history further marginalizes the Black subject as it normalizes Whiteness as "good" and assumes Blackness, and Black people, as the perpetual "Other." By refusing to acknowledge the historical roots of race and racism in Canada, the historiography presents race as "real"; it assumes that Whites were here "first." According to former Prime Minister William Lyon Mackenzie King, as "native Canadians," "a country should surely have the right to determine what strains of blood it wishes to have in its population," and immigration was, and is, not a "fundamental human right," but a privilege.[1] Mackenzie King and others assumed that a fabricated belief of Whiteness equated to the virtues of Canadian identity and Canadian nation-building. It is this belief of White privilege juxtaposed against Black undesirability in Canada that is crucial in understanding Canadian immigration policy. What historical factors led to the belief of Black Barbadian inferiority? How did human beings from the African continent become Black? What does it mean to be a Black Barbadian? The premise of this work is to understand the migration experience of Black Barbadians. To truly comprehend their racialization in the Canadian immigration system one must understand that the "Black" qualifier is a historical and social construction. Their exclusion and marginalization was not because they were black in colour, but "Black" in existence; it was a belief entrenched in Western political thought, Christianity and liberalism, but also rooted in the misrepresentation of African identity during the Transatlantic Slave Trade and developed to maintain socio-economic and class divisions throughout the Americas. Canadians adopted the negative homogenization of the Black

Barbadian that the British perfected during the Transatlantic Slave Trade and the institution of slavery in the West Indies.

"White Canada": Blackness, Liberalism and the Liberal Racial Order

The Curse of Ham, and its many misinterpretations, was at the forefront of the racialization and justification of slavery in the New World. There have been attempts to emphasize its importance as a leading cause in the explanation of Black oppression. David Brion Davis (2006), Jonathan Schorsch (2004) and Anton L. Allahar (1993) discussed the importance of the Biblical text and its misinterpretations, which condemned Blacks to a condition of perpetual servile exploitation. Davis argued that there was, and is, no direct link to race or colour in the Biblical text. Nevertheless, the Curse became the foundation and justification for anti-Black racism and slavery. Davis admitted that the Curse of Ham was "not a racist script," but the enslavement of Africans transformed its meaning. Goldenberg reinforced Davis' argument and stated that Biblical commentators "conveniently" forgot the wording of the text. Oppressors conveniently interpreted the text to fit their own bigoted views. Davis summarized the previous thoughts and concluded that the Curse became "absolutely central in the history of anti-black racism," and "no other passage in the Bible has had such a disastrous influence through human history" (Davis 2006: 65, 67).

The Curse of Ham is arguably the foundation for the negative codification of dark skin colour and Blackness as the textual Curse justified Negro slavery. Schorsch (2004: 153, 135, 137) listed 38 authors between 1400–1700 who cited the Curse to explain the "servitude" of Blacks and/or the cause of "Human Blackness," including Gomes Eannes de Zurara (1453); Elizabeth Cary (1613); and John Milton's *Paradise Lost* (1667). Schorsch (2004: 161) concluded that the Curse explained the "perpetuity" of Black servitude and the "origin of their physiognomy" (facial/ bodily features). Evidently, according to Schorsch, one cannot lay blame on the Jewish people for the devastating and dehumanizing effects of the Curse of Ham. However, Anton Allahar challenged Schorsch's argument that "the association between blackness, evil, and punishment" is made explicitly through the Curse (Allahar 1993: 46). Whether the Jewish interpretations of the Curse included Blackness or facilitated the enslavement of Blacks, Allahar argued that those arguments were irrelevant. According to him, generations of Christians came to understand the Curse as "punishment in a specific way and acted on the basis of that understanding" (Allahar 1993: 47). Views on Blackness became synonymous with slavery (Allahar 1993: 42).

It is clear then that the roots of the negative ideology of Blackness and Black identity preceded the Transatlantic Slave Trade and slavery in the British West Indies. Ideas of Black inferiority preceded the enslavement of Africans and those of African descent. There was the concept of the "monstrous" races in medieval art and thought, which linked the idea of "Blackness" to the creative imagination of the unknown (darkness) in Greco-Roman ideology as it created the belief of the Other as an inferior being (Allahar 1993: 42). The ideology of Blackness and its negative connotations were thus historically defined concepts and "Black" as a pejorative term was subsequently applied to justify African enslavement in the Americas. African and African-American slaves were "historically linked to inferiority, ugliness, and Blackness," which subsequently facilitated the creation of universal stereotypes — the racialization — of slaves where black or darker skin colour became negative phenotypic codifiers (Davis 2006: 65–67). Through this historical process "being black came to signify inferiority," as "being" Black — the reified and subjective ideological manifestation of inferiority and servitude — became the ubiquitous representation of those of African descent (Allahar and Cote 1998: 71). This concept was supported by the Biblical "fact" of the Curse of Ham and also through Christian ideology that justified the European enslavement and degradation of Africans and African-Americans. The effects of an environment dominated by Christian doctrine and "the mentality of the enslaver all housed in his black, ex-slave's body" created a Western society where "being black was devalued and despised, even by black people themselves" (Allahar 1993: 81).

Religion and Christian doctrine were used to justify Black African enslavement throughout the Americas. Jack Gratus (1973), Peter Kolchin (2003), Davis (2006), Allahar (1993), Roger Bastide (quoted in Allahar 1993: 48), and Kyle Haselden (1964) argued that the Church and Biblical interpretations demonized and "racialized" the Black African, which subsequently permitted and encouraged his eternal enslavement. The Biblical justification for "White domination" began within the institution of slavery. Through his interpretations of Exodus and Leviticus, the Bible and, subsequently, Christianity, Reverend Raymond Harris (1788) supported slavery. Nevertheless, leading abolitionists such as William Wilberforce, Thomas Clarkson and Thomas Buxton believed Blacks (in Africa) were heathens "needing conversion, and needing the benefits of white Christian morality" (Gratus 1973: 15, 141). Furthermore, three religious arguments (supposedly) justified chattel slavery: Hebrews owned slaves and Jesus did not condemn slavery; the Curse of Ham; and slavery was God's plan to expose "heathens" to the "blessings of Christianity" (Kolchin 2003: 192).

That being said, Davis analyzed the creationist theory justification for Black servitude and believed it to be a contradiction. In theory, Islamic and Christian doctrine did not tolerate enslavement based on colour, and racial difference was irrelevant (Davis 2006: 48). Bastide disagreed with Davis and contended,

"Christianity as a doctrine or body of thought is replete with examples of racial stratification and colour prejudice" (quoted in Allahar 1993: 48). Allahar (1993: 52) asserted that Christianity as an ideology was "a unique justification to the enslavement of Black Africans," and a rationalization "used to explain away any guilt that might have been incurred (by enslavers and those implicated within the institution) along the way." Ideological beliefs, facilitated by Christian doctrine, justified the paradox of hypocrisy of Barbadian and New World chattel slavery. Nevertheless, Haselden (1964: 51) postulated that the Church's discrimination and subjugation of Blacks during and after slavery were "embedded within moral consciousness." He contended that the Church officially endorsed the enslavement and inferiority of Blacks and cited the Bible as its justification. He wrote that "prolonged exposure and need to rationalize slavery" through discrimination subsequently became a part of the Christian religion (Haselden 1964: 51). Prior to the proliferation of the institution of chattel slavery, Haselden (1964: 51) argued that there was a "code of morality justifying the dehumanization of Blacks." Christianity, the Curse of Ham, and medieval art and thought are central to the history of anti-Black racism throughout the Western and Christianized world. These ideas of Black inferiority proliferated throughout the Great White North.

Several scholars of Black Canadian history, specifically Afua Cooper in *The Hanging of Angélique: The Untold Story of Canadian Slavery and the Burning of Old Montreal* and James W. St. G. Walker's *The Black Loyalists: The Search for a Promised Land in Nova Scotia and Sierra Leone, 1783–1870,* have identified the presence of Canadian anti-Black racism since the early eighteenth century; a decidedly British and French — not American — colonial form of anti-Black racism that paralleled the rise of discrimination in Barbados and the British West Indies. I contend that there was not an explicit process of transfer of racial attitudes in Canadian society from Barbados, but it was a shared British anti-Black sentiment. I seek to explain how, when and why Black Barbadians were negatively codified to contextualize the racist attitudes held by British colonial subjects throughout the Empire. I also construct a theoretical and historical parallel of British racial attitudes in the Atlantic World, specifically between the roots of the ideological and physical creation of Black identity during slavery in Barbados, and how the liberal racial order influenced anti-Black sentiment and racialized silos in Canada.

The liberal racial order and the process of transfer of anti-Black attitudes to Canada are exemplified when one deconstructs the rigid geographical and ideological nation-state boundaries of place and space. If imagined geopolitical barriers are challenged and redefined, it is much easier to contextualize anti-Black racism in an Atlantic paradigm. The concepts of the ship and the Black Atlantic first argued by Paul Gilroy in *The Black Atlantic: Modernity and Double Consciousness* and "The Black Atlantic as a Counterculture of Modernity" further support a transnational and globalized framework of Black identity formation, skin colour, ethnic and national belonging, and racial attitudes throughout the Atlantic World. Gilroy (2003) argued that creolization, the ship and the Atlantic Ocean each facilitated the making of Black people in the Western World; historical and modern transnational movements created Blacks who subsequently fit outside the paradigms of modernity and nationality. National and diasporic belonging existed in the absence of political boundaries. Gilroy's definition provides a foundation to "rethink" and "reconceptualize" Black identity formation and considers the transnational ties of racial attitudes throughout the British Empire and how it influenced Canadian immigration policy and the admission and settlement of Black Barbadians and West Indians.

Liberalism, liberal ideology and a liberal democratic society were the ties that bound Barbados, the British West Indies and Canada and their historical conceptions of racial hierarchies. Barbados and Canada experienced the paradox of liberalism as equality did not extend to all, nor was the system designed to work in such a manner. It was not a question of what Black West Indian immigrants wanted, but of what the dominant Canadian liberal ideology was willing to give. A liberal society promoted itself to be a free and fair system, with equal opportunity for all. However, the dominant ideology of liberalism managed to "mask reality" and convinced "all citizens that they live in a middle-class society with few extremes," particularly in the mid- to late twentieth century (Allahar and Cote 1998: 27). Black needs and wants became irrelevant when Barbadian, West Indian and Canadian societies appropriated dominant liberal democratic ideology. They, like all minority groups, became tools to a system in which they had no control. Liberal ideology was a process by which ideas were constructed and imposed to support the views and motives of the dominant class in society. Ideology facilitated the use of power and authority over the masses. Max Weber (quoted in Allahar and Cote 1998: 32) argued that power "was simply the ability to issue a command and have it obeyed, even if it goes against the will of the person or persons commanded to execute it." Liberal ideology was thus used as a form of social control, whereby the White British "elite" in Canada and the West Indies manipulated and created a "reality" that was favourable to their particular interests.

The British West Indies and Canada were areas "where white, male, Anglo-Saxon, Protestant, wealthy, middle-aged, and older heterosexuals hold power in the leading institutions," which was altruistically supported by historical "facts" (Allahar 1995: 18). Furthermore, liberal ideology was bolstered by its functionalist argument of natural inequalities in society. Functionalist liberalists argued that "social inequality is a fact of life" and has "existed in all known human societies and is therefore thought to be inevitable" (McLellan 1986: 6). Once the ideological "fact" of "Black" and "Blackness" was conflated with functionalist liberal ideology,

Black people were deemed perpetually inferior in a system designed and dependent on social inequalities. Social inequalities served "the political functions of social order and control" and through the power of liberal ideology "no systemic injustice explains their inequality, instead, those who do not get ahead have failed themselves. What is more, they themselves believe this to be so" (McLellan 1986: 15). Canadians and Canadian society were firmly entrenched in liberal philosophy and anti-Black racial attitudes and social inequality prior to the mass immigration of West Indians in the mid-twentieth century. It was a philosophy and ideology fraught with contradictions and one that did not support or welcome Black West Indian immigrants and Canada's growing racialized population during the late nineteenth and twentieth century (McLellan 1986: 22).

Liberal internationalism and liberal nationalism supported this theoretical framework on liberalism and the restriction of immigrants. Liberal internationalism posits "a strong positive link between the state and the rights of non-citizens, forged by liberal ideas of equality and freedom alongside cognate international norms" (Anderson 2013: 7). Liberal nationalism is "rooted in a more insular interpretation of state sovereignty that supports a narrower range of rights that non-citizens can claim against the receiving state," and it is focused on much more race-based exclusionary immigration policies (Anderson 2013: 7). Liberal nationalism effectively promoted a "White Canada" nation-building project from 1887 to the *Immigration Act* of 1952. Christopher G. Anderson provided the overlooked example of the Canadian Senate's liberal internationalist attempt to defeat and repeal the racist liberal nationalist *Chinese Immigration Act* of 1885 and the conflict between the "rights-restrictive" border control policies of the two ideologies up to the 1960s. Anderson (2013: 10–11) argued that these historical developments in Canadian immigration history and the "tensions between control and rights … did not simply unfold through interest group politics or the courts but were more the product of robust parliamentary debate over what it meant to be a liberal democracy." Canada's liberal founding principles and liberal democratic political culture firmly contributed to its immigration policy and how the state excluded Black and non-White peoples (Anderson 2013: 7, 9).

The conflation of liberal ideals with Canadian state institutions in the late nineteenth and early twentieth century subsequently produced "a tendency to replace the vocabulary of race and distinction with legal phraseology that was self-consciously race neutral and ostensibly universal in its application" (McKeown 2008: 9). The point to emphasize is that Canada may not have explicitly used race as a barrier to immigration since racialized border controls were normalized; "neutralized language obscured the racial origins of migration control and projected them into the universal standards of the international system" (McKeown 2008: 9–10). It was the accepted norm to exclude migrants based on race in a liberal state. This was most apparent with anti-Asian border controls in the 1880s to "white settler nations." These controls "were created by white settler nations around the Pacific that saw themselves as the forefront of the liberal freedoms of the nineteenth century ... Ideals and practices of self-rule were also the foundation of exclusionary policies" (McKeown 2008: 7). The Canadian state excluded Asians and non-Whites to protect late nineteenth-century ideals of liberal "freedoms." These individual freedoms for Canadians were measured through "an effective political community ... [which] required membership controls, whether to protect the existence of liberal institutions or merely as the right of a free, self-governing people" (McKeown 2008: 7). The techniques used to control and exclude Chinese migrants in the late nineteenth century became the template and foundation for immigration laws in Canada and other White settler nations. With respect to the exclusion of Chinese migrants, exclusionary immigration policy was a reflection of the battle between "civilized" liberal and "free" Canadians as opposed to the "uncivilized" Chinese (McKeown 2008: 13–17).

Non-Whites were not welcomed in Canada at the turn of the twentieth century. Canadian bureaucrats deliberately and arbitrarily excluded Black Americans and Blacks from the West Indies. Permanent civil servants in the Immigration Branch, most notably W.D. Scott, Superintendent of Immigration Branch prior to the First World War, ignored "Parliamentary statute and public principle ... [and] appointed themselves guardians of Canada's racial purity," and kept Canada "White" — a "White Canada" (Schultz 1982: 53). Immigration Branch officials were the gatekeepers of Canada's "Whiteness." Anti-Black immigrant racism in the twentieth century was most apparent with the exclusion of African-American farmers from settling in Alberta and Saskatchewan since their "loose habits, laziness, sexual appetites, lack of manliness and mental deficiencies would pollute the pure stream of Canadian morals" (Schultz 1982: 54). This is important as Canada actively sought farmers from the United States during this time but did not want Black American emigrants. In 1909 Scott essentialized Blacks as a homogenous group of "Africans" and stated that "there are certain countries ... and certain races of people considered as suited to this country and its conditions, but Africans, no matter where they come from are not among the races sought, and hence, Africans no matter what country they come from are in common with other uninvited races, not admitted to Canada" (Schultz 1982: 54). Scott's anti-Black or anti-African sentiment effectively eliminated the right that Black Barbadians and West Indians had as British subjects to emigrate to Canada. Moreover, Scott and the Immigration Branch used "bureaucratic barricades" to bar Blacks when official immigration policy proved insufficient. The case of the schooner *Yolanda* that disembarked at Saint John in August 1912 carrying thirty-five Black Barbadians was an excellent example of racialized barriers. Port authorities seized the vessel claiming that it violated the *Passenger Act* as it did not provide the required deck space for each adult on board. Other ship captains feared they would face the same arbitrary prosecution — and the cost of returning their Black passengers back to the West Indies — and hesitated to carry other West Indian migrants. Canadian bureaucrats found creative means to bar the "West India nigger," including the constructed belief that Blacks were destined to become public charges. Complaints came from shipping lines including the Royal Mail Line that stated their passengers should have been admitted since they fulfilled all the immigration requirements and were medically fit (Schultz 1982: 56).

The 1910 *Immigration Act* allowed the Governor in Council to exclude potential immigrants based on race; however, Scott refused the entry of Black West Indian emigrants even when their labour was needed and requested. Due to a labour shortage, the Dominion Coal Company guaranteed employment and sought permission to import 150 West Indians to work in Glace Bay, Nova Scotia, in 1915. Scott refused this request on the grounds that there was "absolutely no hope" of Black foreign workers. The superintendent held the position that his role and the role of the Immigration Branch was to keep "Canada a White Man's Country" (Schultz 1982: 58). Schultz (1982: 59, 61) argued that a "small clique of officials" at the Immigration Branch "came to see themselves as guardians of the gates," destined to keep Canada "White" by enforcing its "own version of the Canadian mosaic." There may not have been an official "White Canada" policy; however, protected by civil service tenure and "the tradition of anonymity," Immigration Branch officials "bent public policy to suit the whim of their private prejudice" (Schultz 1982: 62). Arbitrary decision making, personal bigotry and exclusionary immigration policies contributed to Canada's anti-Black immigration policy and its unofficial status as a "White Man's Country."

Constructing Black Barbadian Identity and the Transatlantic Slave Trade

The classification of human beings during the Transatlantic Slave Trade precipitated the homogenization of African identity, which facilitated the negative codification of the African-Barbadian and her Black identity. Slave traders and planters recognized African "cultural variants," but they used a "simplified cultural nomenclature or typology derived from the two general tendencies" (Handler and Large 1978: 26). These aforementioned tendencies were also described as "identifying nationalities customarily shipped from a particular African port by the name of the port," and through the selection of "one ethnic or linguistic term to identify a much larger group" (Handler and Large 1978: 27). Moreover,

these tendencies make for confusion and overlapping terminology ...

overlapping variants make it difficult to equate ethnic identifications with particular coastal regions of the slave trade ... The most common European error was to use a narrow, or ethnic, or linguistic name, or a costal shipping point, to stand for a larger and more diverse assortment of peoples. (Handler and Large 1978: 27)

I argue that this careless "European error" is at the root of the misappropriation of African and Black Barbadian identity; Whites negated vibrant cultural variants to expedite the dehumanization of their human chattel. Eltis et al.'s *The Trans-Atlantic Slave Trade: A Database on CD-ROM* identified nine African coastal region slave embarkation ports. These included The Bight of Benin, The Bight of Biafra, The Gold Coast, Senegambia, Sierra Leone, South-east Africa, West-central Africa, Windward Coast, and Africa unspecified. The significance is that from the outset of their study the researchers identified only nine possible origin variants if Europeans used a coastal shipping point "to stand for a larger and more diverse assortment of peoples," thus limiting the historical possibility of the cultural heterogeneity of Barbados-bound African slaves (Handler and Large 1978: 77). While Eltis et al.'s study does not claim to represent ethnic origins, it is possible that embarkation points, similar to the misappropriation of Coromantee identity, could have been misinterpreted by slave traders to represent and classify multi-ethnic groups. The 200-year English involvement in the Trade witnessed the embarkation of 433,336 slaves en route to Barbados with the successful delivery of 359,178 captives. The following table highlights slave distribution, with respect to specific African slaving ports, destined for Barbados.

The identity and origin of over 40 percent of the total number of slaves shipped from African coastal regions were unidentifiable. The initial stages of the Barbadian Slave Trade, 1601–1700, highlighted a slight increase of Africans from the Bight of Benin followed closely by unspecified African regions. Barbados was settled by the English in 1627 and the first major slave cargo was landed from *Marie Bonadventure* in 1644, captained by George Richardson (Eltis et al. 1999).

In 1770, during the height of trade to the Island, 9,411 Africans were destined for transport. One must be aware of the addition of the Windward Coast as a slaving port.

The tables highlighted the diversity of West African embarkation ports and carelessly classified origins of African-Barbadians. Barbadian slave traders and planters arbitrarily homogenized and constructed the multi-ethnic, linguistic and geographical backgrounds of Africans. This practice continued with the ethnic identities of African slaves. Throughout the late seventeenth and eighteenth centuries, Barbadian planters preferred slaves of the Gold Coast whom they described as Coromantees. They were "in general ... looked upon to be the best for labour"

Table 1-1 African Slaves Destined for Barbados by Embarkation Port[2]

Region	Slaves	Total Percentage of Slaves
Bight of Biafra	36,967	33.30
Africa unspecified	25,807	23.30
Gold Coast	13,281	12.00
Windward Coast	10,717	9.66
Senegambia	8,111	7.31
West-central Africa	7,606	6.86
Sierra Leone	5,626	5.07
Bight of Benin	2,666	2.40
South-east Africa	123	0.11

Table 1-2 African Slaves Destined for Barbados by Embarkation Port, 1601–1700

Region	Slaves	Total Percentage of Slaves
Bight of Benin	33,903	29.50
Africa unspecified	30,604	26.60
Gold Coast	16,346	14.20
Bight of Biafra	14,422	12.60
West-central Africa	8,683	7.56
South-east Africa	5,387	4.69
Senegambia	4,882	4.25
Sierra Leone	681	0.59

Table 1-3 African Slaves Destined for Barbados by Embarkation Port, 1751–1775

Region	Slaves	Total Percentage of Slaves
Bight of Biafra	36,967	33.30
Africa unspecified	25,807	23.30
Gold Coast	13,281	12.00
Windward Coast	10,717	9.66
Senegambia	8,111	7.31
West-central Africa	7,606	6.86
Sierra Leone	5,626	5.07
Bight of Benin	2,666	2.40
South-east Africa	123	0.11

(Handler and Large 1978: 25). A wealthy Barbadian planter circa the 1670s or 1680s noted, "I have observed ... the Caramantines, and Gold-Coast slaves, have always stood and proved best on my plantations" (Handler and Large 1978: 25–26). The seventeenth-century idea of "Coromantee" and slave origins were consigned and fabricated identities as there was no identifiable proof to confirm the ethnic identity of African slaves if the only recorded evidence identifying slave origins was their embarkation port. Those involved in the Trade thus initiated an accepted practice of misappropriating African, African-American and Black identity; no factual truth could confirm the specific ethnic and geographical origins of slaves destined for Barbadian plantations. African slaves were identified by the region from which they left for the Middle Passage and not by their homeland, ethnicity or nation. Furthermore, throughout the seventeenth century, over one quarter of all African-Barbadians came from an unidentified African port of origin. This further supports the argument that the institution of slavery constructed the identity of Black Barbadians, since slave traders used inaccurate generalized African regional descriptors as a means for logistical and accountable convenience. The diachronic social ramifications of the misrepresentation of Africans in the Americas did not inhibit the economically profitable Slave Trade and institution of slavery in Barbados. If the Coromantee was perceived to be a suitable and profitable planta-tion slave, all suitable and profitable plantation slaves became Coromantee. James Knight, a former slave who won his freedom in Scottish court, stated in 1742:

> The Gold Coast Negroes, though they generally go under the denomi-nation of Cromantus, are of different Provinces or Clans; and not under the same Prince or Chief, nor do they speak the same language. Of these, the Coromantines, Fantuns, Shantus and Achims are mostly esteemed. (quoted in Hart 1985: 8)

Richard Hart (1985: 8) argued in *Slaves Who Abolished Slavery: Volume II: Blacks in Rebellion* that there was no conclusive evidence of a distinct Coromantee "tribe"; it was a generalized region in which Africans of different ethnicities were bought, sold and shipped to the Americas. Slave traders and owners ascribed an ethnic identity that reflected desired personal and physical characteristics. The previous tables highlighted that Africans destined for Barbadian plantations embarked at various ports throughout the continent were of different ethnic and linguistic ori-gins; however, once in the Caribbean, a constructed and perceived generalization of African and Black identity supplanted their true regional and ethnic origins. The African's physical deracination facilitated the ideological perception, construction and ascription of their Black Barbadian identity.

The commodification of African-Barbadian Black identity began with the homogenization of African origins. By the mid-eighteenth century, most Black Africans in Barbados originated from what are present-day Ghana, Togo, Dahomey, western Nigeria, and the adjoining regions (Handler and Large 1978: 27). The evidence presented highlighted this area at the peak of African slave transports to Barbados between 1751 and 1775 as the Bight of Biafra at 33.30 percent of slave exports. However, it must be acknowledged that an unspecified region of African slave shipments followed closely at 23.30 percent of the total figures. Moreover, African imports over the course of the seventeenth century favoured the Bight of Benin at 29.50 percent, while unspecified African origins trailed by less than 3 percent at 26.60 percent. Seventeenth- and eighteenth-century Barbadian planters may have favoured Coromantee slaves from specified regions such as the Bight of Biafra or the Gold Coast, but conflicting and inconclusive evidence highlighted the inaccurate classification of African identity. Throughout the course of the Slave Trade, 41.40 percent of African slaves in Barbados held no recorded origin. Slave traders and plantation owners may have held the Coromantee in high esteem, or believed that their product was genuine "Coromantee," but no conclusive evidence validated their claims. Furthermore, the Coromantee was not a homogenous African ethnicity. It included peoples such as the Adangme, Ashanti, Dahomeans and Ewe, Edo, Fanti, Ga, Ibibio, Ibo, and Yoruba. White generalizations and codifications of the African-Barbadian began with the convenient classifications of a majority of African ethnic groups as Coromantee — preferred Barbadian slaves — followed by the Whydah, or Ouidah (Handler and Large 1978: 27). By the turn of the nineteenth century and the introduction of the Slave Registers, defining regional or ethnic variations ceased to exist; White Europeans normalized "African" as the identifier for Blacks originating from the ethnically diverse African continent. A critical assessment of Eltis and his colleagues' work highlighted the possibility of nine slave African regional origins. Nine regions that — following the data — revealed the presence of only nine different African ethnicities, or "types," of Africans in Barbados. A near majority of Africans had no specified origins, nor identifiable ethnicity. Barbadian Black African origins were inconclusive and contrived; slave owners and traders ignorantly preferred "Coromantees" and "Gold-Coast slaves," and subsequently classified and codified their property. Slave traders and owners acknowledged the presence of African heterogeneity, but marginalized African identity for the expediency of an omnipresent and unified slave group. The custom facilitated the practice of White European consigned slave identities; it precipitated the ideology of negatively commodifying African-Barbadian slave and Black identity based on skin colour.

This late eighteenth-century Barbadian negative representation of African-Barbadian slaves was recorded by Scottish Abolitionist William Dickson of Moffat, Dumfriesshire, the Private Secretary to the Honourable Edward Hay, Governor of

Barbados from 1783–1786, in his *Letters on Slavery*. Thomas Clarkson and William Wilberforce befriended him for advocating the end of the Slave Trade. Dickson was described as "the Thomas Clarkson of Scotland"; Wilberforce believed he was "indeed a most intelligent and worthy man" (Dickson 1789: iii).

Dickson's *Letters on Slavery* (1789: iii) set out to "lay before the Public a free and impartial sketch of negro slavery as it now exists in the island of Barbados." He showed "how it would be affected by the abolition of the slave-trade; and to prove by arguments, founded on *facts*, the natural equality of the natives of the immense continent of Africa to the rest of mankind" (Dickson 1789: iii). Dickson questioned late eighteenth-century ideological views of "Black," "Blackness" and White superiority in Barbados based on the biological "fact" of colour. With respect to ideas of White supremacy and Black inferiority, Dickson (1789: iii) wrote in Letter IX of his *Letters on Slavery*, "I call colour (the principal difference in the varieties of men) a very equivocal mark of superiority." He continued, "The white man reasons thus, the negro's *colour* is different from mine, *ergo* I am naturally *superior* to the negro (author's emphasis)" (Dickson 1789: iii). He then stated, "May not a copper-coloured man, or a *black* man thus demonstrate the natural superiority of men of *his* own colour, to all others (author's emphasis)?" (Dickson 1789: iii). Dickson did not accept that the idea of skin colour could be the irrefutable mark of superiority or inferiority. The late eighteenth-century abolitionist challenged the irrational logic behind White superiority. He (1789: iii-iv) wrote, "Philosophers ... have gravely reasoned on phoenomena [*sic*] which never were ascertained or which never existed, and have perplexed the world with systems useless and incongruous in themselves, contradictory to one another," towards an "injured race of men." With similar unproven, illogical and fallacious arguments, Dickson argued Africans and Blacks — theoretically — had the right to discriminate against Whites due to their light skin tones. The institution of chattel slavery, the Slave Trade and African colonization disproved the aforementioned theory and Dickson's argument, but the sentiment must not be dismissed. White superiority was not an irrefutable fact.

Dickson showed that discrimination based on one's Blackness and black skin colour was flawed and he challenged the arbitrary nature of associating colour and ideas of virtue. Dickson (1789: 62) stated, "The ideas of intellect and of colour have a mutual dependence in minds which pretend to be superior to that of our black philosopher — The whites paint the devil black, and the negroes paint him white; but do such chimeras prove the devil to be either black or white?" He (1789: 63) continued, "A man may associate his idea of *blackness* with his idea of the devil, or with his idea of *stupidity*, or with any other of his ideas he thinks proper; but he ought not to reason from such arbitrary associations." Arbitrary reasoning created the ideological justifications for the debasement of Black peoples and the degradation through the creation of Black identity. Dickson (1789: 63) concluded:

And, if it appear, that there is no *connection* or *relation* of any kind whatever, between ideas which, some prejudiced, and weak minds have absurdly, unaccountably and unphilosophically *[sic] associated*; how, in the name of common sense, is it possible to infer the one from the other?

The author qualified the absurd nature of ideological manifestations of eighteenth- and early nineteenth-century bigotry. Respect for laws, morals and human decency did not apply to Africans and those of African descent in Barbados and throughout the Americas. Blacks were legislated to a position of subaltern servitude; a belief held throughout the British Empire and its ties to the Black Atlantic, the liberal racial order, liberalism and Western political thought. Dickson's work captured the peculiar, inconsistent and hypocritical nature in which some — and the author was clear to praise the decent and moral residents of the Island — White Barbadians conveniently aided in the "virtual murder" of Blacks.

White hegemonic power facilitated the marginalization of Black Barbadians. What must be acknowledged is that the misappropriation of African-Barbadian and Black West Indian identity crossed geographical and generational boundaries. The British liberal racial order, firmly rooted in Canada and the West Indies, empowered White supremacy allowing them the right to exclude racialized groups from British North America and the Canadian nation-state. The careless misrepresentation and generalization of African and Black identity in Barbados was representative of anti-Black sentiment throughout the British Empire in the Americas. However, one's black skin tone should not have equated to one's socioeconomic position in society, but historically, this proved to be false. Colonial British North America and Canada's liberal racial order and anti-Black liberal ideology were the foundations for the common British West Indian negative perceptions of Blacks and Black Barbadians. White nativism also allowed the state to perpetuate exclusionary immigration policies based on racial characteristics throughout Canadian history. I have set out to explain Black identity formation in Barbados and position how Black Barbadians challenged an established British liberal racial order in Canada. It provides a foundation to understand the historical mechanisms that created and facilitated the misappropriation of Black Barbadian identity and, subsequently, how during the mid-twentieth century Canada continued to discriminate against British subjects in the same fashion they did Black Loyalists in the late eighteenth century, Black refugees during the mid-nineteenth century, and Black American settlers in the West at the turn of the twentieth century. Canadian anti-Black immigration policy worked within the fabricated concept of "Black" identity and the ideological process of codifying Blackness that began prior to the generalization of African origins during the Transatlantic Slave Trade. Whites discriminated against all Blacks, but Blacks attempted to distance themselves from their "Black" identity. Black Barbadians fought for recognition as worthy and deserving immigrants that could, and did, contribute to Canadian nation-building. This process is highlighted by an examination of female Emigrant Ambassadors. These women deconstructed gendered, racialized and class-based immigrant categories and challenged White Canadian perceptions of Black identity in households throughout the country.

Black Barbadian Colonial Identity

To further understand the position of Black Barbadians in the international migration system during the mid-twentieth century, it is important to contextualize their status, and more importantly their identity, as British colonial citizens. Despite the belief and teaching of a common British identity, not all British imperial citizens were created equally; colour, colonial status and geography determined one's relationship to the metropole. However, the late nineteenth- and early twentieth-century British social imperialist and philanthropist, Thomas Sedgwick, argued that movement throughout the Empire facilitated and consolidated a common imperial identity. Sedgwick stated that to "move from Britain to New Zealand was no different from moving from Cornwall to Cumberland" (quoted in Gorman 2006: 179, 185). What is important is that Sedgwick qualified this argument by stating that this common imperial identity was restricted to Anglo-Saxon imperial citizenship in British settlement colonies. Canada attempted to balance the racialized exclusion of fellow British imperial citizens; however, Canadian nationalist and racist attitudes prevailed, and non-Whites, particularly Chinese "members of the Empire," were indiscriminately excluded. The differential treatment of non-White British imperial citizens and their "racial exclusion without naming race" was exemplified by the "inconsistency in one of the putative principles of imperial citizenship — equal treatment of British subjects under the law," through the exclusion of Indian passengers in 1914 on the *Komagata Maru* (Gorman 2006: 161). As British subjects, Indians had the right to intra-imperial movement; however, racialized Canadian liberal and colonial nationalism circumvented imperial citizenship and British colonial commonalities (Gorman 2006: 161). As a case study of Black Barbadians, non-White colonial peoples were taught to believe they were British and were rightfully entitled to the privileges of other White British colonial peoples. Nevertheless, their imperial citizenship outside of the Island and the West Indies was validated and authenticated by their skin colour.

Barbados was, and is, distinctively British in culture and customs. John Western (1992: 22) stated that "of all the formerly British Caribbean islands, none is more British than Barbados. Both Barbadians and non-Barbadian West Indians will tell you this, though likely with rather different imputations: the Barbadians with pride and satisfaction, the others with mirth and exasperation." This may have contributed to the sense that Barbadians believed themselves to be "exceptional" or simply "different" from other West Indians as they could exceed qualifications of such exclusionary immigration regulations as the *Commonwealth Immigrants Act* of 1962, which will be discussed later in this monograph. Western (1992: 87) argued that the Barbadians in his study, "formerly pretty representative of a wider collectivity of Afro-Caribbeans, have with the passage of time become an above-average group." Frank Springer, who migrated to the United Kingdom in the 1950s, said that Barbadians have "a completely different set of values [from other West Indians], different dispositions, different interests and enthusiasms," and that Jamaicans "are a completely different breed of West Indians" (quoted in Western 1992: 33).

Not only did the English differentiate between Barbadians and other West Indians, but the Barbadians Western interviewed openly stereotyped other West Indians. Barbadians referred to the "small-islanders" of the Windward and Leeward Islands as "country cousins" and that Barbados provided their teachers, priests and police in the "old days" (Western 1992: 198). One interviewee admitted that "Trinidadians are mercurial, we're historically prior (and thereby superior) to them because we peopled Trinidad and Guyana significantly, *and* (author's emphasis) they're mixed with Indians down there too. And Jamaicans are, well ... Jamaicans!" (quoted in Western 1992: 198). Tony Gill, an employee of British Rail at the time of Western's study, also expressed his "consciousness of Barbadian superiority," and argued that Barbadians not only settled Guyana and Trinidad, but as a result of the "good education in Barbados" there were Barbadian teachers throughout the Caribbean teaching other British colonial subjects (quoted in Western 1992: 199). This migrant-generation Barbados "chauvinism" and "Little England" British identity was validated by an English traveler named Quentin Crowe. Crowe (quoted in Western 1992: 199) wrote:

> I was not sorry to go. The island was the most English we had seen and although the people, for the most part, were far better off than those on other islands, it distressed me that so many of our worst traits had survived so vigourously. The colour bar, the pomposity of asking people to wear [tuxedos] for Christmas and what they call Old Year's Night, the general philistinism.
>
> It is a smug and snobbish island ... so [pious] an island.

Barbadian "Englishness" and their unique West Indian-British identity were also exemplified in the following exchange between Western (1992: 22) and a successful Barbadian businessman during the 1950s:

"You must appreciate the Englishness of the Barbadian. That's why we can love the English despite the hassles. We are what we are."

"But it was forced on you against your will originally," [Western] said; "yet are you saying it *is* you now?"

"Of course … We're us. What do you want us to be? Spaniards? French? No. Why should we change? Nobody's going to force us to change again, oh no…"

Audley Simmons, a former employee of London Transport, recalled that Barbadians were "brought up so English. When we got here [London, England], I was amazed in the cinema at the end of the film, we were the only ones who stood still for the playing of 'God Save the Queen.' Everyone else was rushing for the exits!" (quoted in Western 1992: 28). Barbadian Londoner Gladstone Codrington, a high-ranking British official, revealed why Barbadians assimilated well to English society. He stated that "*Barbados is a more conservative society than England* (author's emphasis)" (quoted in Western 1992: 200). D'Arcy Holder, a former London Transport employee, asserted that she could recall all three verses of the British national anthem. She also pinpointed Barbados' diplomatic watershed moment at the beginning of the Second World War that internationally recognized the West Indian island as "Little England." The Barbados legislature had sent a telegram to Neville Chamberlain on September 3, 1939, that stated, "Stand firm, England; Barbados is behind you" (Western 1992: 31).

Upon their arrival in London during the late 1950s and early 1960s, Barbadians were confronted by their idea of "Englishness" and their own British identity. In a revealing letter to Western, Springer wrote:

> I always had this desire to go to England, "the omnipotent Mother Country." The land of my great heroes like Sir Walter Raleigh, Lord Nelson, Robin Hood, Sherlock Holmes, The Saint, Sexton Blake, D.H. Lawrence, Charles Dickens, Shakespeare, G.B. Shaw.
>
> England to me was the land of wit, intelligence and the sophistication of Noël Coward.
>
> Little did I know that fact and fiction were two different ball games. The England that I encountered was more Dickensian. They were nothing romantic about the cold chilling winds, the dense fog, and the endless row of ugly building with a conformity of chimney stacks continuously belching out black smoke. None of this endeared me to the rather charmless country that I first encountered. (Western 1992: 56)

Springer was quite startled by this first encountered with his "fictitious" and ideological home. The "omnipotent Mother Country" was an idea that he, and arguably most Barbadians, had of England. This was not a result of ambivalent ignorance, but due to what Springer and other British colonial subjects were taught to believe. This differential attitude of the Barbadian British colonial Self and subjected English identity was also expressed by Audley Simmons. She stated:

> We're different from the English working class. They're not interested in bettering themselves. They just want food and steady wages. If I started as a worker I'd want my child to work hard at school and become a teacher, and *his* child to be a professional, a lawyer or a doctor. (quoted in Western 1992: 139–140)

Her comments highlighted the Barbadian emigrant's ambition and, most importantly, she represented the Barbadian desire for social mobility through generational status.

The Black Barbadian in England during the 1950s and early 1960s did not wish to overthrow an oppressive system and society, but work and fit within it. One may argue that Black Barbadians simply wanted to be recognized by their British identity and not their skin colour or colonial status. Barbadians were "prepared to be members of a small minority among white neighbours, for as they (Black Barbadians) rationalize it, this is a white country" (Western 1992: 160). These young Barbadians displayed their individual autonomy and left for England "as individuals, for themselves (and perhaps for their immediate family members, yes), individuals who wanted to get on in the world" (Western 1992: 160).

Unlike Western's focus on the "fictitious" or "real" British identity of Barbadians upon their arrival and settlement in London, England, Austin Clarke's *Growing Up Stupid Under the Union Jack: A Memoir* focused on his life in Barbados and his upbringing in the British education system as a British colonial subject. Austin Ardinel Chesterfield Clarke was born on July 26, 1932, and emigrated to Canada in 1955. He and Reginald Eric Taylor grew up in the same area and attended St. Matthias Boys' Elementary School during the 1930s and 1940s. The pursuit of education to escape poverty was central to both of their respective childhoods.

Taylor's life was not one of privilege or of status. He grew up in one of the many early to mid-twentieth-century segregated Barbadian neighbourhoods and started school at the early age of three in 1939, since his mother worked as a domestic servant. His father alternated between careers as a painter and carpenter, and he and his family lived in and owned their own home, but his parents were among the poorest. Taylor attended the open concept St. Matthias Boys' school where students were assigned to classes according to their ability and not age. Unfortunately, the introduction of age grouping by the Barbadian Government in 1945 devastated school enrollment; students were forced to leave elementary school once they reached the age of fourteen. By the age of twelve, Taylor left St. Matthias Boys' school in search of employment. His parents wanted him to attend secondary school but were unable to pay the necessary school fees. Between the ages of twelve and twenty he acquired two unpaid apprenticeships in carpentry and auto mechanics and several short-term paying jobs including work as a painter (Taylor 2010).

At twenty, Taylor found work in the diesel department at Barbados' Central Foundry and worked on the engines of fishing boats. He earned the meager starting salary of $13.50 a week. By 1960, news reached him and his colleagues at Central Foundry that the Barbadian Government was actively recruiting persons interested in accepting work in England at a salary considerably higher than they currently received. This included work for British Rail, hospitals, restaurants and London Transport, both on the buses and underground on the subway trains. Taylor was recruited and set sail for Southampton, England, on January 28, 1960, on the French Liner SS *Colombie*, and arrived February 8, 1960. While in England he earned his qualifications in mechanical engineering and he continued his emigrant journey to Canada where he settled in 1967. Taylor's love for education and his industrious perseverance led to an undergraduate degree and Master's in Education at the University of Toronto, all while working fulltime as an educator in the Peel District School Board. This was from a man who left school at the age of twelve (Taylor 2010).

As a Black Barbadian student, Clarke (2005: 3) recalled that to grow up and become a civil servant was beyond his "wild dreams"; it was a mark of privilege and progress to be dressed "like the white Colonial officers who ruled and ran [Barbados]." Clarke's colonial mentality and allegiance to the Crown as a British subject went beyond his education. Similar to Holder's comments, the Second World War solidified young Barbadians' British identity. Clarke (2005: 12) remembered, "And now the Germans were ruling these same waters and waves, and killing fathers, brothers and uncles from our village. And as black Britons we wanted to do something about it." Clarke also reiterated the watershed moment that forever identified Barbados as "Little England" when the Barbadian legislature, specifically Sir Grantley Herbert Adams, founder of the Barbados Labour Party (BLP), told Chamberlain and King George VI, "Go on, England, Little England is behind you" (quoted in Clarke 2005: 42–43). According to the author, approximately three hundred to four hundred Barbadian men volunteered for the Barbados Volunteer Force. Clarke (2005: 56) wrote: "We were English. The allegiance and patriotism that our leader, Mr. Grantley Adams, had imprisoned us with had been cabled to the Colonial Office in London. We were the English of Little England. Little black Englishmen."

Their "English education" remained the defining feature of Clarke's and many young Barbadians' colonial British identity. Clarke's mother epitomized the reverence for education — albeit a colonial education — in Barbados. Clarke remembered that his mother told him, "You must learn, son. You hear me? Learn. Learning is next to godliness" (Clarke 2005: 37). However, one of the several issues that Clarke experienced with his English education was that he and his Black Barbadian peers at Combermere School for Boys, a school for middle- and lower-middle class Barbadians, were taught that the best things came from and were made by the English. Not only were Barbadians taught in schools that England was the epitome of civilization, Clarke and his colleagues were taught "nothing" about Barbados. Clarke (2005: 80) wrote:

> We learned about the Battle of Hastings; the Battle of Bannockburn; about Kings who lost their heads; about Kings who kept their heads; and about Kings whose wives lost theirs … I knew *all* (author's emphasis) about the Kings; the Tudors, Stuarts and Plantagenets; and the Wars of the Roses; but nothing was taught about Barbados.

Moreover, the author and his fellow Combermerians were taught by English school masters to act superior and discriminate against fellow Barbadians since they were educated in and expected to perpetuate British class attitudes. Clarke (2005: 56, 80) recalled that "we lived in Barbados, but we studied English society and manners," and that he was "more at ease in England, the Mother Country, than in Barbados." Clarke stated how *his* British history shaped his British identity: "I just loved and cherished my past in the *History of England* book. I did not use it as a stepping stone to the Civil Service or the Department of Sanitary Inspection. I decided instead to live it, to make it a part of me" (Clarke 2005: 56, 80–81). Using Clarke and the Barbadian Londoners as a case study, one can argue that Black Barbadians did believe themselves to be British. One may dispute the subjectivity of oral or autobiographical history; however, it is difficult to undermine Clarke's account that the curriculum taught British history. I argue that similar to Clarke, most Barbadian children adopted British history as their own. More importantly, this section has highlighted that Barbadians did not simply adopt a British identity because it was the only identity they knew and were taught in schools; they had a British *habitus*. One can argue that the only difference between the British of "Little England" and the British in the "Mother Country" was their skin colour.

The socially and historically constructed identity of Black Barbadians contributed to anti-Black Canadian immigration policies. White Canadians shared the British constructed liberal racial order and, subsequently, its negative perceptions of Blacks and Black Barbadians. Similar to the presence of climate discrimination in Canadian immigration, Canada used fallacious and constructed stereotypes of Black Barbadians and West Indians as reasonable means of exclusion. This Canadian belief of Black inferiority, which paralleled the negative construction of African-Barbadian identity, dictated their anti-Black and anti-Black Barbadian immigration policy. Mobilizing White hegemonic power operated throughout geographical time and space.

Historical and geographical boundaries must be challenged to understand the diachronic nature of racialization. The historiography on race and anti-Black racism in Canada rarely examines the ideological roots of identity construction and the ascription of negative codifiers that dictate institutional and personal discrimination; we must historicize race. This negation normalizes Whites and Canadian Whiteness and assumes that all "non-Whites" or racialized groups are excluded — physically and ideologically — simply because the British liberal racial order defined difference as inferior. While nationalist primordial attachment did play a significant role in Canadian xenophobia, the Slave Trade, the institution of slavery and colonialism throughout the Americas constructed the Black African as a picayune pejorative stereotype; an individual and collective that should be hidden, excluded and dominated by White hegemonic power. Moreover, the Black Barbadian's colour superseded her or his British identity. The historiography on Canadian immigration must examine the concept of the undesirable and homogenized non-White immigrant — in this case the Black Barbadian — in conjunction with the construction of Whiteness and the concept of a "White Canada" that dictated immigration policy up to 1962. Race is one of the organizing principles that influenced migration; however, one must acknowledge codependent binary identities. As White slave traders generalized the heterogeneity of people from the African continent, they simultaneously created the White race to perpetuate the inequality of phenotypic difference to maintain hegemonic rule in society. During the early twentieth century, race continued to authenticate imperial citizenship as a means to maintain socially and politically constructed White nationalist sentiments. Early to mid-twentieth-century Canadian immigration policy was a manifestation of the state's need to maintain White hegemonic rule by the exclusion of all Blacks and racialized groups; individuals that could, and did, challenge the fallacy of White "natural" supremacy. Barbadian Emigrant Ambassadors and the Autonomous Bajan were the antithesis of Canadian perceptions of ideological Black identity and forced Canadians policy-makers and the public to redefine the historical negativity assigned to Black Barbadians and West Indians. One must challenge Black inferiority stereotypes and argue that through Barbadian Government initiatives, the pursuit of education and upward social mobility through academic success became Barbadian cultural characteristics. This provides a foundation that uplifts and redefines Barbadian collective migration agency. No longer can one accept that Barbadians simply left the island because of an ancestral forced migration *habitus*; late nineteenth- and early to mid-twentieth-century Barbadian emigration was a deliberate movement supported and encouraged by the Island's government.

Notes

1   William Lyon Mackenzie King, "The Diaries of William Lyon Mackenzie King, February 13, 1947," *Library and Archives Canada* <www.collectionscanada.gc.ca/ databases/king/001059-119.02-e.php?&page_id_nbr=29395&interval=20&&P HPSESSID=kjrmhp00c9o1angknic2bhtke2> [accessed January 4, 2013]; William Lyon Mackenzie King, "The Diaries of William Lyon Mackenzie King, May 1, 1947, page 396," *Library and Archives Canada* <www.collectionscanada.gc.ca/databases/ king/001059-119.02-e.php?&page_id_nbr=29662&interval=20&&&&&&&& &&PHPSESSID=kjrmhp00c9o1angknic2bhtke2> [accessed January 4, 2013].

2   The data from this table, and the following two, was collected from Eltis, Behrendt, Richardson and Klein 1999.

Chapter Two

THE POLITICS
OF EDUCATION

Any suggestion that Caribbean migration can somehow be characterised as uncoordinated and essentially chaotic, has to be firmly rejected. (Pot ter 2005: 27)

The Barbadian political environment between the 1930s and the 1960s facilitated the emigration of Barbadians during the postwar period. I argue early twentieth-century Barbados displayed a democratic political culture that was fundamentally based in the socio-economic uplifting of its Black population. It was the educational reforms instituted by the Barbadian Government beginning in the 1920s that became the platform for the Emigrant Ambassadors' and the Autonomous Bajans' transnational pursuits. Education in Barbados was at a premium and revered by both its government and its citizens. Education was the foundation for socio-economic mobility, and the Barbadian Government instituted several policies to ensure access to education for all Barbadian youth during this period. One must underscore the government's overwhelming support for education, its financing of elementary and secondary school studies, as well as its support for students willing to partake in post-secondary education overseas through scholarships and bursaries. The framework is provided for the study's argument that a highly educated population in an overpopulated British West Indian colony created avenues for social mobility abroad. Along with its power to deconstruct stereotypes of Blackness, educational capital was a means for emigration. The government supported the education of its citizens under the premise that they would contribute to the betterment of their country as individuals and as a collective. However, with limited opportunities on the Island, most Barbadians used their education capital as a means to emigrate.

The Rise of Black Barbadian Democracy, 1938–1966

The Barbadian House of Assembly was first established in 1639, making it the third oldest legislative body in the British Commonwealth after the British Parliament and the Bermuda House of Assembly. With the signing of the Articles of Agreement in 1652 with Barbados and the Government of Oliver Cromwell, the Barbadian Government was appointed a Governor, Council, and Assembly. In 1881, Barbados gained significant control over implementing its own government policy with the establishment of the Executive Committee. For the first time in Barbadian history, local members of the Assembly, the Governor, his official advisers, four members of the of the House of Assembly, and one member of the Legislative Council were "given the opportunity to advise on official policy" (Hoyos 2003: 174–77). Free Blacks were first given the right to vote for members of the House of Assembly in 1831, and further reductions in voting qualifications in 1884 allowed (mostly) disenfranchised Blacks with an income qualification of £50 the right to vote (Hoyos 2003: 174–77).

Late nineteenth-century Barbadian politicians were described as the "proudest aristocracy in the Caribbean" (Hoyos 1963: 8). Local Black politicians in the early and mid-twentieth century fought to deconstruct the oppressive oligarchy of White male rulers. Sir Grantley Adams, the Oxford-trained "gradualist liberal reformer" lawyer and arguably one of Barbados' and the Caribbean's most prominent and accomplished politicians, spearheaded the launch of the Barbados Labour Party (BLP) in October 1938. The leaders "set about the task of forming an organisation to lead and represent working-class opinion" (Beckles 1990: 170). The BLP, later to be known as the Barbados Progressive League, and finally reverting back to its original name, was "a political organisation designed to 'provide political expression for the island's law-abiding inhabitants'" (Beckles 1990: 171). The BLP was a "middle-class-led organisation vying for a mass base in order to confront and eventually reduce the oligarchal political power of the consolidated merchant-planter elite" (Beckles 1990: 171). Through gradual reforms, the Barbados Progressive League and Adams argued it was in the best interest of the ruling class elite in the long run to grant concessions to the working class. The BLP's official slogan — "Three units, one arm: raising the living standards for the working class" — explicitly summarized its defense of the working class (Beckles 1990: 175).

Adams and the BLP fought for universal voting rights. With the implementation of the 1943 *Representation of the People Act*, "the number of persons now able to vote increased by some 510 per cent, and women, for the first time in the colony's history, got the franchise" (Beckles 1990: 178). By 1950, Adams and the BLP gained the majority in the House of Assembly and pushed for adult suffrage. The BLP-backed bill passed, and in April 1950, "property or income requirements for both voting and House membership were removed" (Beckles 1990: 185–186). The Barbados Labour Party acted as the catalyst for voting amendments and full representation of Barbadian colonial citizens. Enfranchisement precipitated political independence. On February 1, 1954, Barbados earned a full ministerial government, where "a semi-cabinet system was put into operation ... and the Governor was bound to accept policy decisions made by ministers. As far as Adams was concerned, the island was now enjoying a practical degree of internal self-government" (Beckles 1990: 189). The Black working classes during the 1950s now had a democratic voice within a gradually reforming colonial parliamentary system. Barbadian political culture on the eve of independence in 1966, and during the period which many of the emigrants represented by this study left the Island, was one of class and labour reforms and equality for all citizens.

Fractures within the Barbados Labour Party during the 1950s problematized the class-based, and consequently race-based, nature of Barbadian labour-centric politics. By 1952, Errol Barrow, a fellow BLP member, "was reported as making frequent critical comments on Adams' conservatism and illustrating that he had the intellectual capacity and stamina to cope with Adams' assaults" (Beckles 1990: 190). Irreparable differences led to the creation of Barrow's Democratic Labour Party (DLP) on April 27, 1955. The DLP was "the long-awaited organisation to counter Adams' growing conservatism and softness on the colonial question" (Beckles 1990: 193). The DLP represented the Black working class and the Black middle class, and the party was favoured by the urban youth. On December 5, 1961, precipitated in part by the impending collapse of the West Indies Federation, the DLP "took the Barbados Labour Party out of office with a clean sweep" (Beckles 1990: 195). In 1965, following yet another failed attempt of West Indian political unity with the "Little Eight" federation of the Leeward and Windward Islands, Barrow pushed for total Barbadian autonomy and independence. His leadership during the early 1960s focused on development through foreign investment and free secondary education for all Barbadians, which was achieved in 1962. Under Barrow and the DLP, a Barbados campus of the University of the West Indies was opened in October 1963 in Cave Hill. The DLP's "commitment to the educational development of the population improved considerably the government's image, locally and overseas" (Beckles 1990: 197). Several features characterized Barbadian politics and its political culture on the eve of colonial independence in 1966. These included autonomy and development through class-based social reforms; a reinterpretation of Blackness, Black self-rule, and Black Power; and education (Beckles 1990: 190–200). Hilary McD. Beckles (1990: 201) postulated:

The black community certainly appeared more confident in its expression of its hitherto stultified nationalist sentiments. The rapidly expanding professional black middle classes, in particular, became the advocates of a revived radical political ideology that demanded the imposition of government pressure upon the white corporate elite in order to liberalise employment policies. In addition, black power activists urged the government to use its fiscal and legislative power in order to democratise the ownership of economic resources.

A political culture characterized by Black conservatism within socio-economic and race-based reforms marked Barbadian political and racial stability as opposed to the respective turmoil of Jamaica and Trinidad in the 1960s (Henry and Miller 2009: 261–267). Despite its progressive race consciousness, the DLP "remained cautious on the question of white economic and racial domination in Barbados" (Beckles 1990: 204). The Barbadian Government went so far as to prevent influential Trinidadian-born Black Power activist Stokely Carmichael from speaking in Barbados. Furthermore, the 1970 *Public Order Act* not only "sought to suppress the black power movement, but also to escalate police surveillance of known black-consciousness radicals" (Beckles 1990: 204). The class-conscious ideals of both the BLP and the DLP superseded the seemingly militant aspects of the Black Power movement; however, the development of a Black professional class constituted "perhaps the most noticeable social feature of the post-independence era" (Beckles 1990: 207). Capitalizing on the political socialist ideals of the global Black Power movements of the 1960s, Barbadian Black Power was synonymous with Black leadership, mobility and socio-economic empowerment within the structures of a White-dominated capitalist system. The government's expansion of the White-controlled corporate sector, foreign multinational corporations and banking and finance institutions facilitated the growth of an influential Black middle class. It appeared Barbadian class consciousness ostensibly superseded Black consciousness, but socio-economic reforms and the access to education for all classes and colours of Barbadians uplifted a race and a nation. The universal access to the elementary, secondary and tertiary education systems acted as "evidence of the basic egalitarian nature" of the Barbadian social order (Beckles 1990: 210). Barbados of the 1960s and beyond was a country where "working class families were able to produce individuals who could be found within all social groups" (Beckles 1990: 210). Prime Minister Barrow contended that independence was not exclusively political or economic, but an "intellectual process," and argued that citizens should always look critically at the "mirror image of themselves" (Beckles 1990: 210). Black Barbadians in Canada during this period not only cherished but also appreciated the political process due to the fact that most of them understood disenfranchisement during their lifetimes.

The Barbadian Education System

The pursuit of education and the Barbadian education system were two driving forces behind the emigration of a highly upwardly mobile population during the mid-twentieth century. Barbadian Government domestic policies had focused on the education of Blacks and all Barbadian children since the late eighteenth century. These policies in turn contributed to the Barbadian Government's emigration schemes and their selection of Emigrant Ambassadors. Barbadian officials were confident that these educated individuals were well-suited to represent themselves and the Island as "exceptional" migrants. Prior to a discussion of the history of Barbadian emigration schemes, it must be established that the individuals involved were not illiterate degenerate objects devoid of any means to contribute to the betterment of a twentieth-century post-Emancipation Barbadian society — a pejorative "Black" identity that was thoroughly discussed in Chapter One. They utilized their education capital to capitalize on opportunities abroad in the face of limited opportunities at home. During the late nineteenth century, overpopulation of an unskilled labouring class precipitated earlier discussions of sponsored emigration. However, late nineteenth-century Barbadian officials feared the loss of highly skilled labour through emigration. During the mid-twentieth century, Barbados experienced a "brain drain" of a highly educated and upwardly mobile population, following the implementation of a comprehensive education system. The out-migration of this class of the population plagued Barbados throughout its history. Throughout its post-Emancipation history, Barbados trained and educated a population that was not confined to the Island's geographical boundary of 166 square miles; Barbados operated within a system which saw education as a means for self-empowerment and growth within a liberalized and globalized environment. In his memoir, Austin Clarke (2005: 211) wrote of the importance of a successfully completed education for the social mobility of young Black Barbadians:

> So we prepared ourselves for this [Cambridge University Senior Cambridge Examination overseas], the most important event in our lives. It could determine whether we were going to be sanitary inspectors for the rest of our lives or were going to get into the Civil Service, not the Department of Customs, which buried men alive from drink, but the "Col-Sec's Offices," and rise to positions of power and hold confidential files under the soiled arms of our white shirts. Perhaps to be given an OBE (Order of the British Empire) at age fifty, with one foot in the grave …
>
> This examination determined whether we would qualify and go up to England by boat, third class, tourist class, with a borrowed winter coat, and enter one of the Inns of Court, and after eighteen months' studying the law, return and flood the country; and get MP behind our name.

It determined whether we would be able to enter a British university. It meant life and could mean death. If you were not lucky and careful and had failed, it meant that for generations afterwards people would whisper when you passed, and say that you had wasted your mother's money and had not got your Senior Cambridge.

Education was not taken for granted, and educated and skilled Barbadians capitalized on these opportunities first throughout the Caribbean basin, the United States, the United Kingdom, and finally to Canada. The Barbadian Government facilitated the emigration of its people to various locations abroad, but the early twentieth-century emphasis on education provided the foundation for the Autonomous Bajan to challenge the racialized structures of the international migration system. The Government of Barbados provided both the education and the schemes necessary to assist the emigration of Barbadians during this period. Despite not being able to afford to attend secondary school at the time, Reginald Eric Taylor benefitted from the Island's emphasis on the right to education for all of its primary school–aged children and the belief that education was a vehicle to self-empowerment and upward mobility. He then capitalized on his government's sponsored recruitment schemes to England for Barbadians to work for London Transport in 1960. While in England, he took every opportunity to improve his education, skills and qualifications as an automotive engineer. Another Barbadian London Transport employee, John Simmons, stated that "most of us (Barbadian emigrants) wanted to use LT (London Transport) as a route out and up, I mean, for example to do night school" (quoted in Western 1992: 226). Taylor was not only a "model" emigrant, but he exemplified what education meant to a culture that inculcated the Barbadian Government's belief that academic success was the means for upward mobility. The "culture-of-academic success" or the "culture-of-education" is a more appropriate description as opposed to the misrepresentation of a "culture-of-migration" when describing Barbadian culture during the mid-twentieth century. The pursuit of education is a fundamental Barbadian characteristic that contributed to and enabled the emigration of an upwardly mobile population. Any discussion on Barbadian emigration push factors must begin with the history of education on the Island to contextualize the positive and internationally marketable characteristics of the Autonomous Bajan prior to his and her migration abroad.

Education as a means for Barbadian social mobility and prosperity originated in the late seventeenth century. The "philanthropic efforts of private individuals and by the humanitarian interest of the Churches" founded the Barbadian education system (Ministry of Education 2000). The majority of the older existing public schools were initially founded for the education of White Barbadian children during slavery. Elementary schools for newly emancipated Black slaves on the Island grew out of the Anglican, Moravian and Methodist Churches' efforts to deliver a Christian education. John Elliot and Rowland Bulkley donated the considerably large sum of $1,000 for the establishment of a school for poor White children in 1686. In 1709, Captain Francis Williams donated one hundred acres to launch a charity school for White children, which became the Foundation School in Christ Church. The establishment of First Grade schools continued in the early to mid-eighteenth century as Thomas Harrison, a "merchant planter," founded the Grammar School for Boys, or Harrison College, in 1733. By 1745, the Codrington Foundation established the Codrington Grammar School, which subsequently became the Lodge School. In 1710, the Codrington Foundation was established under "the will of Sir Christopher Codrington," a colonial governor and planta- tion owner, after "two estates in St. John were bequeathed to the Society for the Propagation of the Gospel to provide a College for the training of missionaries" (Ministry of Education 2000). The first school for Free Black or Coloured boys was established in 1818 in Bridgetown. School fees covered administrative and operational costs, while the Missionary Society salaried a school master. The girls' equivalent was established in 1827. The education of Black Barbadian former slaves increased after Emancipation in 1834 as churches founded schools near or on their properties. Between 1835 and 1845, the British Government granted funds for the education of former slaves, and by 1844, there were 48 Anglican, 4 Moravian, 4 Wesleyan, and 149 private schools and a total enrolment of 7,452 students. By 1846, the Barbadian Legislature provided the first state education grant of £750. Government expenditures and its involvement in education increased exponen- tially with the passing of the first *Education Act* in 1850. The Act established the education committee that included a part-time inspector who served as its execu- tive officer. The £750 education grant increased to £3,000 per annum, and by 1878 the new *Education Act* fixed the spending at £15,000. At the turn of the twentieth century, the Barbadian colonial government officially recognized 169 elementary schools with an enrolment of 24,415 children and 532 students attending the three First Grade and five Second Grade schools, respectively. The First Grade schools provided teaching of particularly high standards, which enabled "boys to sit for open scholarships at English Universities" (Ministry of Education 2000).

The historical emphasis on education continued to expand during the twenti- eth century with the growth of an established freed Black Barbadian citizenry in search of avenues for self-improvement so as to emancipate themselves from the shackles of legislated ignorance during slavery. The 1927 *Colonial Report* recorded that the highly educated population needed employment outlets to succeed and for the chance for social mobility. With limited opportunities in Barbados due to its geographical size and population density, emigration was a means for the edu- cated to seek socio-economic mobility and prosperity. Colonial officials reported:

The aptitude of the Barbadian as a skilled worker is abundantly in evidence, and it is by the development of this feature that he can hope to advance if, as may easily be the case, he should some day meet with disappointment in securing employment in Barbados of a kind of sufficient to place him on a higher social plane than that from which, in the peculiar circumstances of life in his over populated country, he may otherwise find it difficult to emerge. For the present the education system provides for each succeeding vacant junior clerkship in the Public Service a comparatively large number of well-educated candidates of whom some have reached to the highest educational standards attainable locally and many have for considerable periods been unsuccessful in obtaining clerical appointments.[1]

By the late 1920s, the free elementary education system was considerably successful in providing the training needed for a highly intelligent and skilled middle-class workforce. The system was — and continued to be — a success. The *Colonial Report* described how it prepared countless Barbadians for the public service, and many pursued their education as a way to secure meaningful employment and improve their social standing on the Island. However, the lack of employment opportunities in Barbados curtailed the aspirations of young Barbadians and their newly attained educational capital. Education was a means for mobility and an avenue to escape poverty and destitution, and the public service epitomized societal success. A new class of highly educated and unemployed youth emerged during the late 1920s and beyond; youth desperately sought means to be placed "on a higher social plane" as described in the 1927 *Colonial Report*.[2] The education system worked, but it also facilitated the push for young Barbadians to emigrate to search abroad for the meaningful employment and financial opportunities that Barbadian society could not provide. Barbados thus exported its most valuable commodity — its highly skilled and educated citizens. Education was the foundation for Barbadian progress, development, independence and, most importantly, its history of emigration.

The Barbadian Government maintained and funded the Island's elementary schools. The Board of Education managed the elementary schools through nine individuals appointed by the Governor and seven elected by members of the Legislature. In total, the Board recognized 129 elementary schools and three First Grade schools. The First Grade schools included the boys' Harrison College and Lodge School, and the girls' Queen's College. These schools provided teaching at particularly high standards, which enabled "boys to sit for open scholarships at English Universities."[3] By 1927, the government abolished all school fees for elementary children and established St. Michael's Girls' School. In 1928, the government proposed the establishment of a West Indian University.[4] The abolishment of school fees increased the access to education for all Barbadian children and provided equal opportunity and avenues for self-empowerment. Literacy and education became a cultural birthright. Elementary school children educated in the late 1920s and 1930s became the first cohort of mass emigrants in the post-Second World War era. Education provided the opportunity and skills needed to pass the particularly high barriers set for immigration in Britain, Canada and the United States in the 1950s and 1960s. By the late 1920s, Barbadians used education as a means to acquire cultural and social capital that they could exchange for opportunities abroad.

Governmental support of the education system continued throughout the 1930s and 1940s. The government issued £1,330 for university education in 1938, and in 1949, the number of government-funded elementary schools fell slightly to 124.[5] The three First Grade schools — Harrison College, Queen's College and Lodge School — prepared "candidates for the General Certificate Examinations of the Oxford and Cambridge Board at Scholarship, Advanced and Ordinary Levels in classics, mathematics, science, and modern studies."[6] Government schools provided the necessary training and teaching excellence for Barbadians to attend prestigious universities in Britain. More importantly, the government extended tremendous support for post-secondary education during the postwar period. The 1949 *Government Scholarships and Exhibitions Act* provided five Barbadian scholarships; two exhibitions tenable at the University College of the West Indies and two Island scholarships tenable at Barbados' teachers' college. Exceptional academic achievement was paramount as Barbados Scholarship winners attained "a standard equal to that prescribed by the Colleges of the Universities of Oxford and Cambridge."[7] Scholarships were awarded "from the results of the General Certificate Examinations at Advanced and Scholarship Levels of the Oxford and Cambridge Schools Examination Board."[8] Many Black Barbadian students achieved standards on par or greater than those of British pupils. Academic excellence was not judged, nor based on, comparative Barbadian, West Indian or colonial standards, but rather those created and implemented in the British metropole. Barbadians strove for academic success, and the government awarded the best and the brightest with the opportunity to pursue post-secondary education on the Island and abroad. The government mandated access to education and provided the financial support necessary to those wanting to pursue higher education. The Higher Education (Loan Fund) of 1953 was designed to lend financial assistance to students wanting to attend post-secondary institutions. In 1955, $31,976 was loaned to twenty-one students. Of the twenty-one individuals, thirteen students attended University College of the West Indies; five pursued their education in the United Kingdom; two in the United States; and one at Codrington College in Barbados.[9]

By the late 1950s and early 1960s, 116 primary schools were free for both boys and girls aged 5 to 14; education and access to education became the main priority for the Barbadian Government. That being said, male to female enrolment ratios began to show an alarming trend. The male to female ratio was relatively similar for elementary school enrolment and attendance; however, the same cannot be said at the secondary level. More than twice the number of boys (1,017) attended First Grade schools compared to 467 girls. One must note that by the late 1950s and early 1960s, there was only one First Grade school for girls (Queen's College) as opposed to two for boys (Harrison College and Lodge School).[10]

The gender bias was interesting to note because it was in fact educated women who first acted as Barbadian Emigrant Ambassadors to Canada beginning with the Domestic Scheme in 1955. The Domestic Scheme was the "first full-scale recruitment of West Indian women to Canada," initiated by the Canadian Government in 1955 (Silvera 1989: 7). The initial program included women from Jamaica and Barbados. To qualify, the woman had to be between the ages of eighteen and thirty-five; single; have attained at least the equivalent of a Grade 8 education; and able to pass a medical examination. The final applicants were interviewed in the Caribbean by Canadian immigration officials. A number of the women supported their households and children in the West Indies as "sole-support mothers" (Silvera 1989: 7). They were granted landed immigrant status upon their arrival in Canada and had to work in a home for one year. After the year they could remain as a domestic or find work elsewhere (Silvera 1989: 7). Most women under the Domestic Scheme settled in Montreal and Toronto, and approximately 2,250 women came to Canada under the Scheme as of 1955 to the late 1960s. By the 1960s, there was a quota of 280 women a year, with 104 from Jamaica and the rest from the Leeward and Windward Islands, Trinidad, Barbados and Guyana (Henry 1968: 83). The women chosen under the Scheme acted as their government's representatives in Canada to showcase the suit-ability, integration and upward mobility of future Barbadian emigrants. These Emigrant Ambassadors, along with the nurses, teachers and students who also emigrated during this period, challenged and dispelled the racialized myths of the undesirability of Black migrants in Canada while their industriousness and per-severance in Canadian households and public institutions promoted increased emigration outlets that their government desired. Through their exceptional efforts and stalwart dedication, discipline, socio-economic success, and their ability to manipulate both the Canadian and Barbadian patriarchal system for their personal and professional gain, these women as individuals and as a group became the influential catalyst in the liberalization of Canadian immigration. This showed the irony in the misguided belief that women only needed a rudi-mentary elementary education in order to succeed in gendered spheres of work, most notably employment as a domestic. Domestic work became a vehicle for success, pride and nationhood.

Despite the gendered discrepancy at the secondary level, education was the highest government expenditure between 1958 and 1961. For 1958–1959, the Barbadian Government spent $3,254,841; between 1959–1960, they spent $3,644,009; and in 1960–1961, $3,798,221.[11] The education budget included expenditures for tuition fees and teacher training. Effective January 1962, all tuition fees were abolished for all Barbadian children at all government schools, including secondary schools. During this same period, the government pushed for comprehensive teacher training and looked abroad to Canada for assistance. As quoted in the 1960–1961 *Colonial Reports*, Canadian teachers came to Barbados "in the early half of 1961, the Erdiston [Teachers'] Training College (opened in 1948) for teachers has the benefit of services of Dr. F.L. Bates; a Canadian education expert loaned to the West Indies under a scheme for Technical Assistance by Canada to the West Indies."[12] Barbados also produced scholarships to send Barbadian teachers to Canada for further education. These included one Commonwealth Scholarship for teacher training in Canada in 1962, and by 1963 the number of scholarships rose to two. Other teacher training scholarships included two scholarships for technical teachers and five scholarships in Geography for 1962.[13]

To put this in perspective, in 1955, out of a total population of 229,119 Barbadians, 35,577 children were enrolled in primary schools. This equates to approximately 16 percent of Barbados' total population in primary school. Out of that number there was almost complete gender equality in primary schools for boys (18,289) and girls (17,688). In Canada in 1955, out of a total population of approximately 15,601,000, a total of 2,681,000 children were enrolled in grades 1 to 8. This was approximately 17 percent of Canada's total population.[14] Education was, and is, a fundamental feature of not only the government's budgetary expenditure, but the country's collective upbringing of generations of past, present and future Autonomous Bajans and Emigrant Ambassadors.

The Legacy of (Free) Education

Change is inevitable. Free access to education has become a part of true Barbadian social and political identity; however, the economic recession of the late 2000s has put a significant strain on the Barbadian economy and particularly its government expenditures. While this book focuses on education at primary and secondary levels, the downloading of the cost of tertiary tuition to Barbadian students at the Cave Hill Campus of the University of the West Indies (UWI) is indicative of a larger battle of the Island's citizens' right to free education at all levels of their respective academic careers. Some may argue, especially in continental North America, that education at the tertiary level is more of a privilege than a right. This is a myopic view of education as simply an avenue for children's basic literacy and numeracy. An individual can no longer compete in a knowledge economy of the twenty-first century without training — education — beyond the primary and secondary school levels. This is even more crucial for a developing island such as Barbados, where its citizens must struggle to find their place in the global economy. Arguably, a university degree has become what the secondary school diploma was to Emigrant Ambassadors who emigrated to Canada and the United Kingdom. As the world continues to shrink, the Barbadian Government must continue to put its citizens on the starting line of the globalized race for jobs and international development. However, at what cost?

This is a debate that has divided Barbadians on political and generational lines. As it was announced that Barbadians would have to pay tuition at the Cave Hill Campus of UWI at the start of the 2014–2015 academic year, Sherwyn Walters of the *Nation News Barbados* (August 27, 2013) exclaimed that the presiding DLP Government has "slaughtered a sacred cow, spit on the Right Excellent Errol Walton Barrow's grave, attacked poor people and compromised that which is the greatest avenue to the country's progress." Furthermore, Sir Hilary Beckles, pro-vice-chancellor and principal of Cave Hill, argued that "the Cabinet members have had 65 years of free publicly funded tertiary education ... and I do not believe for one moment that a collection of men and women who had ... free public-funded tertiary education at UWI, will in any way, do anything to prevent others from having the same" (*Nation News Barbados* August 13, 2013).

Why would the current DLP Government that gained notoriety as the "poor Black people's party" and presided over the implementation of free tertiary educa-tion in the 1960s — and whose leaders capitalized on said access — end a program that has universally benefitted all Barbadians who wished to go to university? With the country still mired in a deep recession, the current DLP Government has had to weigh the value of tertiary education to determine whether it is a right, as it has historically been, or a privilege. The debates are heated, historical, driven by economics and fueled by ideological principles on the "right" to an education. Numerous Barbadian newspaper articles have weighed in on this contentious issue. One journalist proclaimed that "selfish" Barbadians show little gratitude or responsibility to this "privilege" to the right to free tertiary education. Walters (August 27, 2013) argued that "we [Barbadians] have not trained our graduates of the free into the idea of transcendent payback. And the spiel of 'personal prospects' (social mobility) has reaped what it sowed." Ironically, it was this same idea of social mobility that propelled a generation of Barbadians during the mid-twentieth century — Emigrant Ambassadors — to seek greater avenues of success beyond the Island's 166 square miles. Meanwhile, fast forward to the new millennium, and this same championed attribute is now seen as a detriment to Barbadian society. This is not a demand for the repatriation of foreign nationals, but a call to action for the "spectacular commitment to society, to the national cause" of collective well-being over personal progress (Walters August 27, 2013). Explicitly, the call is for those Barbadians educated at the Cave Hill Campus of UWI to understand that their government gave them this opportunity as a form of domestic policy for the development of the country. This is analogous to the Island's push with the Emigrant Ambassadors as agents of Barbadian foreign policy to challenge discriminatory international immigration policies in the mid-twentieth century.

Education as an ideological concept, and not simply a taxpayer-fueled institution, continues to tear the fabric of its precious past on the Island. It must not be forgotten that education was, and is, a tool to escape the shackles of mental slavery and legislated ignorance. Barbados and the West Indies was "never a place for the intellectual and spiritual development of the forcefully imported population" in a society where "the brothel, rather than the library, was the source of relaxation for the local monied group, while the majority of population was valued only as a source of labour" (Joseph August 13, 2013). Under the cloud of fiduciary responsibility, Barbadian officials at all levels spoke on the need to promote a culture of education in the lives of boys and girls. Referring specifically to the role of education in the lives of Barbados' young female population, Chief Commissioner Ruth Parris of the Barbados Girl Guide Association stated that "it helps the mind to grow and it is in the only way they (Barbadian girls) can make informed decisions when they have to" (*Nation News Barbados* February 23, 2014). Deputy Principal of Deighton Griffith Secondary School, Anthony Alleyne, disaggregated the idea that education and schooling are synonymous. He contended that "there are some who believe that as long as you get 100 percent on a test or get your degree or you get that piece of paper that you have achieved, that you are educated, but it is not just about what you learn but about what you do with what you learn" (*Nation News Barbados* February 23, 2014). His comments speak to the idea that education — arguably, free tertiary education — is a social contract between the government and its citizens, its citizens to society, and Barbadians to one another. Alleyne's statement is further compounded by the rhetoric of "free" education. DLP member Ronald Jones, Minister of Education, Science, Technology and Innovation, postulated the fallacy of "free" education. It was not free, since Barbadian taxpayers funded the system: "education is free to students but a cost to taxpayers" (Headley August 27, 2014). However, the historically marginalized population of poor Black Barbadians must be cautious when the access to free education is threatened: "It is an old elitist instinct to lament the fact that every Sambo has a degree" (Joseph August 13, 2013).

A Canadian audience constantly facing rising tuition fees may not truly sympathize with this debate. For the 2014–2015 school year, Barbadians enrolled in full-time courses are expected to pay the following: $5,625 Barbados dollars (BBD) in the Faculties of Humanities and Education, Social Sciences, and Science & Technology; $8,808 in the Faculty of Law; $16,618 in the Faculty of Medical Sciences — Clinical; and $65,000 in Medical Sciences — Pre-Clinical (*Nation News Barbados* August 13, 2013). In comparison, in 2013–2014, Canadian students enrolled in undergraduate studies in Canada paid $5,079 Canadian dollars in the Humanities; $4,378 in Education; $5,107 in the Social and Behavioural Sciences; $10,030 in Law, Legal Professions and Studies; and $12,438 in Medicine.[15] The average undergraduate tuition in Canada for 2013–2014 was $5,772, and in Ontario, the costliest province, the number rose to $7,259.[16] Tuition rates in Barbados seem to be on par with those in Canada. However, it must be taken into account that Barbados' Gross Domestic Product (GDP) per capita in 2012 was $14,917.10 USD compared to Canada's of $51,206.20 USD in the same year.[17] Furthermore, as of the end of May 2014, one Canadian dollar was worth almost two Barbadian dollars (Central Bank of Barbados 2014). In theory it would then cost a Barbadian twice the amount a Canadian would pay for tuition in Canada — irrespective of international student tuition fees. Meanwhile, the Island's GDP per capita is a third of that of Canada.

This is where Barbados' economic commitment to educating the masses is truly remarkable, most notably at the tertiary level. In 1999, the Barbadian Government spent $51 million BBD with an enrollment of 3,568 undergraduate students at Cave Hill. Following a major expansion in 2003–2004, the number rose to 6,718 in 2007 with an annual cost of $79.3 million BBD. By 2013, 7,200 undergraduate students attended Cave Hill. Government expenditures rose exponentially between 2007 and 2012. Between 1999 and 2007, the Barbadian Government spent $543.2 million BBD on tertiary education for its population, while the figure rose to $636.3 million BBD between 2008 and 2012. Since 2006, the total contribution to Cave Hill by the Barbadian Government exceeded the amount spent on all nursery schools, primary schools, secondary schools, the Barbados Community College, and the Samuel Jackman Prescod Polytechnic combined (*Nation News Barbados* August 13, 2013). It is clear that with the introduction of tuition fees in 2014–2015, Barbados' admirable contribution to its citizens' tertiary educational needs was simply economically unsustainable. It is fair to argue that the government could not compromise its fiduciary responsibility to the access to quality and world-class education at the primary and secondary levels. In 2010, the Barbadian Government's public expenditure per student as a percentage of its GDP per capita was 40.3 percent. Comparatively, it was 22.7 percent at the primary school level in 2007 and 25 percent for secondary school in 2010. Of a total GDP of $4.225 billion USD in 2012 with a population of 283,000, the Barbadian Government's public expenditure on education as a percentage of its total GDP was 5.6 percent.

In terms of its public expenditure on education as a percentage of total government spending, the number rose to 13.4 percent — 15.4 percent in 2004 (Data-Barbados n.d.). In one of the wealthiest countries in the world with a population of 34.75 million and a GDP of $1.780 trillion USD in 2012, the Canadian Government's public expenditure on education as a percentage of its GDP in 2011 was 5.4 percent. Of its total government expenditure, 12.2 percent was spent on education in 2011 — 12.2 percent in 2005 (Data-Canada 2014). In terms of gender, there was a higher ratio of girls to boys in Barbadian primary and secondary schools (104.7 percent) compared to those in Canada (98.9 percent) (Data-Canada n.d.; Data-Barbados n.d.). Barbados spent more of its country's assets, which benefitted more girls than boys, on education compared to Canada, and this economic focus on education must not be overlooked. The Barbadian Government's ideological push for education born in the immediate post-Emancipation era became one of its largest economic expenditures since the mid-twentieth century. This "culture of education" was costly — it continues to be costly even now; however, in this post-recession society, the Barbadian Government must not deviate from its course. It must make changes, including having students pay for at least a portion of their tertiary education with the opportunity for extensive grants and loan programs. Nevertheless, the government must also look to its past. It must recognize that access to free — and possibly now affordable — education in the twentieth century was, and will be in the twenty-first century, the most crucially beneficial investment for its people.

Through their education system, the Barbadian Government prepared its citizens for success and social mobility in the global environment; their education was of a British standard and internationally recognized. Education capital became the means for physical and ideological decolonization. By the 1960s, the government facilitated free and equitable access to education for all Barbadian citizens, and emigration became the result of a comprehensive and well-executed educational strategy. Barbadians succeeded as international migrants with ambitious goals for upward mobility due to a government-facilitated and culturally consolidated emphasis on education. Barbadians were not only educated, but highly educated in a system that to this day still garners substantial respect internationally. Since Emancipation in the mid-nineteenth century, the Barbadian Government played both an indirect and direct role in the emigration of its people. Government initiatives educated an upwardly mobile and transnational population, but Barbadian colonial officials also used emigration schemes to address and alleviate acute social strife caused by overpopulation and unemployment.

Notes

1   Barbados National Archives (hereafter BNA), *Colonial Reports – Annual No. 1422; Barbados, Report for 1927–28* (London: His Majesty's Stationery Office, 1929), 23.
2   Ibid.
3   Ibid., BNA, *Colonial Reports – Annual No. 1422; Barbados, Report for 1927–28* (London: His Majesty's Stationery Office, 1929), 33.
4   Ibid., 7 & 33.
5   BNA, *Colonial Reports – Annual No. 1913; Barbados, Report for 1938–1939* (London: His Majesty's Stationery Office, 1939); BNA, *Colonial Office Annual Report on Barbados for the Year 1949* (London: His Majesty's Stationery Office, 1950).
6   BNA, *Colonial Office Annual Report on Barbados for the Years 1952 and 1953* (London: His Majesty's Stationery Office, 1954), 38.
7   Ibid., 38.
8   Ibid., 38–39.
9   BNA, *Colonial Office Annual Report on Barbados for the Years 1954 and 1955* (London: His Majesty's Stationery Office, 1957), 53.
10 BNA, *Colonial Office Annual Report on Barbados for the Years 1958 and 1959* (Barbados: Government Printing Office, 1961), 50–51.
11 BNA, *Colonial Office Annual Report on Barbados for the Years 1960 and 1961* (Barbados: Government Printing Office, 1962).
12 Ibid.
13 Ibid, 7; BNA, *Colonial Office Annual Report on Barbados for the Years 1962 and 1963* (Barbados: Government Printing Office, 1965), 6, 43, 48; and *Historical Developments of Education in Barbados*, 5.
14 "Canada Year Book 1956," <www66.statcan.gc.ca/eng/acyb_c1956-eng.aspx?opt=/eng/1956/195601810151_p.%20151.pdf> [accessed June 6, 2013]; "Table W1-9: Summary of total full-time enrolment, by level of study, Canada, selected years, 1951 to 1975," <www.statcan.gc.ca/pub/11-516-x/sectionw/W1_9-eng.csv> (CSV Version, 2kb) [accessed June 6, 2013]; "Table W10-20: Summary of total full-time enrolment, by level of study, related to relevant population, Canada, selected years, 1951 to 1975," <www.statcan.gc.ca/pub/11-516-x/sectionw/W10_20-eng.csv> (CSV Version, 3kb) [accessed June 6, 2013].
15 Statistics Canada, "Undergraduate tuition fees for full-time Canadian students, by discipline, by province (Canada)" <www.statcan.gc.ca/tables-tableaux/sum-som/l01/cst01/educ50a-eng.htm> [accessed May 25, 2014].
16 Statistics Canada, "Undergraduate tuition fees for full-time Canadian students, by discipline, by province (Ontario)" <www.statcan.gc.ca/tables-tableaux/sum-som/l01/cst01/educ50a-eng.htm> [accessed May 25, 2014].
17 Data, "GDP Per Capita (Current US$)," The World Bank: Working for a World Free of Poverty <data.worldbank.org/indicator/NY.GDP.PCAP.CD/countries/-XR-BB-CA?display=graph> [accessed May 28, 2014].

Chapter Three

THE AGENCY AND CULTURE OF MOVEMENT

Barbadian Emigration Push Factors

The sending country's social, economic and political factors associated with the historical international migration paradigm are often overlooked, negated and deemed insignificant. With respect to Canadian immigration historiography and immigrants from so-called "less developed" countries, the "pull" takes precedence over the "push," and their motives are either ignored or grossly oversimplified. This aspect marginalizes the agency within the individual's choice to emigrate and creates a hegemonic power structure dominated by the receiving state. Canadian immigration studies must incorporate transnational congruencies and host country sensitivities. The following questions must be asked when studying present day and historical migrations: why would people leave, for what reasons and under what circumstances? Favourable conditions within the host country do not create a magnet for emigrants, nor would one arbitrarily leave the known for the unknown and a possibly precarious socio-economic standing within a new state. Transnational migration is an uncertain, life-changing event, whereby the emigrant's identity, agency and autonomy are challenged through institutionalized structures that both hinder and promote integration. This study of Barbadian emigration contextualizes and creates a specific framework for individual emigrant groups and examines the environments which they left. Studies must consider the social, economic, political and personal determinants, as well as the procurement of the necessary cultural, social and educational capital required for international migration. Studies must also analyze how the sending country prepares its citizens and facilitates avenues for emigration.

The political nature of early emigration from Barbados, including legislated acts and the Barbadian colonial government's decrees for assisted or sponsored emigration, situate the historical migration patterns of Barbadians. The historical documents reveal the government's late nineteenth- and early twentieth-century unequivocal support for emigration as a means to alleviate the burden of over-population and of unemployment. The Barbadian Government regulated the emigration of its population and pursued avenues to settle its people and create labour colonies in other West Indian islands. Emigration to the United States during and immediately following the Second World War and the mass exodus to aid the postwar British reconstruction effort were key historical settlement journeys and sojourns for Barbadians. These movements emphasize the recruitment and selection process for potential migrants destined for the United Kingdom, including the initiation of the British Domestic Workers Scheme. The strategic nature of British migration is paramount in understanding Canada's acceptance of Black West Indian and Barbadian migrants. Canada modeled its Domestic Scheme after that of Britain, and the United Kingdom's *Commonwealth Immigrants Act* of 1962 directly influenced Canada's decision to de-racialize its immigration system that same year. Britain pressured its former North American colony to open its doors to Barbadians as well as racialized peoples from other Commonwealth states. Despite the benefits of this transnational migration, there were considerable negative implications of emigration to Barbadian society on the eve of its colonial independence, November 30, 1966.

A History of Emigration from Barbados

Following Emancipation and the end of apprenticeship in 1838, emigration was a means to solve Barbados' overpopulation and employment crisis. The government sponsored emigration from Barbados in 1860, as "Barbadian planters began to see that the island had a 'super-abundant' population and they took the first steps toward encouraging movement out of the island."[1] Addressing the state of Barbados in the late 1970s, Handler and Large (1978: 14) noted that "Barbados' superabundant population cannot … fairly be attributed to her present demographic character; it is rather historical inertia that is responsible. The island is crowded today partly because it always has been crowded." St. Lucian Nobel Prize-winning economist Sir William Arthur Lewis stated that "Barbados [was] fully peopled in the seventeenth century and [has] been complaining of over-population for nearly three centuries" (quoted in Handler and Large 1978: 14). Barbados' population density since the seventeenth century was due in part to its relatively healthy environment compared to other West Indian islands; the lack of geographic boundaries or "native" inhabitants facilitated easy settlement; and the introduction of sugarcane when slave labour and capital were easy to procure (Lowenthal 1957: 451). One may then argue that due to historical "inertia" and geography, overpopulation is a fundamental feature of Barbadian history, a "problem" that the Barbadian Government began to address with emigration in the mid-nineteenth century.

The *Masters and Servants Act* failed, resulting in overpopulation on the Island. It was designed to produce tenantry in the Island immediately following Emancipation as former slaves were contractually bound to live and work on plantations. The government first proposed migration to other West Indian islands, followed by both South American and Latin American countries, respectively. Following economic decline from the drought in 1863, the Barbadian Government refused to sponsor mass emigration until the twentieth century. In 1863, the July 17 *Barbados Times* newspaper stated that the drought had been "productive of intensive suffering of man and beast," and that the "labouring poor" experienced "severe distress" (Beckles 2004: 95). The newspaper suggested the answer to the drought crisis was emigration because

> there was no possibility of a land reform by which a peasantry could be created. Neither were social welfare measures to be expected from a landed class that had opposed emancipation and continued to see labourers as chattel, in the same category as their animal livestock. (Beckles 2004: 96)

As opposed to larger West Indian islands like Jamaica, with only 166 square miles of densely populated land, Barbados could not support an independent peasantry. Without the net emigration of 104,000 people between 1860 and 1920, Barbados would have had double the population it did in the 1950s — approximately 3,000 people per square mile (Lowenthal 1957: 455). Nevertheless, government-sponsored emigration during this tumultuous late nineteenth-century period did not come to fruition. By 1875, out of a population of 162,000, approximately 3,600, or 2 percent of the population, survived on Poor Relief in Barbados.[2] Barbados could not support its overpopulated and unemployed residents.

Under these difficult conditions, the Governor in Council framed Barbados' first *Emigration Act* in 1873. The *Rules and Regulations* defined an emigrant as

> every labourer, artisan, or domestic servant, and every member of his or her family, the cost of whose passage is paid, or payable by any Government, or by any proprietor or person offering him or her employment, shall be deemed an Emigrant contemplated by these rules.[3]

An emigrant was clearly defined as an individual sponsored by the government or an employer. Government-sponsored emigration schemes were defined in law well before the beginning of the twentieth century. The *Rules and Regulations* stipulated the classification of an emigrant and the voluntary conditions of his or her migration; "the Superintendent of Emigration shall ascertain that every Emigrant is going away voluntarily."[4] Barbados was only thirty-five years removed from the end of slavery and apprenticeship, and the legislated clause of voluntary emigration prohibited the possibility of renewed human trafficking. The document thoroughly outlined the specific duties carried out by the Emigration Office, Emigration Agents and Masters of Emigrant Vessels.[5] It is clear that by the 1870s, Barbadian emigration was a government-regulated, legislated and controlled practice. Since Barbados was such a small country, movement away from plantations following slavery meant migration off the Island. Freedom was exercised through mobility (Marshall 1987: 15–31). Unlike other West Indian colonies, the end of slavery did not result in a complete "overthrow" of the planter class. Compared to Jamaica where most plantation owners were British absentee landlords, in Barbados "a considerable number of estates were owned by local whites" (Hoyos 2003: 127). Through compensation from the British Government, which amounted to approximately £20 per slave, former slave owners adjusted well to a "free" Barbados. This concept of "freedom" in Barbados differed significantly when compared to Jamaica, Trinidad and Guyana. In these colonies, the British were forced to import indentured labourers from Asia, and specifically the Indian subcontinent, to meet labour demands as former slaves left plantations for the cities and formed a Black independent peasantry and free class. In Barbados, former slaves, or "located labour," remained on plantations and worked for their former masters at reduced wages in return for their homes and land allotments. Barbados was dominated by plantations, and its limited and relatively flat geography curtailed the establishment of Black landownership in "uncultivated" lands and mountainous terrain as compared to Jamaica. Former slaves were forced "to continue with their work on the plantations in order to gain a livelihood," and the status quo of White Barbadian landownership remained (Hoyos 2003: 130). For former Barbadian slaves, emigration was effectively a tool for true emancipation.

By 1871 and 1873, "the Barbadian legislature passed an act that actually made provision for assisting certain poor classes to migrate," and "a new policy toward emigration had evolved in Barbados — from a policy of discouragement to one of active encouragement" (Marshall 1987: 16). It was not a "culture-of-migration" if the Barbadian Government classified who was an emigrant and permitted their passage from the Island. The government facilitated the safe passage of its British subjects and effectively regulated the agency of emigration within the structure of a dominant hegemonic colonial government power. At this point in Barbadian history, the Barbadian Government controlled all facets of inter- and intra-island migration, and Black agency in Barbados was restricted by historical "inertia," geography and White landownership. To prevent the post-Emancipation emigration to Guyana, where Guyanese planters actively enticed Barbadians with higher wages, the Barbadian legislature passed a law to "prevent persons enticing inhabitants to 'desert their homes and families and helpless infants'" (Beckles 1990: 112). Barbados effectively restricted emigration:

> [the] law provided that the would-be migrant had first to obtain a ticket of leave from the vestry of the parish in which he resided, which was empowered to refuse the issue of such a pass if it believed that the applicant would leave any dependants unprovided [sic] for. (Beckles 1990: 112)

Workers accused the Barbadian legislature of "tampering" with their rights and agency as Free Blacks to travel and seek employment, and the Governor of Barbados in 1840, Evan John Murray MacGregor, stated that it was not the case. Despite opposition from the pro-planter Barbadian legislature that opposed emigration and the British Colonial Office, by 1840, "hundreds" of predominantly male sojourners emigrated from Barbados for employment in Trinidad and Guyana. By January 1840, "over 2,500 workers had departed for Guiana, and by 1870 at least 16,000 had emigrated to various [British West Indian] colonies" (Beckles 1990: 113). It is interesting to note that Barbadians did not permanently settle in these British West Indian colonies, and seasonal migration dominated the circuitous and temporary sojourns. The Guyanese immigration report of 1883 stated: "They seldom labour for more than limited periods on sugar estates. A large proportion of them arrive in the colony after the end of June when work becomes scarce in Barbados, and return to the island to spend Christmas and crop-time" (Beckles 1990: 113). Between 1850 and 1921, Barbados contributed 50,000 people to the populations of British Guyana, Trinidad and Tobago. During the 1835–1885 "inter-territorial movement" period of West Indian migration, Barbadians migrated in large numbers to Suriname; 3,500 went to St. Croix in 1863 (Marshall 1987: 7). Post-Emancipation emigration was one way of "socio-economic betterment" and arguably not simply a historically conditioned desire to migrate (Beckles 1990: 113).

One must also take into account the historical time period of the 1873 Act, as it was only one generation removed from the end of slavery and apprenticeship in 1838. The parents of many of the individuals affected by the Act, and possibly some of the migrants themselves, lived within the draconian structure of the institution of slavery. Prior to the end of the British Slave Trade in 1807, Barbadian plantations experienced positive population growth rates, making the vast majority of slaves Creole and native to the Island, which was unique compared to other British West

Indian islands. In sum, these migrants had no experience or culture of migration prior to the end of slavery and apprenticeship. Moreover, the superintendent classified the emigrant class and regulated those who left Barbados; culture could not, and did not, dictate emigration. The government introduced emigration schemes to control its "super-abundant" population.

Emigration to alleviate overpopulation became a popular solution by 1895. The *Barbados Emigration Commission Report* of 1895 outlined the possibility of the implementation of reasonable and controlled sponsored emigration for overpopulation. The late nineteenth century was the beginning of sponsored and government-oriented emigration schemes. G. Ruthven Le Hunte, the Acting Governor of Barbados and the author of the *Emigration Commission Report*, outlined possible destinations for Barbadian emigrants and provided the framework for a legislated emigration scheme. The Emigration Committee focused on West Indian host countries, including Trinidad, Tobago, Dominica, St. Lucia and St. Vincent. The scheme concluded that the emigration of Barbadians was a labour and employment initiative. The Committee proposed that emigrants "be encouraged to undertake Cane farming in Trinidad."[6] The need for labour throughout the British West Indies following Emancipation and the exodus of former slaves away from plantations facilitated the settlement of Barbadians abroad. The document highlighted the recommendation by the Committee that "*Labour Colonies* be founded in the Islands of St. Vincent and St. Lucia in which Islands the conditions appear to be most favourable."[7] The Committee recognized the symbiotic relationship between overpopulation and unemployment in the Island and argued "the real object of any Emigration Scheme should be to form permanent settlements rather than to find casual employment for our surplus population — though the latter may be a very useful necessary adjunct to the first."[8] Permanent settlement was designed deliberately as a solution to unemployment and overpopulation.[9]

Late nineteenth- and early twentieth-century Barbadian and West Indian labour migration throughout the Caribbean basin has been examined thoroughly. The construction of the Panama Canal was arguably one of the most well-known labour movements of the period. Beckles argued that the labour required for construction of the Panama Canal created an emigration outlet beginning in 1904 where Black Barbadian male workers "saw an opportunity to reject sugar planters and plantations, and pursue an autonomous path," and where "the migration opportunity was undoubtedly seen by blacks as a chance finally to cast off the yoke of plantation domination" (Beckles 1990: 142–143). The Panama Canal may not have been a program initiated by the Barbadian Government, but the mass migration of Barbadians and West Indians is extremely noteworthy. According to Marshall (1987: 21), three phases characterized the West Indian migration to Panama:

railroad construction (1850–1855), construction of the canal itself (1880–1914), and railroad relocation (1906–1914). Only Jamaicans were involved during the first phase, while the rest of the English-speaking Caribbean followed in 1880 under the French company Universal Inter-Oceanic Company. The patterns of recruitment of West Indians varied as "the movement from Jamaica was mainly individual, whereas from the Eastern Caribbean movement very much depended on recruitment or emigration," and an estimated 130,000 emigrated from the West Indies to Panama between 1885 and 1920, with the majority from Jamaica and Barbados as manual labour, or "pick and shovel" men (Marshall 1987: 21–22). During this period, Barbados' population declined from 171,983 in 1911 to 156,312 in 1921, as approximately 45,000 Black Barbadian contracted and non-contracted sojourners left for Panama despite legislation to control the migration in 1904 and 1907 (Beckles 1990: 143). Alan B. Simmons and Jean-Pierre Guengant described this (1880–1930) period as the "Household Adaptation and Circulation Period," an approximately fifty-year timeframe defined by the continued decline of sugar production and "wage labour opportunities in the region [that] arose with specific developments, such as the construction of the Panama Canal and the building of railways in Central America" (Simmons and Guengant 1992: 109). Male labourers seeking economic opportunities dominated the migration movement to Panama and throughout the Caribbean basin during the late nineteenth and early twentieth century. The Barbadian Government did not help, but attempted to hinder, the passage of their circuitous temporary workers.

The loss of the skilled and educated during the twentieth century was problematic for a colonial state on the verge of independence. However, these fears were rooted in the late nineteenth century and highlighted by the *Emigration Commission Report*. The highly skilled were the most likely and most readily employable sojourners abroad: a "brain drain" of those needed for the socio-economic growth of the Island. Overpopulation and unemployment decreased, but the highly skilled — the artisans and skilled labourers — amassed the social capital needed to work and settle abroad. The Barbadian Government envisioned and had hoped for the resettlement of their growing agricultural proletariat. The loss of the needed middle class reverberated throughout the Island and raised questions about the merits of government-sponsored emigration during the late nineteenth century. The fear highlighted the "risk that attends assisted emigration when inducements are high of losing the best class of workmen, and retaining the worst."[10] Nevertheless, overpopulation defined Barbadian late nineteenth-century social decline. Overpopulation and population density necessitated sponsored emigration. Le Hunte argued that "the only way of dealing with such a problem ... [is] to organize an Emigration Department and its Agencies in the first instance."[11]

He continued:

> Barbados is not like some countries where particular districts only are
> congested and the surplus population have the option of removing to
> other, even waste localities. Here our surplus population have not even
> waste places to turn to, and some other lands elsewhere which they can go
> to and settle or find employment must be found for them and every rea-
> sonable inducement and facility must be afforded to them to emigrate.[12]

The finalized Committee report read:

> It is therefore in our opinion desirable, that some steps should, if pos-
> sible, be taken to provide for the surplus population that now exists in
> this island, and this can be done only by means of emigration, it being
> impossible to advantageously employ, in this island, all those who are
> capable of working.[13]

The Report clearly stated only emigration could solve Barbados' overpopulation
and unemployment crisis. No other solution or recommendation was proposed
other than emigration, and the Report concluded the necessity for sponsored or
assisted emigration schemes. Between 1892 and 1894, the Barbadian Government
assisted approximately 340 people for employment abroad at a cost on average of
£286 a year during the three-year period. During this period, Barbadian officials
aided approximately forty Barbadians destined for Canada. The cost ranged from
$55 to $60 per head to send a single woman to Canada, or a boy for about $10
less. Remittances buffered Barbados' emigrant scheme's economic burden, and
the "Commissions recommend that every facility should be given [to] Emigrants
of transmitting money to Barbados."[14] Nevertheless, there is no record of whether
the migrants were Black or White. It is possible to infer that considering Canada's
reluctance to accept Black emigrants until the mid-twentieth century that these
women and children were poor White Barbadians. Total remittances for Barbadians
in 1894 ranged from £5,433 from British West Indian colonies and £2,001 from
the United States. The Report deemed the remittance figures "striking," and only
about half of the recorded remittances "amount[ed] to a considerable sum."[15]
Remittances, or "Panama money," returned from the men working on the Panama
Canal ("Panama men") had a "profound impact" on Barbados. Migrants were able
to achieve significant socio-economic mobility upon returning to the Island and
were able to buy land (Beckles 1990: 142–143). An overpopulated, unemployed
and newly emancipated population during the nineteenth century necessitated
sponsored and assisted emigration.

The *Emigration Act* of 1904 consolidated government-sponsored emigration from Barbados. The Act highlighted the roles of emigration agents, illegal emigration, and outlined assisted emigration of Barbadians. Barbadian officials mandated every aspect of the emigration process. The Act stated that the emigration agent was "to be licensed by [the] Governor. [There was a] penalty on acting without license or inducing labourers ... to emigrate by falsehood or fraud."[16] Emigration was a contractual agreement between a labourer and agent and as outlined in the Act.

> Every emigration agent who recruits any labourer or artisan for any work, labour, or service in any place out of His Majesty's dominions, shall cause a contract be entered into with such labourer or artisan, and in default thereof shall be liable to a penalty not exceeding fifty pounds.[17]

The contractual agreement permitted work and migration abroad by stipulating that "every contract made in this Island and binding any person to perform any work, labour, or service in any place not within His Majesty's dominions shall be in writing and executed before and attested by a Police Magistrate."[18] Furthermore, "[a] person desiring to leave this Island as a passenger (migrant other than a labourer or artisan, 'recruited under a contract of service by an emigration agent') for any proclaimed place shall make application to a permit officer."[19] The emigration process was subject to strict regulations. It is interesting to note that the 1904 Act limited and promoted emigration to British and former British colonies, while Canada actively refused Blacks from Barbados. There was a significant disconnect between encouraged emigration from Barbados of Blacks and their immigration and settlement throughout "His Majesty's [White] dominions."[20]

The turn of the twentieth century also introduced stringent emigration laws. The laws defined, regulated and protected the rights of potential emigrants. The Barbadian Government facilitated the movement of its people and codified in law the mechanisms needed to migrate, and reiterated the need to dispense financial aid to potential emigrants. The Act stated the "Governor-in-Executive Committee may expend £300 per annum in assisting persons of the poorer class to emigrate."[21] The Committee held the power to select willing emigrants, "who in the opinion of the Governor-in-Executive would be likely to better their condition by so doing, to emigrate from this Island to Canada, the United States of America, or to any of the neighbouring colonies, either British or foreign."[22] The previous excerpt from the *Emigration Act* is an explicit reference to the Barbadian Government aiding in the emigration of the poorer classes of Barbadians. It also mentions that the government would pay for the passage of poorer classes of Barbadians to Canada. This is notable due to the fact that at the turn of the twentieth century, Canada and Canadians restricted Black immigration. However, the question is whether the Barbadian Government was promoting the emigration of White Barbadians. This assumption is doubtful because the previous initiative was directed towards the "poorer class," but it is not improbable that it referred to the poor class of Whites, disparagingly known as Red Legs.

It must be noted that Red Leg identity was characterized as "belonging neither to the white percent of the population ... nor to the black 91 percent of the population, [but] to the lowest echelons of which they are nearest in economic and class terms" (Sheppard 1977: 1). Dr. John Davy, Inspector General of Army Hospitals and resident of Barbados between 1845 and 1848, described Red Leg identity: "Poor Whites, or 'Redlegs,' as they are contemptuously called from the red hue of their naked legs" (Sheppard 1977: 4–6). This was followed by Quintin Hogg's testimony before the West Indies Royal Commission in 1897: "It is a most pitiable thing to see them wandering about with some of the conceit of the white blood, but none of the energy of the European." Hogg made an explicit distinction between white skin colour and European or "White" social characteristics. Poor Whites "formed a class which had no economic role to play" (Sheppard 1977: 5). They were not accepted by higher-class Whites, due to their laziness and arrogance. No legal definition explicitly assigned poor White status or the poor White or Red Leg classifier, but was referred to as a "class comprising all those white groupings outside the pale of the plantocracy and the closely allied business and professional class" (Sheppard 1977: 6).

Despite the lack of a clear racialized statistics, the government also assisted in one's family reunification abroad. Nevertheless, similar to the precedent set in the late nineteenth century, the Barbadian Government both facilitated and restricted the early twentieth-century movement of its people as outlined in the *Emigration Act of 1904*. Government officials had the power to stop the recruitment of emigrants; emigration was at the discretion, implementation and regulation of the Barbadian Government and its legal system.[23] The Act stated:

> The Governor-in-Executive Committee with the approval of the Legislature may from time to time by order prohibit, either absolutely or conditionally, the recruiting of labourers or artificers for emigration to, or labour in, any place out of His Majesty's dominions to be mentioned in such orders, and may from time to time revoke, rescind, or vary any such order.[24]

The Barbadian colonial government of the late nineteenth and turn of the twentieth century implemented strict controls through laws, which clearly classified migrants and determined how they migrated. The government assisted in the passage of the poorer, Black — and possibly White — unemployed and over-populated proletariat. The Barbadian officials aided in the creation and settlement of labour colonies throughout the West Indies, while simultaneously solving their social problems at home. Overpopulation and unemployment dictated the late nineteenth- and early twentieth-century sponsored emigration of Barbadians. While the middle classes benefitted from the policies for skilled emigration, the Barbadian Government also implemented schemes that assisted the movement of poorer Black Barbadians.

The early twentieth century saw little relief for Barbados' social decline due to overpopulation and unemployment. Barbadian planters argued in favour of emigration, believing "only emigration could prevent the degratation [sic] of Barbados."[25] This point is interesting to note and somewhat contradictory (though it sheds light on the gendered aspects of emigration and labour in Barbados) since it was the planters — the landowning elite class in Barbados — that discouraged male workers from leaving the Island for the Panama Canal project and who boasted of a "super-abundant" labour supply of Black workers (unlike anywhere else in the British West Indies since Emancipation). They were forced to use female labourers on plantations following the mass exodus of male sojourners to the Isthmus of Panama in the early twentieth century. The planters' motives were to keep a sustained labour pool on plantations to work in a system of neo-slavery. In one of the first initiatives of the twentieth century and following the gendered lens of emigration, the Barbadian Government, in collaboration with the planter class, founded the Victorian Emigration Society, which sponsored the emigration of Barbadian women. By 1901, the program sponsored approximately two thousand Barbadian female emigrants.[26] The document did not specify the reasoning for the Emigration Society nor the colour of said emigrants; however, eighteenth- and nineteenth-century Barbadian social class and gender relations structured poor White women's lives. The St. John School for Female Industry, a vocational school for young White women supported by the Poor Relief fund and the parish vestry, exemplified the restrictions placed on White women at the turn of the nineteenth century. The school was created ostensibly for the well-being of young poor White women and to alleviate the financial strain and burden on Poor Relief. However, it was used to control the sexual behaviour of these young women who were "existing on the margins of white society" (Sheppard 1977: 5). Poor White women "represented a potentially threatening category whose socio-sexual behaviour ... could seriously undermine and disrupt the ideologies and practices of hegemonic white ruling patriarchy" (Jones 2007: 15). There was a feeling of an "innate" blackness of white women and a supposed altruistic and protective control of female sexuality within the Barbadian slavocracy (Jones 2007: 23). The hypocrisy of "protecting" White women was apparent throughout the patriarchy of the colonized world. Poor White women were subject to physical constraints through the prohibition of socio-sexual relationships with Black men, designed to protect the ideological creation of "Whiteness" assigned and implemented by the White male patriarchal ruling elite (Jones 2007: 15). Seventeenth-century Barbadian sex ratios reflected 150 males per 100 females. Following mass White emigration during the eighteenth century, and following Emancipation, the sex ratio declined significantly. Higher class White men's "natural reaction" was to place White women "protectively upon a pedestal and then run off to gratify passions elsewhere," while White women were held "aloof from the world of lust and passion" (Jordan 1962: 197). One may argue that the sponsored emigration of White women displayed the patriarchal control over female autonomy (Jordan 1962: 197). Scottish Abolitionist William Dickson believed elite White women in Barbados "deserve the first place on the side of humanity — a virtue which many of them carry to an excess, which is not only troublesome to their husbands, but really injurious to their slaves," and he admired their "economy, sobriety, fidelity and attachment to their husbands," as their husbands "live[d] in such habits of intimacy with the female domestic slaves."[27] One may then argue the 1901 Victorian Emigration Society was a derivative of an eighteenth- and nineteenth-century patriarchal ideology to control female agency, White or Black. With respect to White women, emigration could have been a response to White men wanting to hypocritically control miscegenation on the Island. Gender played a significant role in the history of Barbadian emigration. Not surprisingly, the surviving documents do not allow historians to interpret and analyze the marginalized late nineteenth- and early twentieth-century female voice as they focused primarily on the political and economic determinants, specifically labour and unemployment, of emigration.

With respect to labour on the Island and issues of unemployment, the *Colonial Report* of 1927 detailed that "notwithstanding the emigration which takes place annually to Cuba and other West Indian islands there is an abundant supply of labour for the requirements of the Colony."[28] Emigration as a solution to unemployment and overpopulation continued throughout the early to mid-twentieth century. In the first meeting of the West Indies Standing Conference at Barbados, January 24, 1928, representatives from all British West Indian colonies, British Guiana, and Bermuda discussed emigration and the logistics and assistance for emigration settlement schemes and West Indians migrating to non-British West Indian colonies. The representatives proposed the establishment of an organization to help and "serve the interests" of West Indians in Cuba. They discussed the establishment of a permit system for emigrants in foreign countries and a "fund for defraying the cost of relief of destitute West Indians in foreign countries and the cost of their repatriation in certain cases."[29] It was a government-assisted social security and safety net for West Indian emigrants. The Great Depression created pressures for further government involvement for the welfare of British West Indian sojourners.

The Great Depression devastated Barbadian and West Indian economies, specifically the volatile sugar industry that was dependent on the global market. Unemployment reached epic proportions during the 1930s, and possible schemes to stem the effects of the Depression on the sugar industry included "any schemes of migration of labourers or land settlements."[30] Barbados had "an abundant supply of labour" and needed avenues to employ or relocate the unemployed as the "door to emigration [was] closed."[31] Barbados experienced a population increase in the 1920s due to immigration exceeding emigration. There is no explicit evidence for why this occurred, but it is possible that with the completion of the Panama Canal in 1914, fewer Barbadians migrated for work abroad. Each year of the 1920s (notwithstanding 1923 and 1928) "shows an increase of immigration over emigration," and the average net increase of the 1920s was 972 persons.[32]

Canadian merchant ships employed "a number of Barbadian seamen … on ships of the Canadian National Steamships and the Furness Withy Line"; however, by 1932 as the Depression worsened, "the chances of employment for Barbadian seamen were further reduced by the decision of the Canadian National Steamships to carry Canadian crews on their passenger steamers calling at West Indian ports."[33] The economic prosperity and opportunity for Barbadian seamen was intrinsically linked to Canadian and global economic and labour determinants. Moreover, "the causes of unemployment in Barbados are chiefly the discontinuance of emigration to foreign countries, the discontinuance of employment of local seamen by the Lamport and Holt and Canadian National Steamship Companies."[34] The 1933 *Colonial Report* continued on the direct causal relationship of discontinued emigration and unemployment, adding "the decline of the coaling trade of the port, the wide-spread disinclination of the inhabitants to undertake agricultural work. The absence of adequate vocational training in the educational system of the Island is also a contributing factor."[35] By 1934, 4,109 people registered with the newly opened Barbadian Employment Agency as "opportunities for employment … ha[d] practically ceased and Barbados ha[d] to look within for the solution of its problem of over-population."[36] Since the late nineteenth century, Barbadian authorities identified overpopulation as a key problem on the Island and emigration as a possible solution. However, during this Depression period, the historical solution for employment through emigration to countries such as Canada ceased to exist; the global economic Depression thwarted the Island's solutions to alleviate the pressures of overpopulation.[37]

Despite the Depression, the Barbadian Government proposed and enacted several measures for the settlement of emigrants abroad during the late 1930s.

Barbadian colonial officials continued the emigration scheme with the *Recruiting of Workers Act* of 1938. The Act set to "carry out certain Conventions relating to recruiting of workers," and restricted the age of recruitment to sixteen years of age, or fourteen with the consent of a parent or guardian "for employment upon light work."[38] Other employment acts of 1938 included the *Labour (Minimum Wage) Act*, and the *Employment of Women, Young Persons and Children Act* of 1938–42.[39] By 1938, 7,412 people registered with the Barbadian employment agency.[40] The Barbadian Government continued to facilitate and regulate the transnational travels of its people and proposed the creation of labour colonies throughout the British West Indies. Payne noted that the colonial government owned foreign land in the West Indies to settle Barbadian nationals as temporary workers.[41] Barbados became its own hegemonic power within the Caribbean archipelago in an attempt to solve its unemployment and overpopulation crisis. On the eve of the Second World War, the Barbadian Government procured Vieux Fort Plantation in St. Lucia for the settlement of its surplus citizens. The report from the Committee for the Settlement of Barbadians at Vieux Fort, St. Lucia, detailed that the settlement scheme revealed the Barbadian Government's ownership of a sugar factory in St. Lucia. Colonial Barbados owned the land and factory in St. Lucia and subsequently employed their "surplus population."[42] Similar migration and settlement schemes were forwarded in the 1960s with sponsored emigration to Dominica due to overpopulation and the "surplus population" issue in Barbados. The *Report of the Delegation Appointed to Visit Dominica* examined the possible settlement of Barbadians in Dominica in the 1960s. Issues included social services, climate and agriculture, infrastructure, and education and schools — Dominica had a lower standard of education than Barbados. The attitude was favourable towards Barbadian immigrants in Dominica: "Expressions of opinion were in favour of Barbadian settlers especially in view of the reputation of the Barbadian as a farmer and of his reputed general industriousness nature."[43] Dominica suffered a population decrease due to mass migrations to Britain. They needed a population increase through immigration for economic development.[44] Nevertheless, desperate to assuage its growing population and unemployment, Barbados sought avenues to support the country and its people on the eve of the Second World War.

Barbadian Emigration to the United States

During the Second World War, Barbados also benefitted from the United States' sponsored temporary worker initiatives for the Allied war effort. The United States War and Food Administration and the War Manpower Commission by the Anglo-American Caribbean Commission recruited Barbadians and West Indians for agricultural and industrial work for the war effort in the United States.

In 1944, 3,605 Barbadians laboured in the United States; 3,086 were employed in Florida with the United States Sugar Corporation in 1946. By the end of 1947, 188 Barbadians worked in Florida and 516 men were recruited for work abroad, mostly throughout the Caribbean region. The territorial United States employed approximately 17,000 West Indians as well as many other foreign nationals in American-owned bases in the Caribbean, including Antigua and St. Thomas.[45] The Second World War provided many sponsored emigration outlets for Barbadians. Also immediately following the war, there were many opportunities for employment abroad. In 1946, West Indians employed by the United States Sugar Corporation harvested crops on the mainland. The shortage of manpower in the United States, and particularly in the United Kingdom during and following the Second World War, created mass emigration opportunities, most on a temporary basis, for Barbadians and West Indians.[46] However, by 1949, American temporary labour migration slowed down.[47] The early 1950s ushered in a new era of United States immigration as the *McCarran-Walter Immigration and Nationality Act* of 1952 (the *McCarran Act*) defined the country's postwar immigration policy and effectively curtailed Barbadian and West Indian migration. The *McCarran Act* "eliminated racial barriers to naturalization and thereby to immigration"; however, it "retained most of the quota preferences of the 1924 (immigration) law" (Mills 1994: 16). The *Johnson-Reed Act*, the *Immigration Act* of 1924, set a yearly limit of 150,000 immigrants a year from outside the western hemisphere and "then divided the 150,000 into quotas based on a country's share of the total population in 1920" (Mills 1994: 15–16). The *Johnson-Reed Act* restricted immigration "on the basis of national origins, and quotas were set that favored the immigrants from northern and western European nations" (Pedraza and Rumbant 1996: 7). The 1952 *McCarran Act* ostensibly eliminated the overt racialization of American immigration policy; however, the quota system marginalized West Indian emigration flows. Reflecting on the 1924 and 1952 Acts, as he addressed the new U.S. *Immigration Act* of 1965, U.S. Senator Edward Kennedy (1976: 429) stated it was a "reassertion and return to the American liberal tradition." The new Act "peremptorily rejected the racist assumptions of an earlier era, amended those sections of the *Immigration and Nationality Act* of 1952 incorporating the original national origins quota system, and set up individual rather than group criteria for the admission of immigrants" (Kennedy 1976: 429). A comprehensive study of Barbadian migration to the United States is beyond the scope of this book; however, it is worth noting that Barbadians also overcame racist and exclusionary American immigration policy. The global economic and political climate enabled and restricted early and mid-twentieth-century recruited Barbadian labour migration to the United States.

During the postwar period, the United States Embassy in Barbados employed four American citizens and eleven Barbadian nationals to aid in the recruitment and selection of potential emigrants to the United States. By 1968, two thousand Barbadians landed in the United States, as compared to thirty-nine in 1953.[48] A January 27, 1967, article in one of Barbados' national newspapers, "U.S. Cuts Migration Limit on Bajans," stated, "According to Mr. George Dolgin (U.S. Consulate-General in Barbados), the new system is now in effect and immigration by native-born Barbadians is no longer subject to numerical limitation as had been the case before independence," with respect to emigration to the United States (*The Advocate* January 27, 1962).

During the 1950s, Barbadians continued to sign "short-term" — temporary worker — contracts in the United States as unemployment continued to devastate the Barbadian economy.[49] By 1950, five thousand men in Barbados were either unemployed or underemployed. It was also the year that persons emigrating (21,040) exceeded immigration (20,734).[50] The 1952 and 1953 *Colonial Reports* recorded that the "estimated seasonal unemployment during the inter-crop period (the end of May to the beginning of January) is approximately 10,000" Barbadians.[51] It is interesting to note that the number of Barbadian seasonal workers in the United States — cotton and citrus agriculturalists in Florida — increased following the *McCarran Act* of 1952; they numbered 717 emigrants in 1952 and 1000 in 1953. Barbadian workers "were selected by the employers from persons called up by the Bureau of Employment and Emigration maintained by the Labour Department."[52] The Barbadian Government continued to recognize and attempt to alleviate overpopulation and unemployment through sponsored emigration, especially for temporary migrant seasonal work in the United States. Despite the new immigration restrictions of 1952, American employers continued to accept cheap "super-abundant" Barbadian labour, which further perpetuated the class-based temporary status of West Indian migrants. Nevertheless, overpopulation remained a key issue in Barbados, and the "Joint Committee of both Chambers of the Legislature [was] set up in 1951 to study the question of overpopulation."[53] In addition to the recommendation for family planning clinics, emigration once again was a sustainable solution for overpopulation. The Report stated, "The amount of unemployment is considerable. As a result, a flow of emigration began in 1954, and attained considerable proportions in 1955."[54] Under schemes initiated by Barbadian and West Indian governments, 329 Barbadians were placed and signed under contract as agricultural workers with American authorities in 1954. In 1954, a total of 1,003 contracted Barbadians worked in the United States, and the number dropped slightly to 985 in 1955. In the same year, 2,990 migrants left Barbados for employment overseas, with 401 settling in the United States. The previous figures highlighted Barbadians "temporarily or permanently, in search of work."

(See Appendix D for a table of West Indian and Barbadian Farm Workers in the United States between 1956 and 1963.) By this time the Barbadian Government "assisted emigration, in an effort to relieve unemployment, by securing employment and accommodation overseas for emigrants, and by making loans to emigrants for whom those were assured."[55] While the Barbadian Government supported the emigration of its people to the United States, Barbadian migrants relied on their own diasporic networks to aid in their settlement.

The United States federal government did not provide settlement programs for new Barbadian immigrants; newcomers relied on the generosity and benevolence of private organizations including the Barbados ex-police. Most Barbadians settled in New York City and 80 to 90 percent identified as Black. The influx of a new Black ethnic group created African-American and Black West Indian antagonisms. Despite the phenotypic and soft primordial relationship, similar to Anglo-American and continental European strife in nineteenth-century North America, the new ethnic Blacks — West Indians — did not integrate and assimilate with the charter member African-Americans. This was due in part to the divergent histories of the British colonies and the differences in the institution and practice of slavery, but also from White American socially constructed codifications and its compartmentalization of Black ethnicity in the United States. White perceptions of Black and African-American identity influenced the settlement and identity of ethnic Blacks in the Americas and the United States. Black West Indians were seen as "better" in the eyes of White America compared to "lazy" African-Americans. Black Canadians and Black West Indians in Canada experienced a similar de-unifying racist ideology.[56]

Jamaican-born Black political leader Marcus Garvey had addressed the Black West Indian and African-American schism in the United States and had called for a united Black and Pan-African front in a speech at Madison Square Garden on March 16, 1924.[57] Garvey believed that his Universal Negro Improvement Association (UNIA) represented "the hopes and aspirations of the awakened Negro. Our desire is for a place in the world; not to disturb the tranquility of other men."[58] Garvey did not classify Blacks in terms of ethnic or national background; he believed that Blacks were "divided into two groups, the industrious and adventurous, and the lazy and dependent."[59] The well-being of the Black race superseded the divisive nature of historically constructed social and political boundaries. Garvey argued that the industrious, adventurous and socially conscious "awakened Negro" believed that "whatsoever others have done [the UNIA] can do," and the "Universal Negro Improvement Association belongs to this group, and so you find us working, six million strong, to the goal of an independent nationality."[60] Garvey and the UNIA laid the groundwork for an early twentieth-century Black and Pan-African united front, one that struggled for consolidation as the pre-eminent Black political bastion.

During the mid-twentieth century, new waves of West Indian immigrants experienced socio-economic, ideological and cultural backlash from African-Americans as they struggled to maintain their autonomy and precariously marginalized existence in American society. Garvey's position on Pan-Africanism and universal Black self-empowerment challenged the notion of the "better" West Indian immigrants as compared to "lazy" African-Americans, which perpetuated racialized migrant stereotypes. Garvey deconstructed "Black" negative identifications and positioned Blacks as a unified and politicized group with common interests despite their immigrant or "native" status. This disconnect in Black consciousness favoured White American racial hegemony, which was manifested in its immigration policy, where "acculturated Afro-Americans in the United States formed a buffer for white American society, a foil against which the black immigrant/white host interaction could be played, as well as a section of American society into which the black West Indians could be absorbed" (Marshall 1987: 27). Black identity played a pivotal role in the settlement and migration of Black West Indians in the United States; it exploited White American and African-American divisions and also mobilized the Black political class.

The British and American treatment of Blacks during the institution of slavery, and in the late nineteenth and early twentieth century, created the divergent socio-economic and cultural legacy of British subjects and African-Americans, respectively. The ideology of the Black "race" must not be conflated with the factual reality of Black ethnicity. While slavery and discrimination were the common bonds that tied Blacks in the Americas, this generalization exacerbated Black ethnic divisions in the twentieth-century United States and continues to cause strife to this day. Black West Indians and African-Americans both have a history of slavery; however, West Indians "have had greater economic opportunities during and after slavery" (Hao 2007: 180). As opposed to the segregated and marginalized racialized minority of Blacks in the United States, the West Indian Black majority "developed a higher achievement orientation" in the Caribbean (Hao 2007: 180–181). The colonized British subjects experienced greater socio-economic and political autonomy and educational opportunities, particularly in the early twentieth century. However, this "cultural advantage" was lost on the progeny of the mid-twentieth-century charter West Indian emigrants in the United States. American-style racial discrimination eroded the West Indian culture of upward mobility, and "though the first generation of British Caribbean immigrants achieve upward economic mobility and outperform African-Americans, the stubborn U.S. racial hierarchy confines them to the lowest tier" (Hao 2007: 180–181). West Indian immigrants lost "ground because of the downward succession of neighbourhoods and communities and the downward assimilation of the second generation" (Hao 2007: 181). Black West Indians and African-Americans were forced to fight for scarce and oftentimes nonexistent resources. Colour, and White perceptions of Blackness, remained a contributing factor to Black Barbadian marginalization in the United States. The Second World War was a watershed moment for Black Barbadian and West Indian migration; they were enlisted as temporary workers and contributed to the United States war effort and were subsequently recruited to contribute to Britain's postwar reconstruction.

Barbadian Emigration to the United Kingdom

The United Kingdom became the primary destination for Barbadian emigrants following the Second World War. As the colonial master with its desperate need for labourers, Britain was a natural pull for British subjects in the West Indies; the emigration of West Indians to the United Kingdom "was the first movement to a totally white host society" (Marshall 1987: 27). The postwar growth of the British economy "created gaps at the lower end of the occupational and residential ladder to which West Indians and other coloured immigrants have been drawn in as replacement population," and the main "pull" of West Indians to Britain was to fill labour needs (Marshall 1987: 27). The high demand for labour in the United Kingdom during the 1950s facilitated migration outlets, and nearly all emigrants from Barbados left for the British Isles between 1954 and 1955 for permanent settlement. The Barbadian Government initiated several services and put forth legislation in 1955 to aid in the emigration and settlement of its citizens to the United Kingdom, including the Welfare and Liaison Service. The Liaison Service was established for the "benefit of Barbadian emigrants in the United Kingdom," and the service assisted 1,028 Barbadians under the government scheme. It must be acknowledged that Barbados was the only West Indian government that actively encouraged emigration (Peach 1968: 20, 92). The Barbadian *Employment Exchanges Act* of 1955 enabled the "Governor-in-Executive Committee to establish and maintain employment exchanges in such places as he thinks fit ... [and] to meet the expense of persons desiring to travel to places outside the Island when work is available to them."[61] In 1955, 2,754 Barbadian emigrants left for the United Kingdom. Voluntary workers who used the Government Employment and Exchange in 1954 totaled 39 Barbadians selected as student nurses in English hospitals and 361 Barbadians were selected and took employment in the United Kingdom in 1955.[62] The Liaison Service "assisted with the welfare of all Barbadian workers arriving in England."[63] Through sponsored emigration, the Barbadian Government facilitated the permanent settlement of citizens abroad, and "the Government continued to grant loans under specified conditions to Barbadians wishing to emigrate permanently."[64] From 1954 to 1957, 3,049 Barbadians found assistance and most went to the United Kingdom. During that period, $964,807 were loaned by the government; $475,076 were repaid.[65] The 1958 and 1959 *Colonial Reports* noted the Barbadian Government loans for emigration for transportation costs to the U.K. in September 1954: "4,204 loans totaling $1,331,057 have been made of which $922,845 were repaid at the end of December 1959," and "8,438 persons received loans totaling $2,883,875.20 of which amount $2,063,572.86 was repaid up to the end of 1963."[66] The government selected and provided grants to those that qualified to migrate to the United Kingdom.

London Transport was the main employer for Barbadian sponsored emigrants. The selection process was as follows: the Labour Department in Barbados, on behalf of London Transport, administered tests for individuals in Barbados and processed them on site. Following a two-week training course in Britain, the Barbadian candidates began their employment.[67] Reginald Eric Taylor was one of the young Barbadians selected and recruited to work for London Transport. He described his recruitment process:

> One day in early January 1960 one of our Central Foundry colleagues came back during lunch and enquired whether any of us were interested in emigrating to England. Beginning in the mid-1950s Barbados was actively recruiting persons interested in accepting work in England. The available work in England included British Rail, hospitals, some restaurants, and London Transport, both on the buses and underground on the subway trains. The salary in England was said to be in the region of 7 pounds per week (the equivalent of 28 Barbadian dollars at the time).
>
> We universally rejected his offer since at Central Foundry our pay was either $21.50 or $31.50, but he pressed on with his invitation informing that our work would be at Foundry at 24 pounds per week, and not in any of the above mentioned fields. Conversion of British pounds to Barbados dollars means that 24 pounds equal $96.00 Barbados dollars. That salary coupled with the fact that we were being recruited to work in a foundry, five of us from the foundry immediately left to go to the recruitment centre. Our colleague had suggested that we informed them at the centre that he had sent us. That we did on arrival there. Immediately following that first interview they dispatched us to the Enmore Health Centre for health testing. That visit to Enmore was a firm indication that we were about to be selected to travel to England. Significantly, one of our CF colleagues never returned to work after that visit. I distinctly remember that on a visit to the Recruitment Centre one of the managers came to us and asked who is Blenman, stating that I have spoken with your father.
>
> The way things go in Barbados even today in 2010, one usually needs to have a godfather, one to speak for you, in order to make any progress.

There were five of us from Central Foundry who went over to the recruit-ment centre, but the Government was recruiting four (4) persons to go to England. We at CF felt that the guy who never returned to work at CF and the guy whom the manager said "I have spoken with your father" were on the selected list. Now that would have been two (2) of the required four (4). For our last interview, we had to attend another location where we also had to pay a deposit for travelling on the ship to England. I must note that in spite of the fact that they only required four they still had six of us to attend that last interview and to bring the deposit which was about $100.00 BBD. On leaving that interview another of our CF colleagues informed us that he was a personal friend of the interviewer. That sealed it for me. I was one of the remaining three who were not yet selected and upon leaving there I immediately telephoned the character who was speaking for me. He assured that I was selected on the list to travel. That information was confirmed when someone from the recruitment called me next day, gave the news of the aforementioned colleagues, and asked [us] to come over right away.

We went over and had our selection confirmed. We traveled by an upscale French Liner, the SS *Colombie*. We took eleven days to reach Southampton, England. We left Barbados on January 28, 1960, and arrived at Southampton on February 8, 1960. (Taylor 2010)

Taylor was one of the many young Barbadians that took the opportunity offered by the recruitment schemes, and his passage to England was expedited by youthful exuberance and the thought of higher wages abroad. His account is an excellent example of the Autonomous Bajan and how the individual initiated his or her migration overseas as the Barbadian Government simplified and facilitated the procedure for those that were qualified in a specific field. Employed as a skilled worker as a mechanic repairing ship engines in the diesel department at Barbados' Central Foundry, Taylor was qualified to join London Transport immediately and set sail for England within the same month of his first inquiry to go abroad (Taylor 2010). This process was unlike the cases of "exceptional merit" where Barbadian nurses Gloria Ramsay and Pearl Thompson waited seven months and one year, respectively, for admission and employment in their field in Canada in the mid-1950s. Conversely, Barbadian nurses were in high demand in the United Kingdom in the 1950s, and student nurses from Barbados received similar screening and training procedures to those outlined by Taylor. The 1956 and 1957 *Colonial Reports* stated that "a number of" student nurses and other hospital workers left for the United Kingdom.[68] Payne estimated about sixty thousand Barbadians lived in Britain following the Second World War and up to the introduction of the exclusionary and controversial *Commonwealth Immigrants Act* in 1962 that restricted Black West Indian settlement in the United Kingdom. The 1952 *McCarran Act* effectively curtailed permanent Barbadian and West Indian migration to the United States, and along with failing economic conditions in the West Indies, it is believed that these were additional reasons why emigration to Britain increased (Marshall 1987: 26). Audley Simmons, a former London Transport employee, stated that with the *McCarran Act*, "America closed down, and England opened up" (quoted in Western 1992: 46).

The United States accepted high levels of Caribbean emigrants immediately following the Second World War, but the migration flow shifted dramatically after the implementation of the *McCarran Act*. It was shown that prior to the Act, "for every West Indian who migrated to Great Britain, nine went to the United States. After the Act the ratio was reversed" (Pastor 1987: 250). Barbadian emigration was not dictated by unilateral and binary movements of migrants from one country to the next; it worked within the global context of the political, social and economic environment of the receiving countries.[69] Moreover, the bureaucracy of state governments simultaneously facilitated and restricted the international migration of Barbadians across the globe. Individual Barbadians experienced agency as they moved within the structure of the international context of British imperialism, sovereign state diplomacy and national interests. However, the Barbadian Government and its

Table 3-1 Sponsored Barbadian Emigrants in the United Kingdom, 1950–1966[70]

Year	Number of Sponsored Emigrants
1950	20
1954	39
1955	361
1956	835
1957	650
1958	359
1959	464
1960	1,011
1961	978
1962	1,315
1963	499
1964	972
1965	1,350
1966	420

emigrant class understood the confines of the colonized-colonizer relationship and Black-White diplomacy, and thoroughly prepared this newfound ambassador group for the racialized and discriminatory environment abroad, especially that of postwar Britain. Prepared and qualified Barbadians left for Britain in considerable numbers during the 1950s and early 1960s.

The following tables highlight the postwar boom of the number of sponsored Barbadian migrants in the United Kingdom and the specific occupations under Barbadian Government emigration schemes. One must note the rising number of emigrants throughout this period, culminating with the migration boom in 1962, which coincided with fears of the impending *Commonwealth Immigrants Act*. Those seeking work with London Transport declined sharply in 1963, while the recruitment of nurses rose steadily during this period. Similar to the recruitment of West Indian nurses for Canadian hospitals, it is possible that the increase was due to the

Table 3-2 Workers Sponsored by the Barbadian Government Recruited for Work in the United Kingdom, 1955–1963[71]

	1955	1957	1958	1959	1960	1961	1962	1963
Clerks (LCC)	N/A	N/A	N/A	2	N/A	N/A	N/A	N/A
London Transport	N/A	926	108	230	623	638	639	189
London County Bus Services	N/A	N/A	N/A	N/A	N/A	15	N/A	N/A
British Railways	N/A	N/A	44	3	36	80	30	2
Tea Shops	N/A	N/A	N/A	N/A	N/A	N/A	5	48
Catering Assistants	N/A	38	27	8	57	N/A	17	5
Hotel Workers	211	308	58	100	50	15	10	11
Hospital Workers	25	N/A	6	1	34	15	N/A	N/A
Domestics	N/A	38	13	17	33	9	39	9
Nurses	N/A	N/A	103	103	130	200	175	229
Student Nurses	113	N/A	N/A	N/A	N/A	N/A	N/A	N/A
British Army Recruits	N/A	N/A	N/A	N/A	N/A	N/A	400	N/A
Cotton Workers	N/A	N/A	N/A	N/A	30	6	N/A	N/A
Engineers	N/A	N/A	N/A	N/A	4	N/A	N/A	N/A
Laundry Workers	N/A	N/A	N/A	N/A	N/A	N/A	N/A	N/A
Coppers	N/A	N/A	N/A	N/A	N/A	N/A	N/A	3
Other Workers	12	N/A	N/A	N/A	N/A	N/A	N/A	3
Total Gov. Sponsored	361	1,310	359	464	997	978	1,315	499
Total Independent	N/A	4,293	889	2,353	3,330	5,052	2,489	1,891

continuing shortage of qualified nurses in the United Kingdom. The total number of Barbadian emigrants declined significantly in 1963 and fluctuated with a peak in 1965 with the British Government's August 1965 *White Paper, Immigration from the Commonwealth*. Ceri Peach (1968: 59) argued that economic factors, not the British Government's *Commonwealth Immigrants Act* of 1962, "had been responsible for the initial decrease in immigration after the Act had come into force."

Barbadian Government assistance for potential emigrants also included the preparation and proliferation of comprehensive information booklets. The *Information Booklet for Intending Emigrants to Britain* intended to do the following:

> Set out the facts and conditions of life in the United Kingdom. It is not meant to change your mind from going, any more than it is meant to encourage you to go. It merely gives you information which you should have before you go and is meant to prepare you for the kind of life which you may have to live.[72]

The booklet gave advice on the cold and wet climate, English customs, food and accommodation. It also directed new immigrants in Britain on what to expect on their arrival and settlement. The concise booklet outlined and thoroughly explained the British taxation system, healthcare, transportation and avenues to find employment. The guide went so far as to explain simple social customs; simple but potentially embarrassing situations oblivious to Barbadians prior to their arrival in Britain. This included how one was to wait and board a public bus and how to cross the street. It served as a cautionary note to potential female emigrants to avoid "unscrupulous persons" upon their disembarkation in Britain. It also highlighted seemingly mundane details, such as personal hygiene. On baths, presumably due to the colder climate, the piece stated that there is "less need for the daily bath in Britain than in Barbados" and that sometimes a landlord would only allow one weekly bath.[73]

The *Information Booklet* clearly outlined the regulations and responsibilities for sponsored emigrants and procedure for sending remittances. Sponsored emigrants acted as Emigrant Ambassadors and represented their government and country. The Barbadian Government contended that those it selected were to be grateful for their privilege to live and work abroad. The *Information Booklet* reiterated this point and stated to the potential sponsored emigrants:

> If you are going as a "sponsored" emigrant, for whom work has been found by the Government of Barbados, you will have had a great deal of help from the Government, which will have found you your job, shown its confidence in you by selecting you from among the many hundreds

of people who would have liked the job, and probably lent you money for your fare.[74]

The Barbadian Government clearly laid the responsibility on the emigrant in whom it invested. The emigrant was rather explicitly reminded that they were a charge of the state; without the collective aid of their country, the Barbadian would not have been able to leave or find employment while abroad. The burden, pride and industry of Barbados weighed heavily upon sponsored emigrants who knew it was a privilege and a great responsibility to migrate. They were to uphold that respect and remember their patriotic duty in positively representing their country abroad. The Autonomous Bajans and Emigrant Ambassadors represented themselves, but proved to be beacons of positivity and hope for a racialized and colonized island in the heart of the British Commonwealth.

The responsibility for Barbadian expatriates in Britain extended to the social and financial welfare of the families they left behind. Remittances gained through employment in Britain proved to be a vital characteristic of the migration process. The monies returned to the Island buoyed the Barbadian economy and buffered the government's financial burden in supporting the unemployed and destitute. Government officials deemed remittances a dutiful responsibility of all emigrants with family remaining in Barbados, and stated, "If you are leaving dependants in Barbados, please be sure to send them money regularly."[75] "Dependants" were not necessarily children. John Western wrote that "the bond with parents in Barbados was for many years not only an emotional tie but also an economic one. Twenty of twenty-three interviewees had remitted money home to their parents or parent (and some to other family members there) for a considerable number of years after their arrival in Britain" (Western 1992: 135). The *Information Booklet* continued, "If you have a wife and children in Barbados you will have to show that you are in fact maintaining them before you can claim Tax rebate."[76] The leaflet also summarized and cautioned Barbadian immigrants with respect to transcontinental money transfers. It stated:

> When you send money from the United Kingdom to Barbados *do not send bank notes* (emphasis in archival text). This is against the law and the person receiving the notes will have difficulty in changing them. Send the money by postal order or money order (obtainable at any post office) or make arrangements with a bank.[77]

Family accountability remained the individual migrant's priority. In doing so, the financial and logistical investment in sponsored emigration benefitted both the transnational worker, their respective families in Barbados and the Barbadian

Government. Sponsored emigration effectively privatized and transferred some of the government's social welfare responsibility to its people.[78]

Migration was an individual and voluntary choice, but Barbadians exhausted all avenues for preparation prior to their transatlantic migration. This discussion is yet another example of the Barbadian Government's state-controlled, or aided, emigration schemes. The Barbadian Government and the choice and inclination of its people, not simply a Barbadian "culture-of-migration," facilitated migration to Britain. Government officials supported the emigration of their people and acted as a reliable source of information and social welfare. However, Britain's *Commonwealth Immigrants Act* of 1962 restricted and forever altered the migratory patterns of Barbadians and the Island's limited autonomy in directing the ideological and physical return to the colonial metropole.

The *Commonwealth Immigrants Act*

Britain's 1962 *Commonwealth Immigrants Act* "attempted to restrict the flow of (non-white) immigrants from the former [British] colonies, whilst still allowing free entry for other nationalities such as the Irish" (Price 2001: 195). British immigration policies were not influenced by economic determinants, but politically motivated; the Act was a direct response to the political and social antagonisms following the rise in racial tensions due to the increase of non-White immigrants in postwar Britain. The Act was characterized by the implementation of work vouchers: Category A — those who had jobs in the U.K.; Category B — Applicants with skills or qualifications; Category C — those not included in A or B. The vouchers were valid for six months and could be extended for up to another six months "if good reason were shown" (Peach 1968: 51). By 1965, "the total number of vouchers issued was to be limited to 8,500 per year. Category C vouchers were to be discontinued completely" (Peach 1968: 59–60).

The British public pressured its government to restrict its liberal immigration policy and argued against the recruitment of migrants from their colonies following the Second World War. The Act, enforced July 1, 1962, decreed that "all Commonwealth citizens, except, broadly speaking, those born in the United Kingdom or holding United Kingdom passports, came under new regulations regarding immigration and ... penalties regarding deportation" (Davison 1966: 1, 139). The British Conservative Government conceded to "social pressure" and the Act came into effect July 1, 1962. This "social pressure" was racially motivated; "at the time that the Commonwealth Immigrants Bill was debated, it was clear that its purpose was to restrict, not merely regulate, the movement of Commonwealth immigrants and particularly that from predominantly coloured countries" (Peach 1968: 51). The Act and British immigration policy in the 1960s "ignored the country's manpower requirements and [were] designed almost entirely to slow down the influx of nonwhites," and they were influenced by public opinion (Freeman 1987: 188). By comparing the divergent histories of race relations in the United States and the United Kingdom, Gordon K. Lewis (1990: xiii–xix) revealed that

> it was conventional wisdom in 1945 that England was the liberal society and the United States the racist society, and lecturing the Americans was the favorite pastime of the London media establishment. But the last 30 or so years have witnessed a curious reversal of roles. The United States has moved forward, with the civil rights movement and the Great Society legislation, to redress the historic injustices done to its nonwhite minorities, especially black Americans; but Britain, after 1962, passed a number of race relations acts step-by-step making entry for nonwhite immigrants more difficult, with the final end of destroying the old Commonwealth concept of a family of nations.

The Act did not explicitly mention race or Blackness; however, by restricting the entry of what Lewis has described as "nonwhite immigrants," which ultimately affected entry requirements for emigrants of non-White Commonwealth nations, the British Government both succumbed to and facilitated postwar British racial and class mores. British racial tension erupted in the Nottingham and Notting Hill attacks on Blacks and their property in 1958 and 1959, which culminated in the racially motivated murder of West Indian carpenter Kelso Cochrane in Notting Hill in 1959. Black immigrants received unfair negative publicity following the racist attacks, which unfortunately swayed public opinion in favour of barring Commonwealth immigration. Despite Blacks suffering race-related attacks and hate-crimes, "some people used the 'disturbances' of 1958 and 1959 as an excuse to argue for stricter immigration controls" (Dodgson 1984: 31). With the emergence of the British racist youth cult, the Teddy Boys, in the 1950s and 1960s, who assaulted and harassed Blacks in the U.K., a "Black Unity" was created amongst all West Indians and South Asians who never considered themselves Black until they were attacked by the Teddy Boys (Burrowes 2009: 148–50).

The symbiotic relationship of race and class both opened and subsequently closed the door for Black West Indian labour settlement in postwar Britain. Black West Indian racialization and their perceived Blackness correlated with their subjugated subaltern status and immigrant labour class in Britain. This was apparent by the conflation of race and class in Britain and the relationship between White British upward mobility and Black West Indian immigrants. Class must be taken into account when discussing West Indian migration: "West Indian migration has a class character which is the outcome of centuries of colonialism and underdevelopment, beginning with slavery, and which has persisted in the present neo-imperialistic relations still linking Britain and the West Indies" (Pryce and Rambachan 1977: 16). Black West Indians were a subordinate labour class in British society;

> the harsh reality is that the neo-imperialist background of the Commonwealth migration to the United Kingdom in the post-war years has ensured that West Indians (together with Indian and Pakistani workers) are concentrated at the bottom of the occupational structure doing some of the worst jobs in Britain [and] abandoned among the unemployed in periods of recession. (Pryce and Rambachan 1977: 4–5)

It was "postwar affluence in Britain" that saw the "upward mobility of British workers by absorbing many of them into skilled and socially valued positions characterized by higher income," and immigrant labour, specifically Black West Indian labour, was needed to fill "de-skilled" jobs, "deserted by white workers," due to "technical innovation" (Pryce and Rambachan 1977: 17). Black West Indians "fulfilled this role perfectly" (Pryce and Rambachan 1977: 17). Educated and upwardly mobile Black Barbadians and West Indians faced the harsh realities of a racialized split labour market (Bonacich 1972: 547–59).

Economically, Britain needed this Black immigrant class of workers to meet the demands of the labour market and support a growing White "middle class"; it seemed illogical for the British Government to willingly implement a policy that restricted an inexhaustible pool of exploitable and cheap labour. One may then argue that it was racial discrimination that swayed public opinion — a public that benefitted from the presence of non-White immigrants within their borders who performed the jobs British citizens were now "above" — that facilitated the creation of the racialized *Commonwealth Immigrants Act*. Moreover, the economic irresponsibility of the Act precipitated and perpetuated "the mass employment of cheap labour from the Commonwealth in the post-war years [and] ensured the continued growth of the British economy," as West Indians "cheapen[ed] the labour process ... [since] the material cost of their socialization [was] born by their countries of origin and they [could] be used to split the work force along racial lines" (Pryce and Rambachan 1977: 17). West Indian and Asian labourers were "exploited as a 'reserve pool' of labour in the service of British capitalism" to be discarded "at will" (Pryce and Rambachan 1977: 17). This is the relationship between class and race that highlighted the host-land "pull" of West Indian workers as a cheap labour class within a capitalist system, but also the paradox of hypocrisy of their racialization: their subjugation permitted their exploitation and inclusion in the metropole as an underclass, while simultaneously excluding them because of their race. West

Indian emigration to Britain was a tool for capitalism; the push/pull migration factors work under the same hegemonic power of capitalism.

British false consciousness and racial prejudice superseded the realities of their capitalist system; the host society's limited prosperity relied upon a subaltern racialized immigrant class. Moreover,

> the migration of thousands of colonial working class West Indians to Britain in the late '40s, the '50s and the '60s was designed to achieve not just the balance between the international supply and demand of labour, but the perpetuation of the dependency relationship between periphery and centre and Britain's continued exploitation of the Third World. (Pryce and Rambachan 1977: 17)

Restricted social mobility due to racism against working-class Black West Indians was expressed "in the wish, either to re-emigrate to Canada or America, or to return to the West Indies" (Pryce and Rambachan 1977: 22). Racist public opinion swayed government policy, and the British Government subsequently heightened immigration requirements. In a few short years, from the altruistic welcome of the SS *Empire Windrush* in 1948 — the first ship that brought West Indians to the United Kingdom, with a total of 492 semi-skilled and skilled male workers from Jamaica — to the *Commonwealth Immigrants Act* in 1962, the Black presence in Britain regressed to the unwanted Other, unsuitable for settlement, integration and immigration, and a threat to British nationhood (Dodgson 1984: 13–14). Fears and concerns regarding exclusion reverberated throughout Barbados and the West Indies. Barbadian emigration to the United Kingdom declined significantly, and "this decline may be directly attributed to the introduction of the *Commonwealth Immigrants Act* which controlled the entry of migrants into the United Kingdom."[79] Barbadian newspapers, including *The Advocate,* produced numerous articles in 1962 prior to the July 1 implementation of the Act, as they attempted to assuage fears and explain the contentious British immigration policy.

The Advocate discussed local West Indian political concerns and debates on the British *Migration Bill* and the subsequent *Commonwealth Immigrants Act.* The January 1, 1962, *Advocate* article "CCL meet to discuss Migrant Bill" highlighted the Administrative Committee of the Caribbean Congress of Labour's (CCL) discussion of the British immigration bill at a special meeting in Trinidad on January 15 and 16, 1962. Only two days following the CCL article, *The Advocate* (January 3, 1962) published "No hard shocks for our U.K. emigrants, he says," an interview with Mr. Richard Williams, a shipping agent and managing director of Richard A. Williams and Company Limited. The article attempted to ease the tension in Barbados caused by the proposed bill and stated, "The British Government's

Migrant Control Bill will not affect Barbadians to the extent as it will Jamaicans" (*The Advocate* January 3, 1962). Williams contended "only about a third of the Barbadian emigrants will be affected," and there was considerable pressure from the British Labour Party to pass the bill (quoted in *The Advocate* January 3, 1962). The new regulations required potential emigrants to have "(1) a health certificate; (2) a clean police record, and (3) either an assured job or assured living accommodation" in Britain (*The Advocate* January 3, 1962). It is interesting to note how and why the Barbadian press deflected the concerns of its citizens and argued the majority of Barbadians would not be affected by the new regulations. As opposed to Jamaicans, as inferred by Williams, most potential Barbadian emigrants were in good health with valid health certificates, had clean police records, and were assured of employment and accommodation prior to their arrival in Britain. Barbadians saw themselves essentially as a "higher class" of emigrant than most others in the West Indies and Commonwealth; in other words, a government-controlled, culled and vetted group of Emigrant Ambassadors of exceptional merit and distinction.

The Barbadian press further reiterated the supposedly exceptional character of potential emigrants and, most importantly, reflected the success of Barbadians in Britain. *The Advocate's* January 1962 coverage of the British *Migration Bill* and the *Commonwealth Immigrants Act* continued with an interview with Mr. Frank Jeremiah, the Assistant Liaison Officer for Barbados at the Barbados Liaison Service in Britain. Jeremiah stated, "Barbados is the only West Indian territory which has schemes that fulfill all the conditions which are now being demanded by all those in Britain who are against the influx of West Indians to their country" (*Sunday Advocate* January 14, 1962). The previous excerpt elucidated Jeremiah's auspicious prognostication of Barbadian emigration and the Barbadian people as exceptions to the new restrictions. It in turn validated the Barbadian Government's emigration schemes and its direct involvement in the educational training and migration of its people. Moreover, Jeremiah's comments boosted the elitist ideology of Barbadian civil society; compared to other West Indian colonies from which Britain refused to accept immigrants, Barbadians were the exception to the rule. One may argue that Barbadian cultural and social capital negated some of their racialized characteristics as marginalized Black colonial subjects. One may also refute this argument, stating that Jeremiah's comments, published by a national newspaper, acted as political rhetoric created to assuage social unrest to a policy that their Island's government had little or no ability to change. Despite the conflicting positions, an environment of supposed immunity existed in Barbados. It was an environment which masked the insidious nature of British racism and reiterated Barbadian core values — education — as means for social mobility and international migration. Race and class dictated British and North American immigration policy, and Barbadians understood it was only their perceived Blackness that denied them access, integration and settlement. Barbadian educational, cultural and social capital facilitated their continued settlement in Britain and distanced Barbadians from their belonging to the Black subaltern class. The national press acted as a representation of Barbados' sentiment towards the *Commonwealth Immigrants Act* and challenged the racial discrimination embedded within it. I contend that Barbadians believed that their superior education, skills and training could — and should — have negated racist immigration policies. Race superseded all qualifications, and Barbadians had to continually fight an uphill battle to be recognized for who they were as skilled and educated British subjects. It is important to note how pervasive anti-Black racism was throughout the Western World. Colour determined who you were and what you were worth.

The Advocate exposed some of the problems of the proposed *Commonwealth Immigrants Act*. The April 9, 1962, article "Immigration statistics were false" revealed the fear-mongered political manipulation of immigration statistics to create a hostile environment towards non-White or Commonwealth migration to Britain. It argued that "Statistics prompted the British Government to panic-draft the wretched Immigration Bill and thrust it through the House of Commons against all opposition" (*The Advocate* April 9, 1962). The British Government succumbed to "passion prejudice, political casuistry — good honest figures have been skillfully manipulated throughout the great immigration debate to serve those ends. And not by one side alone, though by far the greater guilt lies with the supporters of the Bill" (*The Advocate* April 9, 1962). British politicians successfully doctored immigration statistics to support racist exclusionary measures. They faced a diplomatic quagmire, and international scrutiny, if their immigration policies revealed institutionalized racism. Through the manipulation of immigration statistics, the British defended their policy by stating civil society could not economically support the mass influx of Commonwealth migrants. In 1966, the *Commonwealth Immigrants Act* was "subjected to a certain amount of criticism ... the Bill had been introduced in haste without a fully adequate examination of the statistical argument upon which it had been based ... this was that immigration, particularly coloured immigration, had reached an excessive level" (Davison 1966: 1). Britain's Conservative Party argued immigration from the Commonwealth grew so rapidly a bill was needed to curtail the ominous threat of overpopulation. The Party described Britain as "bulging at the seams" and a state unable to provide either accommodation or employment (*The Advocate* April 9, 1962). Conservatives then argued that political coincidence, not racism, dictated the need for strict immigration controls from the Commonwealth. The *Advocate* article disputed this claim and revealed a study conducted by the Economics Intelligence Unit named "Studies in Immigration from the Commonwealth," which proved immigration from the Commonwealth was in fact much lower than what was tabled in the British House of Commons. In ten years (1951–1961), Britain's actual increase of population was 6,000 persons out of a total population of 52,000,000. On January 23, 1962, the British Home Secretary argued that net immigration into Britain increased from 58,550 to 135,050 in 1961. The jump was arguably the result of mass immigration prior to the impending passage of the immigration bill and the resulting *Commonwealth Immigrants Act* of 1962. However, the information was "misleading" and not a "fair basis for estimating future migratory movements" (*The Advocate* May 1, 1962a and 1962b). Political rhetoric and astute statistical manipulation circumvented the need to reveal the true racist impetus for the Act. Institutionalized racism and ideological discrimination defined British immigration policy.

In the face of the new restrictions on Commonwealth and Barbadian migration, the British Government expedited the arrival of highly qualified and skilled immigrants through the designation of priority vouchers for occupations in high demand in Britain.[80] The British Government decreed:

> [A] Commonwealth citizen to whom the Act applies will have to obtain an *employment voucher* (emphasis in original text) if he wishes to enter the United Kingdom for employment on or after 1st July, 1962, and that any such citizen who wishes to enter the United Kingdom for any other purpose may, if he wishes, apply for an entry certificate.[81]

Those solicited by the British included draughtsman and higher technicians; skilled craftsmen, especially those in engineering and building occupations; experienced shorthand typists; and individuals with university degrees or professional qualifications, especially those in nursing and teaching.[82] However, there was "no guarantee that [the potential emigrant's] qualification" would be accepted in Great Britain.[83] The *Commonwealth Immigrants Act* was an exclusionary measure designed to impede the immigration of Black Barbadians, West Indians and non-White British subjects, yet Barbadian political culture and collective human capital produced the qualifications required for migration. The implications of the Act in Britain for Barbadians is beyond the scope of this study; however, as Britain closed its doors to mass Barbadian emigration, it forced Canada to re-evaluate its ideological nation-building philosophy of "White Canada" and open its doors to racialized migrants. From my perspective, it was likely not a coincidence that in 1962, the year Britain's *Commonwealth Immigrants Act* came into effect, Canada officially de-racialized their immigration policy. British diplomacy coerced the liberalization of Canadian immigration. British officials wanted Canada to "open its gates" and "share the burden" of more Black West Indian migrants since their increased presence in British cities was causing racial tensions and public outcry, which subsequently led to the *Commonwealth Immigrants Act* (Triadafilopoulos

2012: 64–67). It is quite probable that Canada would have changed its immigration policy, but the British Act likely expedited the process. Nevertheless, one must not overlook the consequences at home as Barbadians continued to leave the Island for Britain and Canada.

Emigration and Barbadian Social, Political and Economic Implications

Mass Barbadian emigration caused significant social consequences. In the Migration Lectures in 1968, Lionel Clarke suggested emigration was *the* solution to overpopulation on the Island. Clarke was arguably the first officer of Barbados' Social Welfare Department to comment on the local social ramifications of emigration from Barbados. As a public official, Clarke argued emigration "provided a useful safety valve for over-population."[84] However, this "safety valve" created irrevocable damage to a colonial state on the eve of its independence from Britain. Emigration was Barbados' double-edged sword, one that facilitated the flight of the best, brightest and most educated individuals suited for political, social and economic leadership. Moreover, these individuals emigrated at one of the most crucial junctures in Barbadian history. Clarke postulated:

> The possibly adverse affect on the Barbadian personality of the tendency to escape to another country rather than take part in the building up of Barbados — the symbols of nationhood created with independence had not yet inspired much esteem for local life and heritage.[85]

Simmons and Guengant might argue that the "personality of the tendency to escape to another country" was a cultural trait, or indicative of a "culture-of-migration." While the former clause of the statement may be justifiably debatable, the latter underscored a lack of patriotism as the cause for flight. Centuries of slavery and colonial domination overpowered the budding patriotic and nationalist sentiment throughout the Island, and emigration remained a means for the individual to succeed rather than focus on the betterment of the collective Barbadian state. This was further problematized as Barbadians may have identified themselves as British subjects with a right to migrate to the metropole, but the colonial centre merely recognized them as resources to be exploited in times of need and discarded at will. This "colonial consciousness" was a double-edged sword for Barbadian emigration in an international system dictated by colonialism and racism. Nevertheless, the Barbadian state promoted emigration because it could not sustain its ever-growing populace; however, emigration was seemingly a social and political detriment to the Barbadian national fabric. It was a counterproductive necessity. The Barbadian state needed people to leave, but it became problematic when potential future leaders fled the Island. However, history has shown that people were — and continue to be — Barbados' most valued export.[86]

Emigration provided benefits to Barbadian financial, demographic and employment sectors. Financially, Barbadians employed abroad sent large remittances back home to support their immediate and extended families, which consequently boosted the Barbadian economy. I must reiterate that emigration was a means to alleviate the pressures of an overpopulated colonial island state with a geographic area of only 166 square miles. As migrants left to seek work abroad, local Barbadians occupied vacant job opportunities. However, the seemingly counterproductive nature of Barbadian emigration presented several problems. Young and talented Barbadians left their homeland. While their money returned to the Island in the form of remittances, the vast majority of Barbadian sojourners did not repatriate. With the loss of one or both parents, Barbadian families suffered tremendous consequences. Barbados witnessed several domestic crises including the "disintegration of family life," "behavior problems in children" and "parental deprivation." Moreover, the Barbadian Government promoted emigration as a means to alleviate social strife, but subsequently had to provide financial support in "maintaining and servicing the families of migrants" (Clarke 1968: 23). Barbadian emigration was both a solution and cause of its societal problems.[87] The exodus of educated Barbadians during the mid-twentieth century was a significant detriment to Barbadian society as the Island suffered from the brain drain of its intellectual elite, most notably the loss of its teachers. The emigration phenomenon "provided the large numbers of qualified people that the Canadian educational system had not been able to supply; [it was] wondered whether the loss of teachers from Barbados — 54 in 1964 — represented a serious loss to Barbados."[88] Emigration was thus a double-edged sword but mutually beneficial to all involved; Barbadians needed jobs, Canadians needed qualified people, and Barbados had a surplus of labour. However, Barbados lost its most qualified people to emigration resulting in a brain drain. Several of the best Barbadian teachers realized their full potential as educators in Canada. One may only speculate about their careers in Barbados if they had remained and taught at home, but at the time Barbados could not provide the same opportunities as the United States, Britain or Canada. The Barbadian intellectual elite left because they had to, but many Barbadians and West Indians worked and studied abroad and returned to do great things for their respective independent nation-states, including Barbados' first Prime Minister, Errol Barrow, who studied at the London School of Economics in England. There is no consensus on whether emigration "failed" Barbados. Alleviating unemployment and overpopulation buffered the damage caused by the loss of the Barbadian elite.

International migration does not work within autonomous silos impervious to multiple and overlapping influences. There are numerous "push" and "pull" factors that contribute to the transnational emigration of a people. Barbadians experienced the "push" of a "culture-of-academic-success" precipitated by their government's emphasis of education. They also felt the "push" for upward social mobility, and the claustrophobic effects of overpopulation, as they migrated throughout the Caribbean basin, the United States and the United Kingdom during the early to mid-twentieth century. Following the "closed door" to the United States and the United Kingdom, why did many Barbadians ultimately choose the Great White North? Since the late nineteenth and early twentieth century, the pervasiveness of insidious institutionalized racism in Canada barred the settlement of Black Barbadians and all Black people. Despite openly racist immigration policies, historical, colonial and economic ties "pulled" Barbadians north of the 49th parallel.

Notes

1   BNA, *Migration*, a series of lectures and a panel discussion held at the Centre for Multi-Racial Studies in Barbados between October and December, 1968.
2   Payne, *Migration*, 9–10.
3   BNA, *Rules and Regulations, Framed and Passed by the Governor in Council, Under the authority of the Emigration Act, 1873*, September 23, 1873, 3.
4   Ibid.
5   Ibid., 3 & 6.
6   BNA, *Barbados Emigration Commission*, Report, 1895, 1.
7   Ibid.
8   Ibid., 2.
9   Ibid., 1–2.
10   BNA, *Barbados Emigration Commission*, 3.
11   Ibid., 3 & 8.
12   Ibid., 8.
13   Ibid, 5.
14   Ibid., 10.
15   Ibid., 5, 7, 10, 16.
16   BNA, by authority, revised and consolidated by C.V.H. Archer, B.A. (Cantab.), Barrister-at-Law and W.K. Ferguson, B.A., LL.B (Cantab.), Barrister-at-Law, *Laws of Barbados: Vol.II: 1894–6 – 1906–5, Barbados* (Barbados: Advocate Company Limited, 1944), 443.
17   Ibid., 443–444.
18   Ibid., 443–444.
19   Ibid., 444.
20   Ibid., 448.
21   Ibid., 443–444.
22   Ibid., 443–444 & 446.
23   BNA, *Laws of Barbados*, 446.
24   Ibid.

25   Payne, *Migration*, 10.

26   Payne, *Migration*, 10; BNA, "Report on the working of the Victorian Emigration Society for 1897," *Official Gazette: Documents laid at Meeting of Assembly of 5th July, 1898*, July 21, 1898.

27   William Dickson, *Letters on Slavery* (London: Printed and Sold by J. Philips, George-Yard, Lombard-Street, and sold by J. Johnson, St. Paul's Church-Yard, and Elliot and Kay, Opposite Somerset Place, Strand, 1789), 38 & 93.

28   BNA, *Colonial Reports – Annual No. 1422; Barbados, Report for 1927–28* (London: His Majesty's Stationery Office, 1929), 25.

29   Ibid, 8.

30   BNA, *Colonial Reports – Annual No. 1462; Barbados, Report for 1928–29* (London: His Majesty's Stationery Office, 1929), 5.

31   Ibid., 31; BNA, *Colonial Reports – Annual No. 1544; Barbados, Report for 1930–31* (London: His Majesty's Stationery Office, 1931), 16.

32   Ibid., 6–7.

33   BNA, *Annual Report on the Social and Economic Progress of the People of Barbados, 1931–32* (London: His Majesty's Stationery Office, 1932), 17.

34   Ibid, 17.

35   BNA, *Colonial Reports – Annual No. 1544; Barbados, Report for 1930–31* (London: His Majesty's Stationery Office, 1931), 17; BNA, *Colonial Reports – Annual No. 1595; Annual Report on the Social and Economic Progress of the People of Barbados, 1931–32* (London: His Majesty's Stationery Office, 1932), 17; BNA, *Colonial Reports – Annual No. 1632; Annual Report on the Social and Economic Progress of the People of Barbados, 1932–33* (London: His Majesty's Stationery Office, 1933), 34.

36   BNA, *Colonial Reports – Annual No. 1725; Barbados, Report for 1934–35* (London: His Majesty's Stationery Office, 1935), 34.

37   BNA, *Colonial Reports – Annual No. 1861; Barbados, Report for 1937–1938* (London: His Majesty's Stationery Office, 1938), 17.

38   BNA, By authority, revised and consolidated by C.V.H. Archer, B.A. (Cantab.), Barrister-at-Law and W.K. Ferguson, B.A., LL.B (Cantab.), Barrister-at-Law, *Laws of Barbados: Vol. V: 1928-5–1942-8, Barbados* (Barbados: Advocate Company Limited, 1944), 415 & 417. "Nothing in this Act contained shall affect the provisions of the Emigration Act, 1904." BNA, *Laws of Barbados: Vol. V*, 419.

39   *The Labour (Minimum Wage) Act*, enacted May 6, 1938, and the Employment of Women, Young Persons and Children Act, enacted July 13, 1938. BNA, *Colonial Reports – Annual No. 1861; Barbados, Report for 1937–1938* (London: His Majesty's Stationery Office, 1938), 18.

40   Ibid, 19.

41   *Migration*, Payne, 11.

42   BNA, *The Report of the Committee Appointed to Draw up a Detailed Scheme for the Settlement of Barbadians at Vieux Fort, St. Lucia, 1937.*

43   BNA, *The Report of the Delegation Appointed To Visit Dominica to Examine the Possibilities of a Land Settlement Scheme there for Barbadians* (Bay Street, Barbados: Government Printing Office, 1960), 5; BNA, *Colonial Reports – Annual No. 1861; Barbados, Report for 1937–1938* (London: His Majesty's Stationery Office, 1938), 8

44   Ibid.
45   Payne, *Migration*, 11–12. BNA, *Colonial Office Annual Report on Barbados for the Year 1947* (London: His Majesty's Stationery Office, 1948), 8–9.
46   King, *Migration*, 15.
47   BNA, *Colonial Office Annual Report on Barbados for the Year 1949* (London: His Majesty's Stationery Office, 1950), 10.
48   Sweany, *Migration*, 35–36.
49   BNA, *Colonial Office Annual Report on Barbados for the Years 1950 and 1951* (London: His Majesty's Stationery Office, 1952), 9 & 11.
50   Ibid.
51   BNA, *Colonial Office Annual Report on Barbados for the Years 1952 and 1953* (London: His Majesty's Stationery Office, 1954), 10.
52   Ibid.
53   BNA, *Colonial Office Annual Report on Barbados for the Years 1954 and 1955* (London: His Majesty's Stationery Office, 1957), 9.
54   Ibid., 9 & 20.
55   BNA, *Colonial Office Annual Report on Barbados for the Years 1954 and 1955* (London: His Majesty's Stationery Office, 1957), 9 & 20.
56   Sweany, *Migration*, 35–36.
57   Marcus Garvey, "Speech Before Negro Citizens of New York", at Madison Square Garden, Sunday, March 16, 1924, at 4:00 p.m., pp. 2–11. Reprinted by permission of Mrs. A Jacques Garvey, in Rischin 1976.
58   Ibid., 254.
59   Ibid., 257.
60   Ibid.
61   BNA, *Colonial Office Annual Report on Barbados for the Years 1954 and 1955* (London: His Majesty's Stationery Office, 1957), 9 & 26.
62   Ibid.
63   BNA, *Colonial Office Annual Report on Barbados for the Years 1956 and 1957* (London: His Majesty's Stationery Office, 1959), 14–15.
64   Ibid.
65   Ibid.
66   BNA, *Colonial Office Annual Report on Barbados for the Years 1954 and 1955* (London: His Majesty's Stationery Office, 1957), 14–15; BNA, *Colonial Office Annual Report on Barbados for the Years 1958 and 1959* (Barbados: Government Printing Office, 1961), 19; BNA, *Colonial Office Annual Report on Barbados for the Years 1962 and 1963* (Barbados: Government Printing Office, 1965), 14.
67   King, *Migration*, 16–17.
68   BNA, *Colonial Office Annual Report on Barbados for the Years 1956 and 1957* (London: His Majesty's Stationery Office, 1959), 14–15. The Nursing Selection Committee sent student nurses, mental health nurses, pupil assistant nurses and nursing auxiliaries to U.K. hospitals. BNA, *Colonial Office Annual Report on Barbados for the Years 1958 and 1959* (Barbados: Government Printing Office, 1961), 19.
69   King, *Migration*, 16–17; Payne, *Migration*, 12.
70   King, *Migration*, 17.

71 Information collected from the Barbadian Colonial and Barbados Reports between 1955 and 1963 at the Barbados National Archives, Barbados. BNA, *Colonial Office Annual Report on Barbados for the Years 1954 and 1955* (London: His Majesty's Stationery Office, 1957); BNA, *Colonial Office Annual Report on Barbados for the Years 1956 and 1957* (London: His Majesty's Stationery Office, 1959); BNA, *Colonial Office Annual Report on Barbados for the Years 1958 and 1959* (Barbados: Government Printing Office, 1961); BNA, *Colonial Office Annual Report on Barbados for the Years 1960 and 1961* (Barbados: Government Printing Office, 1962); BNA, *Colonial Office Annual Report on Barbados for the Years 1962 and 1963* (Barbados: Government Printing Office, 1965).

72 BNA, *Information Booklet for Intending Emigrants to Britain*, (n.d.), 1.

73 Ibid., 1, 5, 13–14, 18.

74 BNA, *Information Booklet for Intending Emigrants to Britain* (Broad St. Bridgetown, Barbados: Advocate Co., Ltd., 1955), 1.

75 Ibid., 2.

76 BNA, *Information Booklet for Intending Emigrants to Britain* (Broad St. Bridgetown, Barbados: Advocate Co., Ltd., 1955), 2.

77 Ibid, 23.

78 Ibid., 2, 14, 23.

79 *Colonial Office Annual Report on Barbados for the Years 1962 and 1963* (Barbados: Government Printing Office, 1965), 13.

80 BNA, *Notice to persons wishing to enter the United Kingdom on or after 1ˢᵗ July, 1962* (Barbados: Barbados Government Office, n.d., most likely early 1960s), 1–2.

81 Ibid.

82 Ibid., 3, 5 & 6.

83 Ibid.

84 BNA, *Colonial Office Annual Report on Barbados for the Years 1956 and 1957* (London: His Majesty's Stationery Office, 1959), 12.

85 Clarke, *Migration*, 19.

86 Ibid.

87 Ibid.

88 Panel Discussion, *Migration*, 43.

Chapter Four

BARBADIAN- AND WEST INDIAN-CANADIAN RELATIONS

Canada was part of the New World, an American society. The New World was a slave society, and Canada shared that feature. (Cooper 2006: 11)

White privilege doesn't operate from a level of consciousness. It operates from a position of privilege. Because they're privileged, they don't have to think about stuff. (Hill 2001: 180)

You have kept them out because they are black. If I were a Communist, there is opportunity for me to change and become a decent, respectable Canadian citizen. But I am born black, God has made me that way. You are asking me to undo what God has done? (Moore 1985: 115)

For a period of time during the seventeenth century, Barbados was one of Britain's most profitable colonies (Menard 2006; Mintz 1985). However, as is true for most British possessions in the Americas, colonies did not operate autonomously; trade, people and ideologies existed within a transnational or transcolonial framework. From its first settlement by British colonialists in 1627 and the establishment of one of the earliest parliaments in the Western World, Barbados played a significant role in the Americas. In terms of importance in British relations in the Western

Hemisphere, the small island and the British West Indian archipelago stood on par with, and at times surpassed, the vast British North American territory, specifically during the eighteenth century. Canada and the West Indies have always been important global players in the imperialist international arena. Furthermore, unlike other British West Indian colonies, Barbados was a unique possession: it was the only island in the Caribbean under British imperial rule throughout the entire colonial period. The aftermath of the Seven Years' War displayed British imperial interests in the Caribbean. As victors over the French, the British chose to maintain possession over the highly profitable island of Guadeloupe in exchange for French colonies in modern-day Canada. The British favoured the small but fertile sugar-producing island of Guadeloupe as opposed to the vast territory of what is now known as parts of Quebec, Ontario and Prince Edward Island. Sugar was arguably the most valuable, contentious and destructive commodity during the eighteenth century. Despite the immediate economic value of the West Indian island, at the time, Britain did not see the benefits of complete control over such a large territory in North America; a territory that faced the threat of invasion by a newly independent United States of America in the late eighteenth to midnineteenth century (Chodos 1977: 61).

The United States played a significant role in West Indian–Canadian relations. The loss of their American colonies following the Revolutionary War expedited British imperial and mercantilist control of West Indian–Canadian relations. The British disapproved of the growing trade relations between their current and former colonies during the late eighteenth and early nineteenth centuries. Apprehensive of an American financial monopoly of the region during the nineteenth century, the British pushed for Canada to be its main source of supply for their West Indian colonies. British fears grew out of the West Indian–Canadian relationship that "existed under the long shadow that the United States cast over both areas" (Chodos 1977: 63–64). The United States' hegemony over the Caribbean region played a significant role in the lack of substantial British West Indian–Canadian trade agreements. West Indian colonies were reluctant to enter into trade agreements with Canada due to a "fear of antagonizing America" (Chodos 1977: 64). However, West Indian–Canadian relations did exist prior, during and following the American Revolution. African and creolized Black slaves on British West Indian plantations ate Nova Scotian cod, which was traded for the fruits of their enslaved labour — sugar, rum and molasses. Following the end of slavery, the West Indies also enjoyed the presence of Canadian banking institutions. Financial transactions and banks followed trade routes, and with Halifax a hub for West Indian trade in the late nineteenth century, Canadian banks flourished in the West Indies. The Bank of Nova Scotia opened its doors in 1889 in Jamaica. The bank had a branch in Jamaica even before it had one in Toronto (Chodos 1977: 64, 67).

There were considerable common British imperial links between Canada, Barbados and the British West Indies. Canadian–West Indian relations were also representative of Canada's relationship with Barbados. This association was political, economic and social. Early twentieth-century history of regional trade relations and trade agreements, including the 1908 Canada Conference and the 1920 Canada–West Indies Conference, are examples of the diplomatic deliberations and political debates. They also underscored the symbiotic and codependent relationship. The Canada–West Indies Conference produced the first trade agreement and brought attention to Canada's dominant business and trade interests in the region. It is important to discuss the historical trade relationship as it exemplified Canada's unequal treatment of Black West Indians. Canada willingly conducted business and entered into equally beneficial trade partnerships with the British West Indies, but refused to accept even prominent and influential Black West Indian businesspeople as Canadian immigrants and their social equals. Immigration hypocrisy, and explicit racism, thus became a detriment to cordial trade and social relations. Racism embedded within Canadian immigration policy and racialized institutional instruments designed to exclude non-White peoples undermined Canada's involvement in the West Indies. The xenophobic "White Canada" ideology and legislated policy must be taken into account as a fundamental feature of Canadian immigration policy. It is important to note that Canadian immigration policy excluded Black British West Indians equally regardless of their island origins. While there is a focus on Black West Indians generally, I also provide evidence from Barbados and on Barbadians. Despite the exclusionary rhetoric, West Indian and Canadian voices spoke against the restrictive policy and were skeptical of the official de-racialization of Canadian immigration in 1962. However, the altruism of the new regulations was not solely based on humanitarian grounds, nor was it implemented with conviction; racism and race-based selection criteria persisted, and British immigration policy influenced Canada's desire to accept non-White migrants.

Economic and Political Relations

A complementary relationship, challenged by the omnipresent threat of American economic and political hegemony, characterized early twentieth-century Barbadian- and West Indian–Canadian trade. The chairman of the 1908 Canada Conference stated, "It was true, and fortunately true, that the West Indies and Canada were not completely, but to a remarkable degree, complementary to each other ... Canada had no tropical connexions [sic] whose claims upon her were stronger than ours."[1] Canada needed the West Indies and its agricultural staples, while the West Indies needed Canadian manufactured goods and a large export market. West Indian sugar was the principal product exported to Canada during this period. The following was recorded in the proceedings of the Canada Conference of 1908: "Practically 79 per cent. [sic] of all sugar consumed in Canada has been obtained directly from the West Indies."[2] However, at the turn of the twentieth century, trade prosperity faced several threats. Concerned Canadian businessmen argued that outside influences could impede the trade in West Indian sugar.[3] Officials organized the 1908 Conference for a variety of reasons, but mainly to buffer American interference in Canadian and West Indian relations. The constant West Indian fear of antagonizing the United States' Monroe Doctrine curtailed optimum trade between the two regions (Gilderhus 2006: 6, 16). Moreover, Canadian concerns over the Monroe Doctrine reflected the uncertainty of their autonomy as an independent country or simply an arm of the British Empire during the early twentieth century. The United States' political influence over Barbados and the West Indies dictated most, if not all, trade and political relations. Canada did not possess the economic, military or political power to displace their southern neighbours as the dominant neo-colonial force in the Caribbean. Despite their British colonial and historical ties, West Indians treaded carefully as to not disturb a fragile and potentially devastating relationship with the United States. Nonetheless, delegates of the 1908 Conference proposed several solutions for improved trade relations. The Barbadian delegate to the Conference proposed exempting Canada from raised tariffs set for other countries in order to keep preferable trading relations. This was in addition to the establishment of telegraphic communication between Canada, the West Indies and British Guiana, described as "most desirable for the improvement of mutual trade relations."[4] Political astuteness and diplomacy dictated West Indian–Canadian trade relations.

The Canada–West Indies Conference of 1920 further propelled and solidified inter-regional trade relations as it mandated preferential trade rights for West Indian goods to Canada. This followed the 1908 Conference and the nineteenth-century international economic market where

> preference given to West Indian products in the markets of Canada in the year 1897 (the first extended tariff preference between the West Indies and Canada), though not reciprocated by the West Indian Colonies, gave a distinct impetus to trade between the two sections of the Empire.[5]

Not only were distinct trade opportunities realized, but they also "produced in these Islands a conviction of the goodwill of Canada which has had the happiest influence upon [their] social and commercial relations."[6] Canadian economic interests dictated social and political relations in the West Indies. British imperial links facilitated the ties that bound the Empire in the Americas together. Despite the United States' real and imagined economic and military hegemony throughout the Americas, the former colony of British North America and its British West Indian neighbours maintained prosperous trade. This statement was reiterated by His Excellency the Governor General of Canada at the 1920 Conference, contending, "In this conference, and necessarily, the principle [*sic*] subject for discussion will be the relations between the West Indies and the Dominion ... cementing all portions of the Empire by closer bonds and closer ties."[7] The Prime Minister of Canada in 1920, Sir Robert Borden, stated, "His Excellency has explained all the opportunities for development of trade, and more than that, all intercourse of every kind between the British West Indies and this Dominion."[8]

The 1920s represented a decade of prosperous West Indian–Canadian affairs. The expressed goodwill and auspicious belief in former and continued relations between the two regions culminated in the inauguration of the first Canada–West Indies Trade Agreement of 1920. Article 1 of the Agreement stated:

> The Dominion of Canada affirms the principle of granting a preference on all goods being produced or manufactured of any of the [British West Indian] Colonies aforesaid imported into Canada, which are now subject to duty or which may be made subject to duty at any future time.[9]

Following the 1897 West Indian–Canadian trade preference agreement and the 1908 Canada Conference, the transnational economic relationship and its causal political and social derivatives consolidated the interdependent partnership of the British Empire in the Americas. The benevolent nature of the symbiotic commercial affiliation was expressed during the Canada–West Indies Conference in 1925, by comments made by the Prime Minister of Canada, William Lyon Mackenzie King. He stated:

> Indeed, one has to consider for a moment the relations in which, geographically, we have been placed, to appreciate what it means both to the West Indies in the tropical part of the world, and our own country in the temperate zone, to have the privilege of exchanging the products which each of us is in a special position to produce and manufacture, and to be able to do this without some of the keen rivalries in trade which come where competition is between those who belong to the same zone.[10]

The mutually beneficial relationship was facilitated by geographical and historical circumstance; the British imperial and colonial link laid the necessary foundation needed for it to develop. Nevertheless, as Mackenzie King stated, the West Indies and Canada were in a position to capitalize upon this good fortune (Donaghy 2012: 9). It was an unequal partnership, but Canada needed the West

Indies and the West Indies needed Canada. By the turn of the twentieth century, the United States had annexed the Caribbean island of Puerto Rico. The ominous and omnipresent threat of further American hegemony and colonization throughout the archipelago caused economic and political problems between Canada and the British West Indies. The twentieth-century globalization of international relations, specifically in the Americas, put former and current British colonies in a united position for the common good and common wealth of the British Empire. Mackenzie King pontificated, "Whatever we do in the matter of increasing trade between ourselves will, we believe, not only be serving our mutual interests but will assist in developing a community of interest within the Empire itself, and that is all to the good for all concerned."[11] Canadian leaders were committed to maintaining and expanding trade with the West Indies during the 1920s.

By the late 1920s, Canada was Barbados' chief trading partner and the largest purchaser of the Island's principle staples — sugar and molasses — absorbing Barbados' falling export market to the United Kingdom. The competitive conditions established during the 1920 Conference favoured the Dominion of Canada. The Island's economic stability was dependent on world sugar prices, generally, and Canadian purchasing power and favourable trading conditions, specifically. However, with the onset of the Great Depression in 1929, and the subsequent fall in sugar prices the same year, the Barbadian export market and its economy suffered dearly. This was also caused by the global overproduction of sugar and dwindling markets, causing the product to drop "in price to a level lower than the cost of production."[12] During the global Depression of the early and mid-1930s, the price of sugar remained at levels below its height in the late 1920s, but the price grew steadily. The lowest precipitation levels in recorded Barbadian history in 1930 compounded the economic decline. Nevertheless, Canada remained the largest purchaser of Barbadian domestic exports, sugar and molasses.[13]

Keynesian economics defined Barbadian Government intervention during the Depression. The government avoided a laissez-faire policy during the global economic recovery and came to the conclusion that Canada was no longer a sustainable market for its domestic exports. The Barbadian House of Assembly sympathetically urged the British Government to buy more Barbadian sugar. The Assembly argued it was "the only immediate available means of reducing the heavy loss to producers, and thereby enabling them to continue the cultivation of their lands, provide work for and pay a living wage to the labouring population during the present depression."[14] The plea to Britain did not fall on deaf ears. Although by 1932, Canada remained the largest purchaser of Barbadian domestic exports, "increased preferences on sugar granted by the United Kingdom diverted some of the produce from Canada to the United Kingdom."[15] Canada imported more Barbadian molasses in 1933, but the United Kingdom superseded its former

North American colony in sugar imports. By 1934, 1936 and 1937, Canada once again became Barbados' chief buyer of molasses and sugar. However, by 1938, the British became the largest purchaser of Barbadian domestic products at 46.6 percent of total exports, while Canada trailed slightly behind at 41.6 percent.[16] This was due in part to government-subsidized prices for sugar in the United Kingdom for British consumers and a falling demand for sugar in Canada. Barbadian sugar, rum and molasses featured as premium exports to Canada during the early and mid-twentieth century. Appendix E provides details for the total Barbadian trade and total domestic product exports to Canada between 1927 and 1936.

As Appendix E indicates, trade to Canada decreased significantly during the early stages of the Depression between 1929 and 1931 and rose again up until 1934. The Barbadian economy was at the mercy of a volatile sugar export market while simultaneously relying on heavy imports of foodstuffs. The data collected for Appendix F highlighted the first recorded trade figures for the Barbadian imports of goods from Canada between 1927 and 1936. The relationship persisted for a number of years. By 1938, a "large importation of foodstuffs continue[d] and [was] essential to meet the requirements of the dense population of the Island."[18] As a small tropical island, Barbados was not a self-sufficient society and was dependent on importing a large amount of goods it could not produce. This was due to its agricultural climate and the geographical and logistical truth that the country was not able to sustain the heavy demands of an overpopulated citizenry. The total value of goods imported between 1946 and 1951 underscored Barbados' dependence on Canadian goods and foodstuffs. In 1946, Canadian imports were valued at £1,297,396; in 1947, £1,540,647; and in 1948, £1,670,604. By 1949, the currency changed from British pounds to the British Caribbean or British West Indian dollar. Canadian imports were valued at $6,711,940 in 1949; $5,588,959 in 1950; and $8,314,894 in 1951. The expansion of trade liberalization with North America in 1950 caused the drop in Barbadian imports by over $1 million; staple Canadian imports, salt fish and animal feed, were placed on open general license and ushered in the end of price and market controls and subsidies. However, during this period, flour was the favoured Barbadian import of Canadian goods.[19]

Barbados and Canada enjoyed mutually beneficial, but unequal, trade relations during the early to mid-twentieth century. Barbadian economic livelihood depended on favourable trade agreements with its Commonwealth partner, while Canada capitalized on this relationship to secure a dependable and stable import and export market. Historical imperial and mercantilist circumstance precipitated Barbadian-Canadian economic links and were the ties that bound the former British colony and its British colonial neighbour in the West Indies. This economic partnership in the British Empire in the Americas extended to social relations.

Social Relations

The political and economic relationship between the West Indies and Canada, and specifically that of Barbados, extended into social and even quotidian ways of life. The *Canada–West Indies Magazine* and the Canadian West Indian League illustrate this association.[21] Established in 1911 by the Canadian West Indian League, the magazine was "published monthly, for the promotion of mutual interest of Canada, Bermuda, the British West Indies, British Guiana, British Honduras and other British countries in the Caribbean."[22] The Canadian West Indian League was officially recognized the same year as the magazine. The League spearheaded Canadian–West Indian trade in the 1920s and consolidated the trade agreements of 1897, 1898 and 1912. The Sun Life Assurance Company of Canada, one of the first Canadian organizations in Barbados and the West Indies in 1879, helped form the Montreal-based League. The League was sponsored by Sun Life president T.B. Macaulay who led the organization for over twenty years and "was a life-long champion of West Indian–Canadian friendship."[23] The founding officers included the honourary president, Sir Thomas Shaughnessy; president Macaulay; vice-president A. Delery Macdonald; the executive council of A.L. Bennett, A. Birchall, H.C.M. Cornish, Henry Dalby, Frank Hart, W. Hutchinson, C.E. Neill, J.H. Stockton and E.M. Walcott; secretary W.T. Robson; and treasurer J.K. Keyes of the Royal Bank of Canada, Montreal (*The Montreal Gazette* June 10, 1911). The membership fee for Canadians was $5 per annum, which included a subscription to the magazine. The June 10, 1911, issue of *The Montreal Gazette* outlined seven key objectives of the League, including to "foster a better understanding between the peoples of the Dominion of Canada, the British West Indies, British South America and the British Empire," and establish travel and unite "patriotic citizens" of the regions (*The Montreal Gazette* June 10, 1911). Economically, the League promoted trade and business lines of communication for sustained commercial partnerships. The League, as shown through the economic agreements of the early twentieth century, became a bulwark for Canadian affairs in the West Indies. The relationship was economically driven, but with political and social ramifications.

The League was also heavily involved in chastising the Canadian Government's position on immigration. It argued that their anti-Black immigration policy would negatively affect business and trade in the region. A member of the League, A.W. Macdonald, wrote to the Superintendent of Immigration Branch W.D. Scott on November 16, 1916, complaining that immigration officials "must take steps to clear up the impression that had gotten around that Canada did not want coloured immigrants" (quoted in Schultz 1982: 57). It is clear that the League understood that unfavourable immigration policy was a detriment to prosperous partnerships in the West Indies. The League and its magazine embodied a mutually beneficial relationship to both Canada and the British Caribbean region. The relationship may have favoured Canadian interests, but favourable trade agreements — most notably a positive outlook on Barbadian and West Indian culture and a significant push for the tourism industry — propelled the region's economic growth.[24]

Tourist advertisements revealed the magazine's Canadian publication and distribution base. The May 1937 issue of the magazine included "Honeymoon Tours" for the "Summer Brides of 1937" in Trinidad and Tobago.[25] The advertisement featured photographs of predominantly White women; the magazine targeted Canadians, in Canada, with interests in the West Indies. The West Indies and Barbados were no longer neglected plantation backwaters. This newfound public interest increased visibility and familial and social ties within the British Empire in the Americas. Barbados and the West Indies were strategic political and trading partners; however, the magazine's advertisements, alluding to the "exotic" curiosity of the Other in the tropical paradise of the unknown, emphasized the Canadian public's interest in the region.[26] The magazine provided Canadians "with a better understanding of conditions in the British West Indies."[27] Nevertheless, it targeted Canadian domestic issues and reciprocated the West Indian tourist sentiment and showcased Canada as a suitable destination.[28] The magazine also featured Canadian advertisements, which promoted trade and tourism to and from the West Indies. These included the Canadian National (West Indies) Steamships Ltd., Saguenay Terminals Ltd., and Trans-Canada Airlines.[29] The magazine may have targeted the Canadian public, but as outlined in the 1911 objectives of the League and its magazine, and reaffirmed in the recognition of their twenty-fifth anniversary in the Windsor Daily Star, the readership was of a higher socio-economic and bourgeois business and political class (Windsor Daily Star December 26, 1936). Its audience was comprised of those Canadians who had the capital to invest in the West Indies and had the disposable income to travel to the West Indies long before leisure holidays to the Caribbean were affordable to the masses in the latter half of the twentieth century. The readership was an elite group of Canadians. These Canadians had considerable economic wealth and political influence, as the League facilitated and contributed to many economic trade agreements and commented on political movements in the West Indies during the early to mid-twentieth century.

A special issue of The Canada–West Indies Magazine in 1957 expressed Canadian support for the West Indies. The November volume celebrated the creation of the short-lived West Indies Federation.[30] This is quite significant in terms of diplomatic relations and the history of migration between Canada, the United Kingdom and the West Indies. Following the Second World War, Canada supported the idea of a West Indian federation. Canadian officials and academics, including Senator A. Neil McLean, went so far in supporting Canadian political unification with the West Indies as a "tropical province," and the idea was "worth exploring" if all political solutions in the West Indies failed (Edmondson 1964: 192). Canada begrudgingly took on the financial responsibility of sending aid to the region as a result of Britain's push in 1956 for Canada to support the West Indies Federation (Donaghy and Muirhead 2008: 278–279). While Canada did have historical trade relations with the region, the authors expressed that the state had very little defined foreign policy and merely economic "interests" (Donaghy and Muirhead 2008: 289). British postwar influence, American hegemony in the region, and the ominous threat of Soviet encroachment in the Americas during the Cold War precipitated the need to keep the Federation "democratic" and viable (Donaghy and Muirhead 2008: 282). Member of Parliament George Clyde Nowlan (PC, Digby-Annapolis-Kings) addressed the threat of the spread of communism in the West Indies during the 1950s and argued the area was "ripe for communism" due to the region's poor socio-economic conditions.[31] On the eve of the West Indies Federation, he argued that Canada should pay more attention to the Caribbean.[32] Under Prime Minister John Diefenbaker in 1958, Canada's aid program sent a ship to the West Indies to facilitate the Federation's inter-island movement.[33] Canada's motives in supporting the ill-fated Federation were not reflected accurately by the benevolence expressed by the magazine, but by the state's emerging postwar role as a "middle player" in international relations. Outside political influences and financial aid could not save the Federation from internal fissures.

Once the new West Indies Federation came to be in 1958, some Jamaicans "had begun to question the benefits of federation membership and to express concerns about the future of federation," and by 1961, Premier Norman Manley "announced that a referendum would be held in 1961, so that the people could decide whether or not Jamaica was to remain in the Federation" (Johnson 1999: 122). As the referendum passed on September 19, 1961, "the majority of Jamaicans voted against the island's continued membership in the West Indies Federation. This turn of events has widely been accepted as that which brought West Indian federal political union to an end" (Johnson 1999: 122). Parochialism curtailed West Indian union; political and economic autonomy and the preservation of national and ethnic identities, specifically in the cases of Jamaica and Trinidad, circumvented common colonial histories and future regional collective interests and policies. The West Indies Federation faced several issues including that of differential development, whereby Jamaican politician and delegate at the Montego Bay Conference, Alexander Bustamante, noted it was not possible for countries with varying levels of development to unite. It was unjust that developed islands, specifically Jamaica, would have to support an entire region, thus constituting a drain on its own socio-economic resources as "issues of differential development were to prove beneficial in the campaign for secession" (Johnson 1999: 142, 147). The relationship among the failure of the West Indies Federation in 1961,

West Indian emigration, and the *Commonwealth Immigrants Act* of 1962 must not be understated. With free and uninhibited migration throughout West Indian nations no longer a possibility, it is quite plausible that the British feared an influx of West Indian emigrants following the short-lived West Indies Federation. The end of the Federation added to British external and internal pressures to bar West Indian emigrants and, subsequently, indirectly pressured Canada to de-racialize its immigration policy in 1962.[34] I argue that both Britain and Canada, despite their perceived benevolence for the welfare and success of the West Indies Federation, had a vested interest in a federation that would have facilitated perpetual inter-island migrant flows and thus alleviating the pressure of inter-regional migration.

Canada, displayed in the publication of the special issue of *The Canada–West Indies Magazine* in 1957, supported the ill-fated Federation; however, it is possible that most of the statements were quite political and diplomatic in nature. Canadian historical and future interests in the British Caribbean relied on cordial, if not manipulative, relations. Nevertheless, several high-ranking officials within the Canadian Government commented within the pages of the special issue. The Minister of Trade and Commerce, the Honourable Gordon Churchill, D.S.O., M.A., LL.B, expressed:

> I congratulate the "Canada–West Indies Magazine" on its efforts, over a period of forty-six years, to provide Canadians with a better understanding of conditions in the British West Indies. This issue will undoubtedly outline some of the problems that the establishment of a new unit within this Commonwealth will create, and point the way towards closer associations between our respective peoples in the years that lie ahead.[35]

The Deputy Minister of the Canadian Department of Trade and Commerce, Mitchell W. Sharp, stated, "Canada and the West Indies are old friends and old trading partners. From the second half of the eighteenth century, the two regions have shared the kinship which has arisen from mutual associations, in what is now the Commonwealth."[36] The Right Honourable Lord Hailes, Governor-General Designate, West Indies Federation, echoed this sentiment and expressed a West Indian obligation for a sustainable partnership within the British Commonwealth. Hailes commented, "I am confident that the Federation of the West Indies will not look in vain for friendship and support from the Dominion of Canada as she moves towards her place within our Family of Nations." [37] A cautious air of diplomacy tempered Canadian pleasantries; the politicians appealed to a diverse audience. Businessmen relied on cordial political relations for sustained trade. It is probable that they most likely dominated readership and some may have benefited financially, or lost, from West Indian unification. As previously mentioned, the magazine's mandate was to provide Canadians "with a better understanding of the (economic and political) conditions" in the West Indies (*Montreal Gazette* June 10, 1911).

However, by the 1960s and following the end of the West Indies Federation, West Indian politicians, specifically those from Barbados, appealed directly to Canadian diplomats on political, economic and social terms ostensibly to support individual islands in the aftermath of the failure of the Federation. The Right Honourable Sir Errol Walton Barrow, former premier of Barbados and its first prime minister in 1966, addressed the Commonwealth Partners in the West Indies Conference held in Fredericton, New Brunswick, October 25–27, 1963 (Barrow 1964: 172–187). Barrow pushed for positive diplomatic Barbadian- and West Indian–Canadian relations. The diplomatic partnership extended to social and economic relations, characterized by the burgeoning tourism industry (Hoyos 2003: 8–11). He noted the average Canadian held the power to extend aid to the region. Barrow (1964: 172) stated, "Keep coming down to our area in ever increasing numbers; and [the average Canadian] will never need the rigours of the winter to impel him in our direction after he has been there for the first time." Barrow mentioned the cold and dreary Canadian winters as a justifiable reason to visit Barbados and the West Indies. The politician appealed to the "push" of the Canadian cold climate as opposed to the "pull" of the Barbadian year-round tropical climate. In turn, Barrow asked that the gesture be reciprocated. He wanted the Canadian people to treat his citizens with the same respect and friendliness as was extended to Canadian tourists and sojourners in his homeland. Barrow (1964: 172) stated that Canadians should treat the West Indian student and West Indian visitor to Canada "with the same candour and friendliness that West Indians extend to Canadians in the West Indies." Barrow wanted respect and equality to define the Barbadian and West Indian position in the Commonwealth relationship.

Economically, Barrow underscored late nineteenth- and early twentieth-century West Indian–Canadian trade relations. Barrow (1964: 172) argued that "Canada–West Indies relations … [and their respective] economies are entirely complementary." West Indians and Canadians envisioned an equal partnership. Trade promoted both Canadian and West Indian interests. However, while it benefited both regions, Canada dictated the terms of the agreements. With the exception of Barclays Bank, banking business was "carried on exclusively by Canadian concerns," since historically established institutions controlled the Barbadian financial market and profits flowed back to Canada (Barrow 1964: 178). Canadian banks dominated the Barbadian banking industry and enjoyed a monopoly in Barbadian finance and commerce. Despite the financial security of Canadian foreign investment, by the mid-twentieth century, Barbados began to suffer the effects of unequal North-South trade. During the early 1950s, Canada imported approximately one million gallons of Barbadian rum. However, due in part to their desire to refine the product in Canada, the state placed import taxes on Barbadian rum. Rum sales to Canada declined in the late 1950s and continued to fall. Recognizing the decline in trade, which devastated the Barbadian export market, Barrow asked for further Canadian foreign investment and for the Canadian emigration and settlement of businessmen and investors. Barrow (1964: 180) offered this piece of advice: "Discover some kind of activity that would have afforded them the privilege of living for an indefinite period of time in the West Indian islands, even after they may have retired from their businesses in Canada." Despite having to deal with overpopulation and issues of restrictive Canadian immigration policy, it seems as if Barrow understood that Barbados needed the economic investment that Canadian businesspeople could bring to the Island. Barrow needed to reconcile Barbados' economic development, overpopulation and emigration, and subsequently highlighted the financial advantages and personal merits of Canadian migration to Barbados (Barrow 1964: 180).

Barrow asked the Canadian people, Canadian businessmen and the Government of Canada to appreciate the similarities — parliamentary, colonial and the English language — of the Canadian–West Indian link before looking elsewhere, including South Asia, for investment opportunities. He drew on Canadian–West Indian historical ties and common British colonial kin to propel future foreign relations and foreign partnerships. The task was difficult, but Barrow pushed for a bond which he knew his country needed for its economic survival. He emphasized the gesture was to be reciprocated by Barbados in maintaining "traditional [trading] markets" in Canada, which included importing Canadian flour (Barrow 1964: 183). Barrow reaffirmed faith in the loyalty of the West Indian partnership as he played on Canada's sovereignty and national identity during a period where the British Government pushed for closer Canadian economic and social ties in the West Indies. Barrow (1964: 174–175) contended that "Canadians are better disposed to the Caribbean than he could ever convert the British people to be." As colonized kin in the British Commonwealth in the Americas, Canadian, Barbadian and West Indian commonalities overshadowed those of their imperial master, Britain.

The unequal power dynamic problematized a seemingly cordially relationship. Did Barrow and his West Indian colleagues downplay their subordinate trading position to gain favourable economic concessions from the Government of Canada? Was Canadian trade with the West Indies voluntary? Was it coerced by the United Kingdom that saw Canada as a suitable outlet for its West Indian migrant "problem" following the Second World War? Did Canada see its relationship with Barbados and the West Indies as a market suitable for neo-colonialism similar to American interests in the region? The physical presence of a colonial master, and the hundreds of years of an indoctrinated colonial mentality, curtailed Barbados' independence and autonomy on the international stage prior to 1966. Despite the

British meddling in its foreign affairs, Canada, as a sovereign state, determined its unequal partnership with its West Indian neighbour. Canada, as is true and expected for most financially dominant players in partnerships with the economically weak, defined the physical and ideological terms which Barbadians were forced to accept. What must be noted is the fundamental fact that marginalized Barbados and the British colonies in the Caribbean — race. Race and racism underlined a divisive hegemonic threat to Barbados and the West Indies; a pathology of race dictated Canadian foreign relations, and specifically its policy towards immigration, with the country and the region.

Race, Colour and the Ideological Paradox of Canadian Immigration

Exclusionary and discriminatory policies defined Canada's history of immigration. Canada openly restricted and regulated the entry of non-White and non-Christian immigrants. Following the Second World War, prominent Jewish Canadians decried Canada's policy against Jewish immigration in favour of enemies of war. The presidents of the Canadian Jewish Congress and the Jewish Immigrant Aid Society, respectively, argued:

> We understand that in a number of [Jewish immigrant] cases, rejections were ordered because of petty dealings with Japanese occupation forces in order to eke out a living and officially labeled as "trading with the enemy"; [however] … this also raises a question of equity. Many Germans and nationals of other countries have been admitted to Canada who not only "traded with the enemy" but actually and directly helped this enemy bearing arms against Canada.[38]

The authors postulated that Canada's obdurate selection and restriction of potential immigrants defied reasonable logic and weighed heavily on ignorant public opinion. They stated that "immigration is admittedly a difficult matter on which there are many views. One may differ — indeed as we do — with the basic approach to immigration policy that is predicated on the basic assumption that it reflects the majority opinion."[39] They continued, "In accepting this view we are not nevertheless prepared to admit that the present policy is being equitably administered nor is it being implemented in accordance with Canada's great reputation as a Western Democracy."[40] In response, Minister of Citizenship and Immigration, Walter Harris, justified Canadian immigration policy stating, "[it] is to foster the growth of the population of Canada through immigration, ensuring careful selection and favourable settlement of such numbers of immigrants as can be successfully absorbed into the national economy without fundamentally altering the character of the population."[41] The Minister's convoluted response did not address who or what was the "character of the population"; however, through his omission, one may assume that enemies of the state during the Second World War could be "successfully absorbed" into Canadian society as opposed to Jewish migrants. J.V. McAree's 1949 article "Jews are Victims" in the *Globe & Mail* (Toronto), described "Nazis on Toronto Streets":

> J. Sinclair also says that the discrimination against Jews by the Canadian Government has been well known. He adds: "There are in Canada thousands of Nazi collaborators and Fascists who entered as DPs. I know of several Canadian veterans who were in prisoner-of-war camps, and recognized their Nazi guards in Toronto ... Even Adolph Hitler could enter Canada under the present stupid immigration plan. Few Jews, if any, have been allowed in as miners, lumber-men or domestics. Any German slut who served well in Nazi brothels can enter Canada as a domestic."[42]

A paradox of hypocrisy defined Canadian immigration policy; Canada permitted the settlement of those who fought against Canadian core values. The state allowed the killers of thousands of Canadians to live next to their victims and benefit from the same freedoms the former enemies tried to dismantle. Meanwhile, the Canadian state restricted the entry of Jewish victims of known genocide and crimes against humanity. How did Nazis and their sympathizers not alter "the character of the population," as argued by the Minister of Citizenship of Immigration? Similar to the Jewish case, xenophobia forced Black emigrants, Black West Indians and Black Barbadians to navigate and circumvent this racist and illogically discriminatory Canadian immigration and settlement pretext. A pathologically ambiguous, anti-Semitic and racist ideology defined Canada's immigrant selection process. The idea of who should be a Canadian, and the negative codification of one's race, religion and, specifically, one's legacy of slavery and colonial subjugation as Black, perverted Canadian immigration policy.

This was an anti-Black, xenophobic, "White [Anglo-Saxon Protestant] Canada" postwar policy supported by all levels of government including Canada's Prime Minister, William Lyon Mackenzie King (Razack 2002; Stasiulis and Jhappan 1995). It was a situation where "making Canada white and attracting white immigrants to populate the Dominion were almost universally viewed as key parts of Canada's nation-building project," or a "White Canada" (Goutor 2007: 5). In May 1947, Mackenzie King most (in)famously declared that "the people of Canada do not wish to make a fundamental alteration in the character of their population through mass immigration" (Goutor 2007: 13; Avery 1995: 151–52). One can assume, and rightfully so, that Mackenzie King's "character" comment was a euphemism for

"White" Anglo-Saxon primordial attachment to "true" Canadianness. Prior to his public address on Canadian postwar immigration policy, Mackenzie King's diaries revealed that on February 13, 1947, he obfuscated his position on exclusion based on racial discrimination and his fundamental right to bar nationalities and "strains of blood" from settling in Canada. The prime minister stated that there was "a good deal of confusion in the minds of all of us as to where to draw the line and how to draw it in the matter of discrimination between different races and peoples who wish to come to Canada," and he admitted that "there should be no exclusion of any particular race."[43] He continued:

> A country should surely have the right to determine what strains of blood it wishes to have in its population and how its people coming from out-side have to be selected. There is going to be a great danger of the U.N. refusing the idea of justifiable rights of selected immigration with racial and other discriminations.[44]

Mackenzie King was not troubled in his personal and diplomatic stance towards racialized groups in Canada (Bangarth 2002: 99–123). It seemed that he person-ally promoted the race-based exclusion of potential immigrants and the nefarious and illogical fallacy of race and racism, which permeated all levels of Canadian and Western society, and permitted the continued open exclusion of non-White peoples.

In his 1947 public address on Canadian postwar immigration policy, Mackenzie King stated that "the government [would] seek by legislation, regulation, and vigorous administration, to ensure the careful selection and permanent settle-ment of such numbers of immigrants as can advantageously be absorbed in our national economy" (quoted in Corbett 1957: 3). Mackenzie King's position on immigration and the settlement of "desirable" future Canadian citizens remained a racialized reality, one which was not dictated by the national economy, but similar to Britain's *Commonwealth Immigrants Act* of 1962, by the xenophobic fears of the White Canadian population. What is most troubling is that the prime minister delivered these statements immediately following the human rights atrocities of the Holocaust and the Second World War. Mackenzie King addressed the arbitrary selection of immigrants and stated:

> I wish to make it quite clear that Canada is perfectly within her rights in selecting the persons whom we regard as desirable future citizens. It is not a 'fundamental human right' of any alien to enter Canada. It is a privilege. It is a matter of domestic policy.[45]

In the May 1, 1947, entry in his diary, Mackenzie King followed up his House of Commons address delivered the same day and stated that there was no "fundamental right which caused us to admit people that we did not think could be assimilated and which could change the composition of our country."[46] Arguably, this "domestic policy" was fundamentally racist and influenced by public opinion, where the government faced pressure from "old-stock" English-speaking Canadians about restricting immigration from certain ethnic groups. Canadians showed "their strongest prejudices against Oriental immigration, and probably also against Negro and Jewish immigration" (Corbett 1957: 31).

This top-down and bottom-up prejudice unsurprisingly led to the *Immigration Act* of 1953, which came into effect June 1 of that year. The Act, similar to the United States' *McCarran Act*, administered admission quotas from certain countries and new sponsorship requirements. It was not until May 1956 that regulations began to discern individuals that could come to Canada from specific countries (Corbett 1957: 38). This new criteria was a direct barrier to the settlement of new immigrant groups, specifically potential racialized migrants; "nationalities [that had] little or no foothold in Canada [could not] become established here by means of family relationships," and this created and indoctrinated a "geographic bias," ostensibly based on race, for the selection of those "privileged" enough to be allowed to settle and become Canadian in a discriminatory postwar Canada (Corbett 1957: 44–45). This "geographic" discrimination was "compounded by prejudices against social customs, ways of doing business, wage standards, family life, religion and skin pigmentation of the people" (Corbett 1957: 45). This new Act and the Orders-in-Council passed under the Act affected West Indians and, specifically, the settlement of Barbadians in Canada. Barbadians would have had to be sponsored by a Canadian citizen or permanent resident in Canada who was an immediate relative. Barbadians in Canada could only sponsor a "husband, wife, unmarried children under the age of twenty-one, mother, father, brother, sister, fiancé(e), 'orphan' nephew or niece under twenty-one, or a grandparent" (Corbett 1957: 40). If ethnic and national groups did not have a "foothold" in Canada, these groups could not have had a firm establishment in Canada "by means of family relationships." Moreover, women selected under the Scheme had to be unmarried without children. By virtue of its restrictive sponsorship requirements, the 1953 *Immigration Act* deliberately barred the settlement of Black West Indian and Barbadian migrants in Canada. Contradictory immigration policy rhetoric throughout the 1950s both restricted and gradually facilitated the settlement of Black Barbadians in Canada. Canada seemingly opened its doors to more Barbadians and non-White peoples specifically through sponsorship initiatives; however, groups that did not have roots in Canada could not benefit from the supposedly "relaxed" immigration policy. The changes effectively retained the status quo, but they did provide a foundation for future liberalization. Throughout the decade, Canadian officials debated the arbitrary nature of their selection process.

At a meeting held June 19, 1953, Canadian officials discussed known and conflicting issues of racism and discrimination in Canadian immigration policy and practice. The meeting also highlighted the inequities in Canadian and Black West Indian relations with respect to immigration and trade. Canada willingly conducted business with Blacks, but expressed hesitation and bigotry towards the international migration of West Indians. The officials revealed that potential emigrants, "although British subjects, are of coloured blood, and when these applicants are turned down by Immigration, it creates embarrassment for the Trade Commissioner who must deal with the same people in his trade activities."[47] The term "Coloured" and its codified negativity further complicated the hypocritical treatment of Black West Indians. Laval Fortier, Deputy Minister of the Department of Citizenship and Immigration, said that "only close relatives of 'coloured' British West Indians are admissible as immigrants to Canada"; he admitted that "the term 'coloured' has not been fully defined."[48] "Colour" was not defined, and Fortier admitted its irresponsible and ambiguous usage. It was an arbitrary exclusion of people based on an undefined classification of colour and codification of race. Canada did not, and could not, implement a colour-based rubric of eligible immigrants from the British West Indies, because "Coloured" was not a definable term. A reified ideology, with roots in the British liberal racial order, justified exclusion. A June 1, 1953, correspondence note, "Immigrant Entry to Canada of Coloured Persons Bearing British Passports" from the Canadian Embassy in Caracas, Venezuela, to the Under-Secretary of State for External Affairs in Canada, reiterated Canada's obfuscated and ideological discrimination by colour, and stated, "we are under the impression that the entry to Canada of British subjects who are coloured is discouraged, but we are unable to find any reference to this in various documents relating to immigration."[49] The Trade Commissioner in Port-of-Spain, Trinidad, L.D. Wilgress, whose territory covered Barbados, was unable to handle immigration inquiries and was having difficulty dealing with Coloured West Indians. The Commissioner stated, "there is, of course, a serious question of policy in dealing with requests for immigration from many British West Indians of coloured blood."[50] Ad hoc legislation justified an exclusionary and "colour-coded" policy. This policy was further highlighted and problematized in a letter dated August 17, 1953, from P.T. Baldwin, the head of the Admissions Division of the Department of Citizenship and Immigration, to R.R. Parlour, the Assistant of the Canadian Trade Commissioner in Port-of-Spain, Trinidad.[51] The child of a Canadian citizen, if not of the same racial and national origin due to miscegenation, was forced to apply and be admitted through immigration channels. Even if one of the parents was Canadian and White, by definition the child was not Canadian. An excerpt from the letter read:

[Name blanked out] is a Canadian citizen and therefore admissible as a matter of right, but her children would have the citizenship [and racial or colour] status of her late husband and would therefore be seeking admission to Canada as immigrants. They would be admissible to or with her mother, but difficulty might arise when they are examined at the Canadian port of entry, if the mother does not have in her possession evidence of satisfactory arrangements for their reception and support.[52]

The following excerpt is an example of how the Immigration Office treated cases of potential emigrants that "looked" Asian and Coloured, and how the Office handled subsequent issues regarding family reunification and sponsorship.

The colour question and the Asiatic question are difficult; but in our experience the former has never arisen in the case of sponsored applicants — i.e., persons going to near relatives in Canada or to marry. In regard to other (i.e., unsponsored) applicants the criterion of the Department of Citizenship and Immigration is not rigidly ethnic — perhaps necessarily so because a rigidly ethnic criterion would be most difficult if not impossible to apply. An applicant who looks like a Latin American or an Israelite evidently passes muster.

[Furthermore, the] Department of Citizenship and Immigration advised us in their letter of November 30, 1949, file 185402, that a person of pure Asiatic origin, irrespective of place of birth of residence, was Asiatic in an immigration sense, and that the racial origin of a partly Asiatic person was determined by the father's race ... [and] perhaps Brazil will in the near future absorb appreciable numbers of these peoples. If this should happen, the attractiveness of North America may weaken.[53]

It seems as though Canada did not want to trouble itself with "hybrid" immigrants and saw Brazil, the supposed "racial democracy," as a suitable nation-state to handle miscegenation. Conversely, it is interesting to note then that if Canada did not want to "absorb" mixed progeny, and excluded those of non-White phenotypes, that Canada wanted to maintain a "racially pure" society by any means necessary. It is similar to the law of hypodescent, or the One-Drop Rule, in the United States.

There was no logical political reason for aforementioned cases of exclusion, and the hypocritical treatment of West Indians embarrassed Canadian trade officials. Canadian authorities "discouraged" and refused entry to many high-ranking Black, Coloured or "Asiatic" West Indian businessmen or political officials. Authorities contended that "this problem is much more difficult when the applicant is only 1/4 or 1/8 coloured, and especially if he comes from one of the respected and wealthy families of the island."[54] This presented difficulties in maintaining collegial colour-blind relations and established partnerships that benefited Canada economically. Trade commissioners barred their supposed West Indian partners based solely on their colour. The shared responsibilities of trade and immigration officials created an unequal relationship and projected the paradox of Canadian foreign policy; a "partnership" characterized by Canada's willingness to do business in the West Indies, and with Black people, but refusing immigration and restricting human rights and equality in Canada. Nevertheless, trade officials continued to do business with Barbadians. Canadian trade officials stated the policy created "bad public relations [and] hinders promotion [of] Canadian trade ... [These rejection decisions] require explanation."[55] They continued arguing it was "embarrassing," "untenable," and caused "serious damage [to] Canadian prestige."[56] Trade officials wrote that "a trained immigration officer on the spot would be in a much better position to decide on these borderline cases, and then to explain to the applicants the basis for his decision," and protested:[57]

> We realize that, as a rule, persons of coloured races are not encouraged to enter Canada unless their background, or settlement arrangements in Canada are exceptionally favourable. However, it seems an unwritten policy of Canada not to mention this partial colour bar, and I find it difficult to advise prospective negro, or partly negro, immigrants whether they should go to the trouble of submitting applications, and then to explain why their application has been rejected.[58]

The documents and correspondence during the early 1950s emphasized a hypocritical divide in Canadian–West Indian relations. The above evidence highlighted the misrepresentation and picayune definition of "colour" and how it implicated the arbitrary selection of potential West Indian emigrants. It also underscored the fallacy of Canadian benevolence and how Canada deliberately concealed its racist motives.

Canada attempted to justify the restriction of "coloured" or "partly coloured" persons through various inconspicuous and devious means. Canadian authorities stated, "It has long been the policy of the Department to restrict the admission to Canada of coloured or partly-coloured persons."[59] Officials desperately argued, without historical cross-examination of the root causes of inequality and discrimination, that

> this policy has been based on unfavourable experience with respect to negro settlements such as we have in Halifax [and] the generally depressed conditions of the negro in Canada and an understanding that the Canadian public was not willing to accept any significant group of negro immigrants."[60]

The Africville settlement, created and subsequently destroyed by the Canadian Government, was a self-fulfilling prophecy and a contrived and biased example against Black assimilation and integration (Nelson 2008; Clairmont and Magill 1999; Walker 1997). Furthermore, the government capitalized on Canadian xenophobia and fear mongering, specifically the denigrating American rhetoric on the condition of the African-American — an unproven and inconclusive fear of the unknown. Canada facilitated a society hostile towards Black immigrants and Black people, and blamed Blacks for their "depressed condition." Canadian authorities assuaged guilt for the exclusion and restriction of Blacks and Coloureds, arguing that Blacks were not suited as Canadian immigrants, nor were they desired. With the July 1, 1950, implementation of P.C. 2856, Canada instituted a supposed "open door" policy, which "was to be restrictive only in the sense that immigrants would be carefully selected as to their suitability and desirability in the light of Canadian social and economic requirements."[61] With the Order-in-Council P.C. 2856,

> approval was given to certain proposals designed to give effects to the expressed policy of the Government to foster the growth of the population of Canada by insuring the careful selection of as large a number of immigrants as can advantageously be absorbed in the national economy, without making a fundamental alteration in the character of the population.[62]

With respect to the arbitrary exclusion of those deemed "unsuitable" in Canada's open but glass door, the exclusion of Black and Coloured emigrants, P.C. 2856, stated:

> All other immigrants, with the exception of Asiatics, who are excluded under Order in Council P.C. 2115, dated 16th September, 1930, must satisfy the Minister of Citizenship and Immigration, whose decision shall be final, that: (a) they are suitable immigrants having regard to the climatic, social, education, industrial, labour or other conditions or requirements of Canada; (b) and they are not undesirable owing to their peculiar customs, habits, mode of life, methods of holding property, or because of their probable inability to become readily adapted or integrated into the life of the Canadian community and to assume the duties of Canadian citizenship within a reasonable time after their entry.[63]

These obfuscated and arbitrary selection criteria created cases of emigrants of "exceptional merit" — those above and beyond the criteria needed for entry of White emigrants — and facilitated the continued exclusion of whomever Canadian immigration officials simply did not like by virtue of being the "Other."

It is important to note that racism was hidden under ostensibly reasonable, but still illogical, means for exclusion. This included climate discrimination that many Barbadians faced once applying to emigrate to Canada. Mentioned explicitly was that "under this Order-in-Council [Canada] continued to administer strictly the admission of coloured persons."[64] Fortier felt that they could not "place the negro on the same basis as other immigrants under the suitable and desirable sections of P.C. 2856"; Fortier also stated, "Administratively I believe we should coat the pill somewhat by being more specific in rejecting these cases and as I stated at the 36th meeting of DACI, rejections wherever possible should be based on occupational grounds."[65]

Clearly, Canadian officials "coated the pill" of racism by using "occupational grounds" as a difficult tool to contest accusations of discrimination based on one's phenotype. Blacks, Coloured and racialized immigrants represented the scapegoats of the Canadian public's fears of lowering wages and "native" job losses to foreigners; an effective overarching excuse for institutionalized racism and personal bigotry. Donald W. Moore of the Negro Citizenship Committee and the Negro Citizenship Association expressed his concerns of this discriminatory policy in the House of Commons in 1953. Moore, a Black Barbadian, emigrated from the Island in 1913. He established a Canadian branch of Marcus Garvey's Universal Negro Improvement Association (UNIA) and a "joint stock venture, the West Indian Trading Company, to encourage Blacks to become entrepreneurs" (High Commission for Barbados to Canada 2010: 138–139). In 1951, he was vocal in founding the Negro Citizenship Association, and he played a key role in pressuring the federal government to relax their immigration restrictions on Black West Indians. Moore was instrumental in supporting the Barbadian, West Indian and Black communities in Toronto and Canada. While he does not focus on the emigration of Barbadians specifically, his work provides an excellent foundation to his political activism and the exploits of the Negro Citizenship Committee and the Negro Citizenship Association in the struggle for the liberalization of Black West Indian migration to Canada. Moore provides several written letters in his text between him and high-ranking officials in the Ministry of Immigration and the Canadian Government. Moore, as a Canadian Negro (see page 137 of his 1985 autobiography on why he referred to himself as a Negro and not "black"), was dedicated to the fight against anti-Black racism in Canada and a racialized and exclusionary Canadian immigration policy. It also must not be forgotten that he was a Barbadian emigrant and that a Barbadian was at the forefront of the push to liberalize Canadian immigration policy and restrictions against all Black West Indians during the 1950s. Some may assume that since he arrived in Canada prior to the influx of Black West Indians in the 1960s that he was a "native" Black Canadian and that his immigrant story is lost in his advocacy for other Black West Indians forty years later. That being said, it is a testament to his success and integration in Canadian society that the historiography represents him as a non-hyphenated and non-immigrant Canadian (High Commission for Barbados to Canada 2010).

At a May 11, 1953, press conference, Moore argued that Walter Harris, the Minister of Citizenship and Immigration, claimed Black people were denied entry to Canada because of the "difficulty to find employment."[66] Moore refuted this reasoning and subsequently presented an example of a Barbadian from Half Moon Forte, St. Lucy, with a Canadian uncle who sponsored him, and who was promised employment by the Canadian National Railways prior to his migration from Barbados. The young man was denied entry despite secured employment, contrary to the theory of rejection based on "occupational grounds."[67] Moore presented a case in which Canada did not follow its own policy and arbitrarily denied entry to individuals based on phenotypic characteristics. Moreover, this policy continued to conflict with Canadian interests and authorities in the Caribbean. Officials in Port-of-Spain argued that irreparable damage caused with "the amount of time devoted to attempts to sooth [sic] ruffled feathers in connection with Canadian immigration decisions seem far too much but appears unavoidable so long as we operate a policy of racial discrimination but do not admit it."[68] Canada's cowardice, reluctance and mishandling of racial discrimination proved to be a disservice for Canadian–West Indian relations. Barbadians understood the devious and manipulative nature of Canadian race relations. George Hunte, the associate editor of Barbados' *The Advocate*, cited Canada's *Immigration Act* "as proof of prejudice in Canada against the black race," and felt that "the coloured majority of the Islands would never voluntarily agree to become a minority through union with another country."[69] The "union" was in reference to unfounded rumours of Canada's interest in annexing Barbados as a province, as well as Prime Minister Robert Borden's consideration of the annexation of parts of the British West Indies in 1917.[70] Barbadians clearly understood the climate of Canadian racism prior to their migration abroad and openly expressed their concerns. The Canadian state may have attempted to "coat the pill" of racism, but patronizing political rhetoric could not mask the obdurate stain of ideological debasement.

The following statistics highlight the emigration flows to Canada from the British West Indies, by race, in 1957: Negro ethnic origin — 497 (43 percent); British ethnic origin — 408 (35 percent); Other ethnic origin — 257 (22 percent). Total: 1,162 British West Indian immigrants in 1957. The numbers highlight that Blacks did not dominate migration from the West Indies prior to the de-racialization of Canadian immigration policy in 1962. Barbados' population at the time was 89.1 percent Black (Layne 1979: 44).[71] Canadian officials feared emigration from the West Indies, but in fact they feared the possibility of mass Black or Coloured immigration; nearly a third of its migrant base in 1957 — and throughout the 1950s

— was White and of British ethnic origin, individuals the state hoped to settle to fulfill its "White Canada" mandate. These numbers also represent the difficulties in determining and understanding race and colour codifiers in the historical record and archival documents when many of the political voices could not justify their seemingly non-discriminatory and non-racist decision making with sound — and recorded — evidence. The insidious nature of racism is an unjustifiable illogical fallacy; its historical subjectivity is an epistemological exercise that historians must interpret and critically theorize.

By the late 1950s, through pressure from West Indian officials, and the fact that it could no longer justify its discriminatory and exclusionary practice, the Canadian Government began to change its racist immigration policy. Canada could no longer arbitrarily discriminate without proven justification as West Indians stood at the forefront to liberalize migration from the archipelago and address the inequity of Canadian immigration legislation and relations. On March 10, 1958, the Acting Deputy Minister of the Immigration Branch, C.E.S. Smith, wrote to the Director, Laval Fortier, that "it has been our long standing practice to deal favourably with British subjects of white race from the British West Indies," and not encourage emigrants outside of the class of domestics, "graduate nurses, qualified stenographers, etc."[72] However, he admitted:

> We are continually being accused of discrimination against the coloured race in this area and our rebuttal has been that there is no racial discrimination and that only persons accepted are those clearly defined in the admissible class and those with *exceptional merit* (author's emphasis).[73]

Even he understood the hypocrisy of the rationalization, admitting, "The facts do not support the statement."[74] Smith's comments reflect the slowly changing public attitudes towards racial discrimination in North America in the late 1950s, specifically on the eve of the Civil Rights Movement in the United States and independence movements throughout the world. It is noteworthy that Ghana, the first "free" Black nation-state, regained its independence from Britain in 1957. The establishment of the West Indies Federation in 1958 must also be noted, as Blacks throughout the former British Empire were now seen to be "fit" to govern themselves as (supposed) equals in the globalized world

Smith highlighted strained diplomatic relations with West Indian representatives and wrote, "[It] is difficult to justify our action in extending favourable consideration to a person of white race when a similar application made by a person of coloured race is refused."[75] With the above evidence of West Indians confronting and challenging the merits of inequitable and racist immigration policies, Smith was "of the opinion [that they] should revise [their] present practice and that, regardless of race, all persons should be given equal treatment, that is, accept only those cases which come within the admissible classes or which have exceptional merit."[76] By no means did Smith propose comprehensive liberalization; however, he acknowledged the preferential treatment of White West Indians and argued that all emigrants would be processed and screened using the same criteria. While it did not open the door for more Black West Indians, it removed the White privilege and the ambiguity and hypocrisy of emigration from the West Indies (Bangarth 2003: 400, 416). A West Indian, regardless of race, was subject to the same Canadian immigration criteria. Laval Fortier responded on April 17, 1958, and wrote, "I am inclined to agree with the conclusion reached by Mr. Smith, but I must say that persons of white race would generally be more readily acceptable to Canada and, therefore, would have better opportunities for establishments than the others."[77] Fortier did not provide any proof, nor evidence or reasoning, for his statement. White primordial ties and indoctrinated bigotry superseded the evidence provided by Smith.

The Canadian federal government actively pursued reified false consciousness of the Canadian "White race" and created the vertical silo of racial hierarchies in Canada. This was apparent in that

> the determination of the federal government to both define and to regulate this complex racialized hierarchy reinforces the point that the powers of racialization only achieve "full structural and systemic power when they are legally defined and enforced by state power." In Canada, that required substantive federal government intervention. (Price 2011: 318–19)

Early to mid-twentieth century immigration policies both necessitated and constructed White Canadian racialized hegemonic state power. Similar to the profound bigotry of Fortier and Smith, leading late nineteenth- to mid-twentieth-century Canadian politicians such as Prime Minister Sir Wilfrid Laurier; his Minister of Labour, Rodolphe Lemieux; Laurier's Minister of the Interior and his Secretary of State, Clifford Sifton and Joseph Pope, respectively; and Prime Ministers Robert Borden and Mackenzie King, respectively, "together with provincial politicians, became architects in the institutionalization of a white Canada" (Price 2011: 20, 318). They created a country where they believed that Whites belonged and racialized people did not; however, Canadian officials could not deny the existence of racialized people wanting to settle in Canada, nor could they justify their racist bigotry following the humanitarian atrocities of the Second World War. Despite this new global approach to humanitarianism following the Second World War, Canadian benevolence towards the "Other," specifically concerning the repeal of the *Chinese Immigration Act* in 1947, "was not a recognition of Canada's racist past:

it was its sanitization … this was not the end of white supremacy, but rather its recasting in different moulds" (Price 2011: 306). Canadian altruism was a façade to placate the United Nations, to manage domestic strife from different immigrant and ethnic groups, and to appease the international humanitarian environment. This appeasement was fallacious and represented by "Colour-Coded Canadian Humanitarianism." John Price (2011: 312–13) argued the following:

> Close to 2 million people came to Canada from Europe in the fifteen years after the war, of whom British immigrants continued to represent the largest single group. The predominance of European immigration, combined with the baby boom in Canada, meant that between 1941 and 1961, the number of Canadians of European (including British) origins increased from 11.2 million in 1941 to 17.7 million in 1961 — an increase of 6.5 million people of European heritage in this twenty-year period.

With Canada's postwar focus on the Atlantic — Eurocentrism or Atlanticism — the above statistics raise the question of why the Canadian public and Canadian officials feared Black immigration when the White population numbers grew exponentially within a twenty-year period (Price 2011: 312–13). Black West Indians and Barbadians challenged the ideological construction of a "White Canada" and refused to accept their exclusion based on a reified anti-Black and, most importantly, a pro-White Canadian immigration policy.

Canadian immigration officials were then forced to debate the question of Black and Coloured West Indian settlement in Canada throughout the 1950s. In the Government of Canada's file on "Coloured Immigration: Policy & Instructions" and its review of immigration from the British West Indies, dated January 14, 1955, officials argued that its policy towards Black West Indians was restrictive; they admitted it was due to a racialized White patriarchal belief of Black inferiority supported by the Canadian public's xenophobic and illogical fear of the Black Other. The following statement from the January 14 review characterized Canadian contempt towards Blacks and Coloured West Indians:

> It is not by accident that coloured British subjects other than the negligible numbers from the United Kingdom are excluded from Canada. It is from experience, generally speaking, that coloured people in the present state of the white man's thinking are not a tangible community asset, and as a result are more or less ostracized. They do not assimilate readily and pretty much vegetate to a low standard of living. Despite what has been said to the contrary, many cannot adapt themselves to our climatic conditions. To enter into an agreement which would have the effect of increasing coloured immigration to this country would be an act of misguided

generosity since it would not have the effect of bringing about a worthwhile solution to the problem of coloured people and would quite likely intensify our own social and economic problem. I think that the biggest single argument against increasing coloured immigration to this country is the simple fact that the Canadian public is not prepared to accept them in any significant numbers.[78]

The idea that "coloured people in the present state of the white man's thinking are not a tangible community asset" clearly highlighted Canadian ideological bigotry. White Canadians thought Coloured people could not contribute to Canadian society and would naturally "vegetate to a low standard of living." Climate discrimination was yet another fallacy, as Canadian policy projected the fundamental xenophobic and anti-Black principles of society. With respect to climate discrimination, Section 38 of the *Immigration Act* of 1910 "provided the cabinet with the requisite authority to prohibit the entry of immigrants belonging to any race deemed unsuited to the climate or requirements of Canada" (Knowles 1997: 85). Harris, who Moore chastised in 1953 for his "difficulty to find employment" argument against the immigration of a Barbadian national, had raised the issue of climate "unsuitability" towards another Barbadian the previous year. In a 1952 letter written to Joseph Noseworthy, the Co-operative Commonwealth Federation (CCF) Member of Parliament for York South, Harris "spoke plainly of the Department's attitude in dealing with immigration of negroes from the British West Indies," and the letter addressed the case of Miss Braithwaite, the Barbadian granddaughter of a Canadian citizen (Corbett 1957: 52). Braithwaite was denied entry, and Harris cited the climate as a factor. The Minister stated:

> In light of experience it would be unrealistic to say that immigrants who have spent the greater part of their life in tropical or subtropical countries became readily adapted to the Canadian mode of life which, to no small extent, is determined by climatic conditions. It is a matter of record that natives of such countries are more apt to break down in health than immigrants from countries where the climate is more akin to that of Canada. (Corbett 1957: 53)

Despite Harris' ignorant bigotry citing his "experience" of tropical and subtropical "modes of life," and Miss Braithwaite's lack of Canadian environmental "cold weather" capital, he had the power and arbitrary right to deny access to any individual he simply did not want in the country. Harris did not have a record of Black West Indians who "broke down in health" due to the weather; Frank Oliver and Sifton, Ministers of the Interior, had cited the climate as a means for Black exclusion since the turn of the twentieth century. If Blacks were perpetually denied entry based on climate, Harris cited a self-fulfilling and nonexistent fallacy as proof to Black Barbadian climate unsuitability. Canadian officials did not need evidence or proven logic to necessitate the exclusion of potential Black and West Indian immigrants in Canada; the normalization of White supremacy gave them the right to exclude based on race.

Canadian authorities manipulated unproven and unsubstantiated "facts" to validate their racist and exclusionary agendas. Officials argued Canadian immigration policy was "one of selective immigration," and due to the fact of it being selective, it was "regarded by many as being restrictive, thus [Canadian authorities were] vulnerable to charges of discrimination. The establishment of an agreement which would provide for a quota of Negroes would have the effect of rendering [their] restrictive policy more obvious."[79] The Department of Foreign Affairs validated the charges, and revealed the absurdity of "[arguing] that the restrictions [were] not aimed at coloured immigration as pointed out," and that it was "a correct criticism. Nobody [would] be convinced that the proposed restrictions [were] not based on colour. To try to make it appear so is an insult to the intelligence of the coloured people."[80] R.G.C. Smith, from the Office of the Commissioner for Canada at Port-of-Spain, Trinidad, reiterated the White Canadian public's contempt for Blacks:

> From my own experience here, I have found that when talking of Canada's immigration policy it has always been best to acknowledge the colour problem, to say that it is not Government policy to encourage or acquiesce to racialism in immigration or in anything else, but that public opinion based on years of prejudice cannot be changed over night, that the unfortunate fact remains that in a period of unemployment if two people apply for a job, it will be the white man who will be chosen as a general rule, that it is to avoid pockets of coloured unemployment that we must restrain immigration.[81]

Canadian authorities were aware of those that accused and challenged their exclusionary immigration policy towards Black West Indians, but wanted to keep the decision making arbitrary in order to evade charges of explicit race-based discrimination and to sanitize the omnipresent racism in Canadian society. One Canadian official unabashedly admitted that "despite legislation forbidding discrimination, [they] believe it would be unrealistic to suggest that discrimination is not being practiced in Canada at the present time."[82] A possible solution to challenge discrimination fueled by ignorance was the theory of the Autonomous Bajan and the Emigrant Ambassador; "to admit such coloured persons who, because of their qualifications, are likely to become exceptional citizens and thus render the Negro more generally acceptable in Canada."[83] Those of "exceptional merit" were to become part of an initiative that was designed to be a "long term programme ... worthy of serious thought and one which adds weight to the suggestion that Negro immigration to this country be increased."[84] Despite the rhetoric, the review concluded that "the disadvantages outweigh the advantages and [they] would recommend that no action be taken in this regard this year and the matter be reviewed again when considering the 1956 immigration programme."[85] Canadian officials also argued that "while restrictive, our policy with respect to Negroes has never been one of absolute exclusion; for example, Negroes who are British subjects within the meaning of Regulation 20(1) (exceptional merit) have always been admissible to this country."[86] In essence, Blacks and Black West Indians had to prove their individual worth. Canadian societal and authoritative reductionist and racialized structures forced Blacks to display the exceptional qualifications of a heterogeneously distinct "race," one encompassing a plethora of cultures and histories. This idea was further problematized by the fact that throughout the early to mid-twentieth century, Barbados produced a highly educated and upwardly mobile citizenry that was denied entry to Canada based on their Blackness. If Canada was serious about their admission based on "exceptionality," the state would have recognized the educational qualifications of Black Barbadian applicants. Racial ideologies dictated Canadian xenophobia and, subsequently, its immigration system. Institutionalized racism perpetuated discrimination within an intentionally ambiguous Canadian immigration policy.

Black Barbadians in Canada also challenged the racist immigration policy. Barbadian-born Moore continued his 1953 House of Commons crusade against the restriction of Black West Indians based on "occupational grounds." He and Stanley Grizzle D.C., as Director and Secretary, respectively, of the Negro Citizenship Association (NCA), along with a delegation of supporters briefed Prime Minister Louis St. Laurent, Minister of Citizenship and Immigration Walter Harris, and officials of the Government of Canada on April 27, 1954, in Ottawa (Grizzle 1998: 99).[87] Moore and Grizzle exposed the prejudiced Act:

> The Immigration Act since 1923 seems to have been purposely written and revised to deny equal immigration status to those areas of the Commonwealth where coloured peoples constitute a large part of the population. This is done by creating a rigid definition of British subject: "British subjects by birth or by naturalization in the United Kingdom, Australia, New Zealand or the Union of South Africa and citizens of Ireland." This definition excludes from the category of "British subject" those who are in all other senses British subjects, but who come from such areas as the British West Indies, Bermuda, British Guiana, Ceylon, India, Pakistan, Africa, etc.[88]

Along with the previously highlighted preferential treatment towards White West Indians, and Whites throughout British colonies worldwide, Canada denied and refused the recognition of British subject status for all racialized people — a policy unique to Canada. Similar to Black Barbadian colonial identity, a Black West Indian may have been born in a British colony, as a British colonial subject, analogous to a White person in Australia or New Zealand, but the colour of one's skin was the only reason for his or her marginalization as a true British subject. They were denied the same rights as other British colonials. Furthermore, speaking on behalf of the NCA, the authors refuted Canada's climate theory and stated, "Negroes have for a century and a half moved into Canada from tropical areas, and have taken up life here with no great problems of adjustment to climate."[89] The *Proposal for Controlled Emigration from Barbados for Specified Types of Workers* also indicated that "although Barbados is in the Tropics, its people have shown themselves to be well able to withstand cold climates."[90] Prior to their 1954 brief to the Prime Minister and the Minister of Citizenship and Immigration, on June 22, 1952, during the first public meeting of the NCA in Toronto, Moore (1985: 102) "told the world" gathered at a church how P.C. 2856 and the Canadian Government "had taken away [his] British citizenship, how they decreed it was impossible for [him], born in the tropics, to withstand the rigours of the Canadian winter, and how [West Indian emigrants] could never become assimilated into Canadian culture." It was at this meeting that the NCA adopted the resolution to demand from Prime Minister St. Laurent and members of his government the immediate removal of P.C. 2856 from the Act (Moore 1985: 102). The letter written by Moore (1985: 102–03) and the NCA dated June 27, 1952, stated:

> May I further impress upon you the extreme importance of immediately revoking the discriminatory Order-in-Council. The Canadian public is fast becoming aware of the extremely unfair attitude of immigration officials towards prospective Negro immigrants. This Committee has a considerable number of proven cases of gross discrimination on record. We are prepared to release them for publication should the attached resolution prove fruitless.

Harris, the Minister of Citizenship and Immigration, replied to Moore on July 16, 1952, and said, "I would be obliged if you would let me have the names and addresses of the persons concerned so that I may review their cases in the light of your resolution" (Moore 1985: 103–104). It was then that Moore and the NCA were encouraged to push for further reforms to the Act that would allow for the increased settlement of Black West Indians in Canada. This first letter from the NCA set the tone for their challenges against the Canadian Government in 1953 and their brief to the Prime Minister in 1954 against climate discrimination and the "considerable evidence to indicate that the 'climate theory' [was] completely erroneous" (Moore 1985: 112). Moore and Grizzle cited examples of West Indians who served with the British army across the globe in varying climates without difficulty or serious affliction from cold weather. In his autobiography, Grizzle said that he wrote to the University of Toronto's Department of Physical Hygiene, the Director of Research for the Department of Health and Welfare Canada, and the Dean of Medicine at Howard University, and none could provide evidence that cold weather climates damaged the health of people of African descent (Grizzle 1998: 100–101). Grizzle (1998: 100) concluded that "the opinions of our federal leaders were disproved." The NCA also refuted the widespread idea that Blacks could not assimilate to Canadian society, and subsequently exposed Canadian barriers to integration. They claimed that "the customs, habits, modes of life, or methods of holding property in the West Indies are essentially the same as in Canada, and no change is necessary when these people become part of the Canadian way of life."[91] The only difference, Moore and Grizzle asserted, was Canada's reluctance to accept Black, Coloured, non-White, or what we would now refer to as "racialized" West Indians. Racism was the only logical explanation, and Grizzle (1998: 102) argued for the immediate eradication of the "Jim Crow Iron Curtain" of Canadian immigration policy. However, the NCA did not attack or polemicize Canadian racial doctrine; Moore and Grizzle provided possible and reasonable solutions. They requested that the Government of Canada

> amend the definition of "British Subject" so as to include all those who are, for all other purposes, regarded as "British subjects and citizens of the United Kingdom and Commonwealth"; make provision in the Act of the entry of a British West Indian — without regard to racial origin — who has sufficient means to maintain himself until he has secured employment; delete the word "orphan" from the regulation which provides for the entry of nephews and nieces under 21; make specific the term "persons of exceptional merit"; and set up an Immigration Office in a centrally located area of the British West Indies for the handling of prospective immigrants. (Grizzle 1998: 102)

Black West Indian–Canadian immigrants, Black West Indians in the Caribbean, and Canadian authorities in the West Indies and Canada all contested the unfair nature of Canadian immigration policy. In the House of Commons on June 26, 1954, Co-operative Commonwealth Federation (CCF) leader and member of Parliament (Rosetown-Biggar) Maj. James Coldwell openly discussed discrimination in Canada's department of immigration. Moore, Grizzle and the NCA presented a comprehensive and persuasive brief to the Canadian Government; however, in the House of Commons both on June 2 and 26 of the same year, Harris avoided debate on the NCA brief and refused to address anti-Black racism within Canada's immigration policy.[92] One may argue that all parties involved understood the system was flawed, while inaction and antipathy on the part of Canadian officials underscored the institutional and ideological racism that facilitated the policy. Race and racism dictated Canadian immigration policy towards Black Barbadians and Canadian interests in the West Indies. Race was an integral feature of historical West Indian–Canadian relations. Racial ideology and White hegemonic power defined and built the predominantly Black islands and White Canada's pathology of race; however, Black Barbadians and West Indians challenged their racialization and Canada's discriminatory policy in the postwar period and finally overcame a substantial barrier as the country officially de-racialized its immigration policy in 1962.

De-racialization of Canadian Immigration: The New Immigration Regulations of 1962

Canada's new immigration regulations, or the de-racialization of Canadian immigration in 1962, ushered in a new era for racialized, Coloured, Black West Indian and Black Barbadian emigrants. I in part attribute this change to British immigration policy, and even more so to the changing face of post-Second World War society during the 1960s. This includes the Human, Refugee, and Women's Rights movements, the Civil Rights Movement, Black Power and Pan-Africanism, and decolonization around the globe. The new regulations, which came into effect February 1, 1962, "provided that anyone in the world could apply to come to Canada without regard to his race or country of nationality, subject only to standards of health, character, education, training," as well as "the skills offered by would-be immigrants."[93] Rex Stollmeyer, Montreal Commissioner for the West Indies, remarked:

> The legislation proposed by the Canadian Government to lighten restrictions on immigration will bring a flood of applications from West Indians seeking entry, as it opens the door for a lot of people who couldn't qualify before and there are lots of West Indians very anxious to come to Canada. (quoted in *Sunday Advocate* January 28, 1962)

Stollmeyer stated that "there is much more opportunity [for West Indians] here," and easing the restrictions ushered in a new wave of capable and worthy Blacks from the Caribbean region, where colour and race, ostensibly, did not factor in their admission (*Sunday Advocate* January 28, 1962). Immigrants from the British West Indies gained admission to Canada "under the broadest of the admissible categories provided for in Canadian immigration law. The Canadian

Immigration Act and Regulations [permitted] the admission of immigrants from the Caribbean area in two separate streams."[94] These included immigrants selected under education, skills, training or other special qualifications to "enable them to establish themselves successfully in Canada," and unsponsored immigrants.[95] Unsponsored immigrants included spouses, sons or daughters and their spouses and children if under 21 years of age, brothers or sisters and if married with their spouses and children under 21 years of age, parents and grandparents, fiancé or fiancée, and "unmarried orphan nephews or nieces under 21 years of age."[96] Canada officially abolished its "White Canada" philosophy and altered the logistics in which Canadian immigration officials operated abroad.

The new regulations assumed the following:

> For all the countries of the world the Canadian immigration authori-
> ties will be able to apply the new criteria of admissibility successfully. It
> should however be pointed out that in many of these countries we have
> no staff of our own … [and] it may well be necessary to open new offices
> in countries where no Canadian immigration officers presently are opera-
> tive (e.g., West Indies, Spain, Japan); and to strengthen staff elsewhere,
> to assume these new and difficult responsibilities.[97]

The admission from the Minister of Citizenship and Immigration that there were no immigration officers based in the Caribbean to serve the region and its people underlined the institutional structures that prohibited West Indian emigration to Canada prior to 1962 and neo-racism throughout the 1960s; its racialized and geocentric immigration policies did not necessitate permanent staff in the region. Eventually, Kingston, Jamaica, was decided as the logical site that would serve the region, which included Barbados. However, the proposal was not finalized due to geographical, travel and logistical issues in an attempt for one immigration office to serve the entire Caribbean. As in the case of the failure of the West Indies Federation, this exemplified the logistical difficulties in homogenizing the West Indies as one geographical and ideological entity. Travelling missions thus served the region yearly following the new regulations of 1962 up to and including 1966. During this period, West Indian emigration experienced "the most noticeable effect" of the new immigration policy, indicating that West Indian people were ready, willing and capable to migrate and settle in Canadian society.[98] West Indian applications "began to build up as soon as the new regulations were announced and in June of [1962] an Immigration team was sent from Ottawa to the Caribbean to examine 311 family units which had been tentatively selected on the basis of 'paper screening.'"[99] Canadian immigration fielded a total of 3,025 applications after the new immigration regulations came into effect.[100] However, the increased application numbers did not translate to a flood of new Canadian immigrants of West Indian background. In 1961, "1,249 persons came to Canada from British and other West Indian islands. In 1962, after the regulations were changed, the figure was 1,586. So far this year (1963), 1,542. These increases are disappointingly small and raise some questions."[101] The total number of immigration cases approved in Barbados: 15 cases of 19 persons; total number of immigration cases refused in Barbados: 23 cases of 53 persons. In Jamaica: 120 cases and 251 persons approved as opposed to 181 cases and 427 persons refused.[102]

Did the new immigration regulations merely provide hope for Black West Indians, but not change the rigid racialized structure of Canadian immigration policy? More West Indians applied, but the acceptance figures did not reflect the increased pool of potential emigrants. The regulations and the rhetoric may have changed, and Canada explicitly denounced race-based immigration procedures; however, one may argue that prior to the implementation of the Points System in 1967, the arbitrary selection criteria associated with Canadian immigration policy perpetuated the exclusion of Black West Indians. West Indians continued to accuse, and rightfully so, Canada and its immigration officers of institutional racism and personal bigotry.

With the new regulations, applications throughout the Caribbean increased exponentially. There was a significant change in the "racial content of the [migration] movement."[103] In 1950, "only 19 percent of the persons admitted from the West Indies were Negroes while in 1963 the figure had jumped to 70 percent."[104] This increase was most present in Jamaica. Roy W. Blake, the Canadian Government Trade Commissioner in Kingston, Jamaica, stated that only one week after the implementation of the new regulation, "the news about the revision of Canada's immigration laws first appeared in the Jamaican press on Saturday, January 20, and naturally more emphasis was placed on the lifting of the colour bar than on the necessity for skills."[105] Blake revealed that February 8, 1962, was their "fourteenth working day since then and [they] handed out over 1000 forms; in other words there [was] an average of 70 persons coming to [their] office each day regarding emigration."[106] However, the increase in applications did not abate the racial discrimination charges, specifically from potential Jamaican emigrants. G.C. McInnes, of the Office of the High Commissioner in Kingston, Jamaica, wrote to the Under-Secretary of State for External Affairs:

> West Indians have long been unhappy about Canadian immigration restrictions. This attitude may have been diminished by the new immigration regulations, but the frequency with which the subject is raised with us here is ample evidence that it is far from eliminated.[107]

The possibility remained that it was simply the amount of time it took for the changes to come into effect, especially in changing the attitudes of Canadian immigration officials; however, McInnes argued that irrespective of colour, potential Jamaican emigrants did not meet the requirements of the new regulations. He refused to admit to Jamaican race-based exclusions and stated, "Jamaicans in general are reluctant to recognize the deficiencies which make them unacceptable as immigrants."[108] McInnes contended that Black Jamaicans were not victims of racial discrimination, but he further racialized Blacks by hypocritically arguing that "generally speaking, negro Jamaicans tend to attribute their inability to meet standards accepted in Canada and other countries to racial prejudice."[109] Not only did Jamaicans rightfully claim "racial prejudice," which McInnes failed to disclose was a fundamental principle and legislated policy of Canadian immigration prior to 1962, but he recklessly postulated, "[Black Jamaicans] refuse to recognise that common Jamaican attributes, such as irresponsible parenthood and indolence, are not regarded with indifference elsewhere."[110]

Similar to climate discrimination, Canadians officially stated that Black Jamaicans were not denied admission because they were Black, but due to their Blackness — specifically their Jamaican culture. They were "bad" parents according to White Canadians and therefore inassimilable to Canadian society. The rhetoric and insidious nature of cultural prejudice was, and is, analogous to racial discrimination. Officials could no longer exclude based on race; however, perceived cultural determinants remained valid means to refuse Black West Indian applicants. McInnes revealed the hypocritical paradox of Canadian xenophobic and racist ideology — how to reconcile gradual institutional changes with personal attitudes towards Blacks and West Indians. Canada managed to circumvent their new regulations and used new condemning language and negative "Black" codifications and connotations first constructed within the historical British liberal racial order. "Irresponsible parenthood" and "laziness" became euphemisms for the West Indian's supposed inability to assimilate to Anglo-Saxon Canadian family values, frontier culture and Canada's cold climate. The problematic nature of McInnes' rhetoric justified the perpetual exclusion of West Indians, and Jamaicans in particular, through denigrating characterizations. He presented unsubstantiated and detrimental claims as truths and misrepresented Canadian racist beliefs as "common Jamaican attributes." He argued that by nature and cultural "attributes," Jamaicans could not, and should not, be allowed in Canada. During the five-year period between the official de-racialization of Canadian immigration policy in 1962 and the implementation of the Points System in 1967, officials in Canada and the West Indies continued to debate the issue of the consolidation of structural racism and indoctrinated personal bigotry embedded within the new "liberal" migration scheme.

The October 1963 Commonwealth Partners in the West Indies Conference, attended by both Canadian and West Indian political leaders, including Barbados' Premier Barrow, highlighted several issues on emigration from the Caribbean and the new regulations. The conference was held under the cloud of the failure of the West Indies Federation and Barrow asking for a strict implementation of Canada's 1962 immigration reforms from Guy Favreau, the Minister of Citizenship and Immigration, and Prime Minister Lester B. Pearson. They had emphasized that "immigration policy [would] be free from the stigma of racial discrimination" (Edmondson 1964: 188–89, 194). Barrow was also seeking more foreign aid for Barbados and the West Indies from Canada. By November 14, 1963, Paul Martin Sr., the Secretary of State of External Affairs under Prime Minister Lester B. Pearson, revealed that Canada would increase its aid to the West Indies in the 1964–1965 fiscal year. Barrow and the speakers agreed overpopulation and unemployment were catalysts for emigration:

> Population pressure was very great in the islands, especially in Barbados where unemployment averaged close to 15 percent of the labour force. Population was increasing so rapidly that a very high rate of economic growth was needed just to provide enough jobs to keep pace with the increase.[111]

Canadian trepidation regarding the impending British *Commonwealth Immigrants Act* compounded the West Indian immigration question by 1961. Canadian authorities contended, and rightfully so, that the U.K. Act would

> inevitably increase the pressures on us to allow more West Indians into Canada … We can expect, therefore, that whatever move the British take in this field, almost regardless of whether the restrictions are real or token, this will develop pressures on Canada.[112]

In the first six months of 1962, prior to the implementation of the Act, Britain accepted forty thousand West Indian emigrants. In the six months that followed, the number dropped drastically to only four thousand. The "closed door" of British immigration opened an avenue for West Indian migration to Canada as the latter state was forced to readjust its philosophy on race-based selection criteria. Canada faced external pressures, most notably from the British, to accept more West Indian migrants, irrespective of a historical Canadian immigration practice to perpetually exclude Black West Indians (Duval 2005: 245–61).

Despite the 1962 rhetorical and piecemeal liberalization of Canadian immigration, conference attendees pressed for further reforms.[113] The majority of the Canadian speakers at the conference felt that the state maintained a discriminatory and colour-based immigration policy towards West Indians due to the arbitrary and obstinate decision-making of the immigration officer.[114] Furthermore, "a strong feeling" persisted among Canadian representatives of the perpetuation of two immigration standards, "one for whites and another for blacks."[115] The "feeling" was legitimized by statements from Blake regarding potential Jamaican emigrants. He highlighted the language used in the letter of refusal to Jamaican applicants, and the sentence, "you do not come within the categories of persons being admitted to Canada."[116] Blake noted the line was "particularly offensive to unsuccessful applicants," and that the denied applicants felt that the word "category" referred to "colour," and despite the diplomatic rhetoric, Canadian immigration policy remained as it was prior to 1962.[117] Whether it was legislated, arbitrary, or perceived and interpreted, racial discrimination remained a fundamental feature in Canadian immigration policy following its official de-racialization in 1962.

Since Canadian bureaucrats, including Canadian Trade Commissioner Blake, openly criticized the de facto racist immigration policy, the question arises: why did nothing change? Formally, Canada de-racialized its immigration policy in 1962. It was the arbitrary nature, or personal bigotry, of Canadian immigration officials that circumvented the new regulations; more than a year and simple legislation was needed to change attitudes and personal racism. With the evidence presented earlier on complaints filed by trade officials with respect to being "embarrassed," and Canada's hypocritical and conflicting foreign and immigration policy that caused "serious damage [to] Canadian prestige," there was also a disconnect between what was happening "on the ground" in the West Indies and Canada's economic interests in the region as opposed to what was being designed and implemented in Canada with respect to its immigration policy. Canadian officials in the West Indies could not disaggregate immigration and economic interests. The comments arising out of the conference clearly demonstrated the confusion between Canadian diplomats abroad who were seemingly sympathetic and understood that Canada's "new" regulations did not immediately change its continued policy to discriminate against Black West Indians. It seems the Canadian delegates, who arguably would have had specific interests in the Caribbean region, understood that although the official policy had changed, the pervasive nature of racist attitudes remained a barrier to immigration.

Premier Barrow continued on this topic as he addressed the Canadian delegation in Fredericton in 1963. Barrow interpreted Canadian immigration practices as a major irritant embedded within Barbadian, West Indian and Canadian relations. Barrow (1964: 184) stated, "One of the more vexing problems of the relationships between this country (Canada) and ours (Barbados and the West Indies) is the question of immigration." By 1962, Canada officially abolished its policy on excluding potential immigrants based on their racial background; however, more needed to be done, and Barbadians took a stand on the true nature of the policy. Barrow (1964: 184) argued, "I am not satisfied that on the question of immigration the Canadian government has ever led from anywhere but far in the rear of public opinion." In the eyes of the marginalized Other in the West Indies, Canadian diplomacy fell victim to racist public opinion. Diplomacy did not solely dictate Barbadian-Canadian relations, but it was also driven by an obdurate society controlled by the social construction of race and the liberal racial order. Barrow presented the staggering figures even after the official de-racialization of Canadian immigration in 1962. In the same year, Barrow argued, the Canadian state accepted only 1,500 West Indian emigrants out of a total of 75,000 successful applicants from other source countries (Barrow 1964: 184). It must be noted that this was a Barbadian political leader, questioning Canadian motives, to Canadians in Canada. His South-North position seemingly did not place him in an authoritative position to debate Canadian immigration policy, but he felt adamant about its injustice. Barrow challenged several of the arguments used to bar his fellow Barbadians and West Indians from entering Canada as permanent residents. While he spoke on the issue of immigration, this open declaration of injustice and inequality exposed a flaw in Barbadian-Canadian relations. I contend that the social construction of race and racism superseded Canadian economic and political goodwill towards Barbadians.

As noted by Moore, Grizzle and the NCA, the harsh Canadian climate was used as a means to exclude potential Barbadian, West Indian and Black American immigrants. Barrow (1964: 184) argued West Indians preferred the Canadian winters over the summer climate in England. By this notion, "one must therefore conclude that the West Indian would sooner come to Canada than go to Britain" (Barrow 1964: 184). Barrow effectively dismissed the idea that Barbadians and West Indians preferred the United Kingdom as a destination over Canada because of a more temperate climate. The Barbadian Premier then proceeded to the critical issue of discriminatory and racist immigration policy:

> To be brutally frank, there is a feeling that in view of the large influx of unskilled Italian and other European immigrants coming into this country, there is either tacitly or explicitly some element of discrimination against the West Indian immigrant. There is no point in telling us in the West Indies that you have unemployment up here if you introduce into this country people who cannot even speak English or French, and who have no skill at all; and at the same time you cream off from the West Indian economy only the highly skilled, the professional and the technical workers that we so badly need for our industrial programme ... Our skilled, our technical and our professional people are the people you are welcoming

now with open arms; and at the same time you are introducing into this country large numbers of people who will probably have to spend two or three years even to begin to understand how to order a loaf of bread or to speak to a taxi driver; and the people who are so culturally close to you in many respects are kept out. (Barrow 1964: 184)

While the language lacked tact and diplomacy, truth was behind Barrow's scathing comments. The only difference between the unskilled Europeans and the Black West Indian migrant was their colour. Barrow clearly elucidated his self-explanatory argument and questioned why Canada, if not for racism in its government and country, would prefer to accept White Europeans as drains on the social system over overqualified Black West Indians. Black Barbadians and West Indians were willing to contribute to the betterment of Canadian society, while their own native countries suffered from their migration. When Canadian officials did select West Indian emigrants — even as domestics through the Domestic Scheme — they took the most qualified Barbadians needed to push forward an emerging new nation-state. It was a brain drain and a system that deprived Barbados of its future leaders. Using Barrow's statement, racism and discrimination perpetuated the idea of a "White Canada," despite the official abolishment of race-based immigration policy in 1962 by Ellen Fairclough, the Minister of Citizenship and Immigration and Canada's first female Cabinet Minister. Political motive did not supplant the ideological ramifications of racism and White superiority in Canada. Barrow knew Canada only accepted and tolerated, as subalterns and inferiors, the best and the brightest Barbadians.

Barbados and the West Indies suffered, but political leaders like Barrow knew their people had the skill and education needed to succeed in a hostile and racist environment. Through his monumental comments, he stood behind his people and his country and challenged the Canadian Government for change. He did not concede or neglect the racism embedded in Barbadian-Canadian relations. Barrow may have gambled on the precarious relationship, but he did so since this was an injustice. He reiterated his position in the Barbadian press in *The Advocate* (September 17, 1967), in an article entitled "Barrow to Press Canada to Relax Immigration Laws." He noted and criticized the Barbadian brain drain to Canada and stated, "Right now, they (Canada) are taking away our skilled people." He continued, "We are hoping for a larger uptake of ordinary workers and in fact they are taking more this year" (*The Advocate* September 17, 1967). *The Advocate* exclaimed, "Prime Minister Errol Barrow said yesterday that he will try to persuade Canada to further relax its immigration laws during his forthcoming visit to Ottawa" (September 17, 1967). Throughout the 1960s, following the official de-racialization of immigration policy in 1962 and prior to the implementation of the Points System in 1967, Barbadian and West Indian leaders continued to challenge institutional racism and the Canadian immigration system.

Canadian foreign policy in the region during this period reaffirmed the idea that Canadian officials wanted to avoid the immigration question by any means necessary. Donaghy and Muirhead (2008: 286) wrote that through Paul Martin Sr., the Secretary of State for External Affairs under Prime Minister Lester B. Pearson in 1963, foreign aid was Canada's primary concern in the mid-1960s. In May 1965, on the eve of the 1966 Canada–West Indies Conference, the Martin administration purposely deflected West Indian pressure to increase immigration levels and did not address Canada's continued racial discrimination of potential Black migrants. As was clear with Barrow's truthful admonishment of the treatment of his fellow West Indians in his statement in Fredericton in 1963, Canada continued to blatantly ignore calls for reform and used the "carrot-on-a-stick" of increased foreign aid to appease the region. In the spring of 1964, Pearson's administration promised its West Indian partners $10 million annually in aid — almost five times the amount from the previous program. The Canadian delegates, led by A.E. Ritchie, the assistant Under-Secretary of State for External Affairs, were instructed by Pearson to only discuss migration schemes for seasonal workers, domestics and industrial apprenticeship plans (Donaghy and Muirhead 2008: 286–87). This admission from the Pearson administration is telling in that it was following the official de-racialization of Canadian immigration policy. It was also after evidence was provided by Canadian officials in the West Indies demanding immigration reforms to maintain favourable trade relations and after the open challenge from Barbados' premier in 1963. Canada did not wish to hide its obstinate stance towards increased Black West Indian migration nor did it care to address the issue as it seemingly attempted to "buy off" their critics with increased financial aid. Nevertheless, Donaghy and Muirhead's position must be viewed critically. Their article focused on Canadian foreign policy in the region and marginally addressed immigration and West Indian diplomatic agency. They did not discuss the de-racialization of Canadian immigration policy in 1962, which was a defining act of foreign policy that forever changed the West Indies–Canada relationship. The authors briefly mentioned the immigration reforms in 1967 as a side note to changes in trade relations. Immigration is a fundamental aspect of Canadian foreign policy, and the article set out to discuss Canadian interests in the Caribbean from 1941–1966, but it did not provide a comprehensive analysis of immigration policy. The authors did not utilize the archival evidence of the relationship between trade and Black West Indian migration. Canadian trade commissioners in the West Indies argued against the racist ad hoc immigration policy as it affected good trade relations with influential West Indians. Foreign policy trade and immigration worked within a racialized paradigm.

The 1966 Canada–West Indies Conference continued the ongoing debate on race and discrimination embedded deep within Canadian institutions and Canadian immigration policy. Canadian authorities argued the following:

> In general we are committed to dealing with West Indian immigrants on a completely non-discriminatory basis. This means that special care must be taken to ensure that the criteria be applied in Europe are applied by our selection teams visiting the Caribbean having regard to characteristic West Indian sensitivity towards real or imagined discrimination.[118]

The assertion of perceived racial discrimination problematized West Indian–Canadian relations and Canada's willingness to address and eradicate the debilitating stain of anti-Black sentiment. The conference's background paper on West Indian immigration, "Immigration to Canada from the Commonwealth Caribbean," epitomized Canada's deliberate disregard and collective amnesia of its colourful and discriminatory past. The paper stated, "aside from the admission of a few individuals under special authorities, there was little immigration from the Caribbean prior to 1955," the beginning of the Domestic Scheme.[119] The falsity and deflected blame of the previous statement was appalling. Black West Indians attempted to migrate to Canada, and some were able to in small numbers; however, the door to equitable immigration was firmly closed. Canadian immigration practice barred Black West Indian — British subjects notwithstanding — settlement. Moreover, Canadian authorities argued West Indians accused Canada of racial discrimination as a cover for ulterior motives. In a memorandum from the Assistant Deputy Minister of Citizenship and Immigration in 1966, it was stated that the charges were a "convenient screen for their real objective, namely a *preferred* (author's emphasis) place in our policies under which we would relax our selection standards and take large numbers of their unskilled and surplus population. The West Indians must realize that this is out of the question."[120]

Canadians accused West Indians of overstating Canada's racist immigration policy. The Canadian Government said that West Indians simply wanted Canada to absorb its unskilled surplus population. The Deputy Minister should have stood down from his defensive stance and realized that there was substantial legal and legislated evidence validating the West Indian claims of racial discrimination in Canadian immigration policy as revealed by the archival evidence used in this chapter.

Meanwhile, Canada continued to celebrate its colour-blind policies and distance itself from the negativity associated with allegations of racial discrimination. The conference concluded that "Canadian immigration law makes no distinction between the racial origins of immigrants. The degrees of relationship of persons admissible as sponsored immigrants do at present vary from country to coun-try."[121] Authorities based their application decisions on "normal and necessary criteria with respect to such matters as health, financial responsibility and absence of criminal record are applied impartially to all applicants without distinction to race."[122] However, the law did not address the personal biases and the racism entrenched within the Canadian immigration system and Canadian institutions. Laura Madokoro (in Webster et al. 2012: 18) questioned whether racism was solely structural and institutionalized and to what degree individuals dictated racial norms. In this case following the end of legislated racism in Canadian immigra-tion policy in 1962, the latter was true as personal agendas determined the fate of potential Black West Indian migrants. The law omitted the "distinction to race," but personal bigotry dictated the interpretation and application of immigration jurisprudence. The law changed, but the ideology remained the same. Within this environment defined by racialized immigration structures and hypocritical policies and actions, Black Barbadian emigrants maintained their sense of self-worth, pride and industry. The individual circumvented the exclusionary barriers, utilized her or his educational capital, and settled and contributed as citizens of the Canadian state.

According to Donaghy and Muirhead (2008: 289), "Canada may have had interests in the Caribbean, but it had very little foreign policy." Canada may have had more "interests" than "foreign policy" in the region, but the country did have a long and lasting historical relationship with the West Indies. From seventeenth- and eighteenth-century colonies within the British Empire in the Americas, to Commonwealth partners in the twentieth century, Barbadian-Canadian relations flourished throughout North American and West Indian history. The institution of slavery and mercantilist opportunities facilitated the growth of economic and political North-South ties; British colonial slaves produced the rum that inebri-ated those in the Maritimes, while Canadian fisheries fed Africans in the West Indies, who eventually appropriated salted cod as a feature of national dishes throughout the region. Naturally, financing systems followed trading routes, and Canadian banks found homes in the West Indies beginning in the late nineteenth century as the Bank of Nova Scotia established a branch in Jamaica in 1889; the significance of this relationship is underscored by the fact that the bank had yet to open a location in Toronto.

Canada was one of Barbados' chief trading partners in the early to mid-twentieth century and highly dependent on this North American export market to sup-port its economy. This relationship extended beyond economics; Canada was invested politically and socially in the British West Indies during the mid-twentieth century and showed interest in the ill-fated West Indies Federation in the late 1950s. During the same period, the issue of exclusionary Black Barbadian and West Indian immigration policies dominated the relationship. Racism, including pronouncements about climate discrimination, and the illogical personal bigotry of Canadian leaders, was a predominant feature of Canadian immigration policy. West Indian officials and political leaders contested this exclusionary practice and won small concessions, including the Domestic Scheme of 1955, prior to the official de-racialization of Canadian immigration policy in 1962 and the implementation of the Points System in 1967. As Sheldon Taylor (1994: 1–8) noted, there were several factors that contributed to the increase in West Indian emigrants to Canada. He argued that pressure from Caribbean trading partners and trade commissioners, the British Government's desire to curtail mass West Indian migration to the British Isles, Canada's role as a growing Commonwealth partner, and the respective West Indian governments that called foul on Canada's racist and exclusionary immigration policy facilitated increased migration of Black West Indians to Canada beginning in the 1940s' postwar boom and culminating in 1962 with the official de-racialization of Canadian immigration policy. Taylor discussed the role of the Domestic Scheme and the emigration of West Indian nurses during the 1950s; however, his work lacked a gendered analysis of West Indian migration (Taylor 1994: 1–8, 214–31).

Black Barbadian and Black West Indian women are central to the migration (her) story from the Caribbean region. Using the concept of the Emigrant Ambassador, Black women overcame gendered and racist immigration policy, hostile working environments, the de-skilling of their labour and downward social mobility, and still managed to spearhead the settlement of future generations of Black West Indians in Canada. The upward mobility through the pursuit of academic success was a fundamental Barbadian cultural attribute, one which challenges Simmons and Guengant's theory of a "culture-of-migration." Barbadian women were at the forefront of the settlement of their fellow citizens, first as Barbadian emigrants, followed by their status as Canadian immigrants, and, most importantly, as Barbadian-Canadians.

Notes

1   BNA, "Proceedings of Canada Conference, 1908," *Minutes of a Meeting of the Canadian Trade Relations Conference held at the House of Assembly Room, on Wednesday the 15th January 1908, at 10:15 a.m.*: 8. The name of the chairman was not specified.

2   Ibid.

3   Ibid., 2.

4   BNA, "Proceedings of Canada Conference, 1908," *Minutes of a Meeting of the Canadian Trade Relations Conference held at the House of Assembly Room, on Wednesday the 15th January 1908, at 10:15 a.m.*: 2–19.

5   BNA, Thomas Mulvey, *Report of Proceedings of the Canada-West Indies Conference, 1920* (Ottawa: Printer to the King's Most Excellent Majesty, 1920), 1.

6   Ibid.

7   Ibid., 4.

8   Ibid., 5.

9   Ibid., 178.

10   BNA, F.A. Acland, *Report of the Proceedings of the Canada–West Indies Conference, 1925, with the Canada–British West Indies-Bermuda-British Guiana-British Honduras Trade Agreement, 1925* (Ottawa: Printer to the King's Most Excellent Majesty, 1926), 2–3.

11   *Report of the Proceedings of the Canada–West Indies Conference, 1925, with the Canada–British West Indies-Bermuda-British Guiana-British Honduras Trade Agreement, 1925,* 4.

12   BNA, *Colonial Reports – Annual No. 1462; Barbados, Report for 1928–29* (London: His Majesty's Stationery Office, 1929).

13   Ibid.; BNA, *Colonial Reports – Annual No. 1462; Barbados, Report for 1928–29* (London: His Majesty's Stationery Office, 1929); BNA, *Colonial Reports – Annual No. 1499; Barbados, Report for 1929–30* (London: His Majesty's Stationery Office, 1930); BNA, *Colonial Reports – Annual No. 1544; Barbados, Report for 1930–31* (London: His Majesty's Stationery Office, 1931), 4–24.

14   BNA, *Colonial Reports – Annual No. 1462; Barbados, Report for 1928–29* (London: His Majesty's Stationery Office, 1929), 4–5.

15   BNA, *Colonial Reports – Annual No. 1595; Annual Report on the Social and Economic Progress of the People of Barbados, 1931–32* (London: His Majesty's Stationery Office, 1932), 16.

16   BNA, *Colonial Reports – Annual No. 1913; Barbados, Report for 1938–1939* (London: His Majesty's Stationery Office, 1939), 4–24; and BNA, *Colonial Office Annual Report on Barbados for the Year 1948* (London: His Majesty's Stationery Office, 1949), 4–24.

17   BNA, *Colonial Reports – Annual No. 1422; Barbados, Report for 1927–28* (London: His Majesty's Stationery Office, 1929); BNA, *Colonial Reports – Annual No. 1462; Barbados, Report for 1928–29* (London: His Majesty's Stationery Office, 1929); BNA, *Colonial Reports – Annual No. 1499; Barbados, Report for 1929–30* (London: His Majesty's Stationery Office, 1930); BNA, *Colonial Reports – Annual No. 1544; Barbados, Report for 1930–31* (London: His Majesty's Stationery Office, 1931); BNA, *Colonial Reports – Annual No. 1595; Annual Report on the Social and Economic Progress of the People of Barbados, 1931–32* (London: His Majesty's Stationery Office, 1932); BNA, *Colonial Reports – Annual No. 1632; Annual Report on the Social and Economic Progress of the People of Barbados, 1932–33* (London: His Majesty's Stationery Office, 1933); BNA, *Colonial Reports – Annual No. 1725; Barbados, Report for 1934–35* (London: His Majesty's Stationery Office, 1935); BNA, *Colonial Reports – Annual No. 1861; Barbados, Report for 1937–1938* (London: His Majesty's Stationery Office, 1938).

18   BNA, *Colonial Reports – Annual No. 1913; Barbados, Report for 1938–1939* (London: His Majesty's Stationery Office, 1939), 13.

19   BNA, *Colonial Office Annual Report on Barbados for the Year 1947* (London: His Majesty's Stationery Office, 1948); BNA, *Colonial Office Annual Report on Barbados for the Year 1948* (London: His Majesty's Stationery Office, 1949), 23.; BNA, *Colonial Office Annual Report on Barbados for the Year 1949* (London: His Majesty's Stationery Office, 1950); BNA, *Colonial Office Annual Report on Barbados for the Years 1950 and 1951* (London: His Majesty's Stationery Office, 1952), 7 and 26.

20   BNA, *Colonial Reports – Annual No. 1422; Barbados, Report for 1927–28* (London: His Majesty's Stationery Office, 1929); BNA, *Colonial Reports – Annual No. 1462; Barbados, Report for 1928–29* (London: His Majesty's Stationery Office, 1929); BNA, *Colonial Reports – Annual No. 1499; Barbados, Report for 1929–30* (London: His Majesty's Stationery Office, 1930); BNA, *Colonial Reports – Annual No. 1544; Barbados, Report for 1930–31* (London: His Majesty's Stationery Office, 1931); BNA, *Colonial Reports – Annual No. 1595; Annual Report on the Social and Economic Progress of the People of Barbados, 1931–32* (London: His Majesty's Stationery Office, 1932); BNA, *Colonial Reports – Annual No. 1632; Annual Report on the Social and Economic Progress of the People of Barbados, 1932–33* (London: His Majesty's Stationery Office, 1933); BNA, *Colonial Reports – Annual No. 1725; Barbados, Report for 1934-35* (London: His Majesty's Stationery Office, 1935); BNA, *Colonial Reports – Annual No. 1861; Barbados, Report for 1937–1938* (London: His Majesty's Stationery Office, 1938). Canadian Goods Imported in 1937 & 1938 (no financial figures were provided for the subsequent years, nor were they listed explicitly following 1938 and the suspension of the Colonial Reports in 1940–1946): Boots and Shoes; Fish: dried, salted, smoked (includes Newfoundland); Flour; Pork salted; Motor Cars; Wood and Timber. BNA, *Colonial Reports – Annual No. 1861; Barbados, Report for 1937–1938* (London: His Majesty's Stationery Office, 1938); BNA, *Colonial Reports – Annual No. 1913; Barbados, Report for 1938–1939* (London: His Majesty's Stationery Office, 1939).

21   BNA, *The Canada–West Indies Magazine*, May 1937 & June 1937.

22   BNA, "Saluting the West Indies Federation," *Canada West–Indies Magazine*, November 1957.

23   Ibid.

24   BNA, *The Canada–West Indies Magazine*, May 1937, 1.

25   Ibid.

26   Ibid.

27   "Saluting the West Indies Federation," *The Canada–West Indies Magazine*, November 1957, 3.

28   *The Canada–West Indies Magazine*, June 1937, 6.

29   "Saluting the West Indies Federation," *The Canada–West Indies Magazine*, November 1957.

30   "Saluting the West Indies Federation," *The Canada–West Indies Magazine*, November 1957.

31   Canada, *House of Commons Debates*, 17 January 1955, 255.

32   Ibid.

33   Ibid.

34   I have to attribute this line of thought to a conversation with Dr. Michele Johnson at the Breaking the Chains Community Partners' Meeting, September 14, 2012, in London, Ontario, Canada. I also have to thank Dr. Margaret Kellow for adding that this move highlighted unusual foresight in the Canadian Government, especially compared to what governments usually display. In 1957, Canada anticipated the 1962 *Commonwealth Immigrants Act* and the impact it would have on the Canadian state's immigration policy.

35   "Saluting the West Indies Federation," *The Canada–West Indies Magazine*, November 1957, 3.

36   Ibid.

37   Ibid., 11.

38   LAC, RG 26, vol. 123, file 3-32-14, pp. 10–12, Submission to: The Honourable Walter F. Harris, Minister of Citizenship and Immigration. President, Canadian Jewish Congress & President, Jewish Immigrant Aid Society. Montreal. November 25, 1952.

39   Ibid.

40   Ibid.

41   LAC, RG 26, vol. 123, file 3-32-14, Letter submitted by the Minister of Citizenship and Immigration, December 9, 1952, to Mr. Saul Hayes, National Executive Director, Canadian Jewish Congress in response to the brief (the one above) submitted November 25, 1952 by the Canadian Jewish Congress and the Jewish Immigrant Aid Society.

42   LAC, RG 26, vol. 123, file 3-32-14, Article by J.V. McAree. "Jews are Victims." *Globe & Mail* (Toronto), September 24, 1949.

43   William Lyon Mackenzie King, "The Diaries of William Lyon Mackenzie King, February 13, 1947," *Library and Archives Canada,* last modified December 4, 2007 <www.collectionscanada.gc.ca/databases/king/001059-119.02-e.php?&page_id_nbr=29395&interval=20&&PHPSESSID=kjrmhp00c9o1angknic2bh tke2>.

44   Ibid.

45   Canada, *House of Commons Debates*, May 1, 1947, 2646 (William Lyon Mackenzie King).

46   William Lyon Mackenzie King, "The Diaries of William Lyon Mackenzie King, May 1, 1947, page 396," *Library and Archives Canada,* last modified December 4, 2007 <www. collectionscanada.gc.ca/databases/king/001059-119.02-e.php?&page_id_nbr=296 62&interval=20&&&&&&&&&PHPSESSID=kjrmhp00c9o1angknic2bhtke2>.

47   LAC, RG 76, vol. 830, file 552-1-644, pt. 1, Minutes of the Meeting Held in Conference Room, East Block, Friday, June 19, 1953, 11:00 a.m.

48   Ibid.

49   LAC, RG 76, vol. 830, file 552-1-644, pt. 1, Note from the Canadian Embassy, Caracas, Venezuela, to the Under-Secretary of State for External Affairs, Canada. June 1, 1953.

50   LAC, RG 76, vol. 830, file 552-1-644, pt. 1, Letter from (Sgd.) L.D. Wilgress to Laval Fortier, June 16, 1953.

51   LAC, RG 76, vol. 830, file 552-1-644, pt. 1, Immigration Branch – File No. 81066. Ottawa, August 25, 1953.

52   LAC, RG 76, vol. 830, file 552-1-644, pt. 1, Letter from P.T. Baldwin, Chief, Admissions Division of the Department of Citizenship and Immigration to Mr. R.R. Parlour, Asst. Canadian Trade Commissioner, Port of Spain. August 17, 1953.

53   LAC, RG 76, vol. 830, file 552-1-644, pt. 1, Department of Trade and Commerce: Inter-Office Correspondence, Mr. M.B. Palmer to Mr. F.L. Casserly, May 22, 1953.

54   LAC, RG 76, vol. 830, file 552-1-644, pt. 1, Memorandum, to Mr. P.V. McLane from Mr. R.R. Parlour, May 6, 1953.

55   Ibid.

56   Ibid.

57   Ibid.

58   Ibid.

59   LAC, RG 76, vol. 830, file 552-1-644, pt. 1, Memorandum to the Minister (from the Director), Ottawa, September 12, 1951.

60   Ibid.

61   W.E. Harris, "Memorandum from Minister of Citizenship and Immigration to Cabinet, Cabinet Document No. 174-50 June 23rd, 1950 (Ottawa)," *Foreign Affairs and International Trade Canada* – Documents on Canadian External Relations <www.international.gc.ca/department/history-histoire/dcer/details-en.asp?intRefid=7987> [accessed October 25, 2012].

62   Ibid.

63   Ibid.

64   LAC, RG 76, vol. 830, file 552-1-644, pt. 1, Memorandum to the Minister (from the Director), Ottawa, September 12, 1951.

65   Ibid.

66   LAC, RG 76, vol. 830, file 552-1-644, pt. 1, Letter from Donald Moore of the Negro Citizenship Committee to Honourable Walter Harris, House of Commons, Ottawa, May 13, 1953.

67   Ibid.

68   LAC, RG 76, vol. 830, file 552-1-644, pt. 1, Excerpt from the Annual Report – Work of the Office – 1952 – Port-of-Spain, Trinidad.

69   LAC, RG 76, vol. 830, file 552-1-644, pt. 1, Letter to the Under-Secretary of State for External Affairs, Canada, from C.W. Dier, Esq., Vice Consul, Caracas, Venezuela, May 7, 1952.

70   Ibid.

71   LAC, RG 76, vol. 830, file 552-1-644, pt. 2, Correspondence to Deputy Minister to Directory, September 12, 1958.

72   LAC, RG 76, vol. 830, file 552-1-644, pt. 2, Deputy Minister (letter signed by C.E.S. Smith – Acting Deputy Minister) to Director, March 10, 1958.

73   Ibid.

74   Ibid.

75   Ibid.

76   Ibid.

77   LAC, RG 76, vol. 830, file 552-1-644, pt. 2, Memorandum for: The Acting Minister – from Laval Fortier to C.E.S. Smith, Ottawa, April 17, 1958.

78   LAC, RG 76, vol. 830, file 552-1-644, pt. 2, *A Review of Immigration from the British West Indies.* January 14, 1955. There was no defined writer indicated for this review. It is quite probable that it was a bureaucrat, maybe even Laval Fortier.

79   LAC, RG 76, vol. 830, file 552-1-644, pt. 2, *A Review of Immigration from the British West Indies.* January 14, 1955.

80   LAC, RG 76, vol. 830, file 552-1-644, pt. 3, Department of External Affairs, Canada. Numbered Letter to the Under-Secretary of State for External Affairs, Ottawa, Canada. From the Office of the Commissioner for Canada, Port-of-Spain, R.G.C. Smith. October 24, 1961.

81 Ibid.

82 LAC, RG 76, vol. 830, file 552-1-644, pt. 2, *A Review of Immigration from the British West Indies. January 14, 1955.*

83 Ibid.

84 LAC, RG 76, vol. 830, file 552-1-644, pt. 2, *A Review of Immigration from the British West Indies. January 14, 1955.*

85 Ibid.

86 Ibid.

87 LAC, RG 76, vol. 830, file 552-1-644, pt. 2, Memorandum: Brief Presented to the Prime Minister, Minister of Citizenship and Immigration, Members of the Government of Canada, by the Negro Citizenship Association, Donald W. Moore (Director) and Stanley Grizzle, D.C. (Secretary). Tuesday, April 27, 1954.

88 Ibid.

89 Ibid.

90 LAC, RG 76, vol. 830, file 552-1-644, pt. 2, *Proposal for Controlled Emigration from Barbados for Specified Types of Workers* (n.d.).

91 LAC, RG 76, vol. 830, file 552-1-644, pt. 2, Memorandum: Brief Presented to the Prime Minister, Minister of Citizenship and Immigration, Members of the Government of Canada, by the Negro Citizenship Association, Donald W. Moore (Director) and Stanley Grizzle, D.C. (Secretary). Tuesday, April 27, 1954.

92 Canada, *House of Commons Debates,* June 26, 1954.

93 LAC, RG 76, vol. 830, file 552-1-644, pt. 4, Memorandum to Cabinet. Re: Opening a Canadian Immigration Office in the West Indies. From the Minister of Citizenship and Immigration (No specified date of revisions. First draft dated November 1962.); LAC, RG 76, vol. 830, file 552-1-644, pt. 4, *Globe and Mail,* November 5, 1963.

94 LAC, RG 76, vol. 820, file 552-1-533, *Immigration to Canada from the Commonwealth Caribbean (Background paper prepared by Canada)* Commonwealth Caribbean-Canada Conference, Ottawa, July 6–8, 1966, June 1, 1966.

95 Ibid.

96 Ibid.

97 LAC, RG 76, vol. 830, file 552-1-644, pt. 4, Memorandum to Cabinet. Re: Opening a Canadian Immigration Office in the West Indies. From the Minister of Citizenship and Immigration (No specified date of revisions. First draft dated November 1962.)

98 LAC, RG 76, vol. 830, file 552-1-644, pt. 4, Memorandum to Cabinet. Re: Opening a Canadian Immigration Office in the West Indies. From the Minister of Citizenship and Immigration (No specified date of revisions. First draft dated November 1962.)

99 Ibid.

100 Ibid.

101 LAC, RG 76, vol. 830, file 552-1-644, pt. 4, *Globe and Mail,* November 5, 1963.

102 LAC, RG 76, vol. 830, file 552-1-644, pt. 4, Memorandum to A/Chief of Operations. From Head, Administration Section, February 28, 1963.

103 LAC, RG 76, vol. 1241, file 5850-3-555, Selection & Processing – General Series – Immigration from Barbados.

104 Ibid.

105 LAC, RG 76, vol. 830, file 552-1-644, pt. 4, Foreign Trade Service. To Mr. D.A. Reid,

Chief of Operations, Immigration Branch, Department of Citizenship & Immigration, Ottawa. From Roy W. Blake, Canadian Government Trade Commissioner, Kingston, Jamaica, February 8, 1962.

106 Ibid.

107 LAC, RG 76, vol. 830, file 552-1-644, pt. 4, Department of External Affairs, Canada, Numbered Letter to the Under-Secretary of State for External Affairs, Ottawa Canada. From Office of the High Commissioner for Canada (G.C. McInnes), Kingston, Jamaica, August 2, 1963.

108 Ibid.

109 Ibid.

110 Ibid.

111 LAC, RG 76, vol. 830, file 552-1-644, pt. 4, Report on the October 25–27, 1963 Conference on "Commonwealth Partners in the West Indies" sponsored by the Canadian Institute of International Affairs (Fredericton Branch) and the University of New Brunswick.

112 LAC, RG 76, vol. 830, file 552-1-644, pt. 3, Department of External Affairs, Canada. Numbered Letter to the Under-Secretary of State for External Affairs, Ottawa, Canada. From Office of the Commissioner for Canada, Port-of-Spain, R.G.C. Smith, October 24, 1961.

113 LAC, RG 76, vol. 830, file 552-1-644, pt. 4, Report on the October 25–27, 1963 Conference on "Commonwealth Partners in the West Indies" sponsored by The Canadian Institute of International Affairs (Fredericton Branch) and the University of New Brunswick.

114 Ibid.

115 Ibid.

116 LAC, RG 76, vol. 830, file 552-1-644, pt. 4, Foreign Trade Service. To Mr. D.A. Reid, Chief of Operations, Immigration Branch, Department of Citizenship & Immigration, Ottawa. From Roy W. Blake, Canadian Government Trade Commissioner, Kingston, Jamaica, February 8, 1962.

117 Ibid.

118 LAC, RG 76, vol. 820, file 552-1-533, Canada–West Indies Conference – Follow-up action. Assistant Deputy Minister (Immigration), Director of Policy and Planning, July 14, 1966.

119 LAC, RG 76, vol. 820, file 552-1-533, *Immigration to Canada from the Commonwealth Caribbean (Background paper prepared by Canada)*, Commonwealth Caribbean-Canada Conference, July 6–8, 1966, June 1, 1966.

120 LAC, RG 76, vol. 820, file 552-1-533, Memorandum to Deputy Minister from Assistant Deputy Minister (Immigration), January 21, 1966.

121 LAC, RG 76, vol. 820, file 552-1-533, *Allegations of Racial Discrimination*, Commonwealth Caribbean-Canada Conference, Ottawa, July 6–8, 1966.

122 Ibid.

Chapter Five

THE EMIGRANT AMBASSADORS

I worked hard on my life. Nothing was easy for me. But at the same time,
I grew up in an environment where resilience was taught, experienced.
And I have operated my life in that spirit. (Keung 2011)

We live in a society where the Black female voice is constantly ignored. Canadian history has deemed (her)story irrelevant and insignificant. We in turn produce Canadian citizens that believe that Black women do not — and never did — exist as heterogeneous building blocks of the Canadian mosaic: she is simply an adjunct to a colourless patriarchal narrative. Black women have been consistently and deliberately erased from the Canadian nation-building narrative. Why? This is done simply because they are Black and female in a society where Blackness and womanhood are marginalized to the periphery of devalued existence and nothingness. The Emigrant Ambassadors are one step in a long process of recognizing the rightful place of Black women in Canadian history.

Like so many other West Indian women, Grenadian-born Jean Augustine saw the Domestic Scheme as a means for greater socio-economic opportunity in Canada. She came to Canada in 1960 and worked as a domestic in Toronto for a year before enrolling in teacher's college and earning her permanent resident status. As the first Black woman elected to the House of Commons and to serve in Cabinet as the Minister of State for Multiculturalism and the Status of Women, she faced barriers to her success in Canada. Despite having completed her secondary education and having taught in Grenada, Augustine recalled the following interaction with a receptionist at a teacher's college: "[She] kept telling me I had to do Grade 13 and pushing my papers back to me. I just stood there. I would not move. She called the next person in the line, then the next person behind. I just kept standing there" (Keung 2011). Eventually Augustine succeeded in her perseverance against discrimination and bigotry; "a supervisory person came by and asked what the problem was. I said I had this letter and that document ... the supervisor looked at them and said, 'Yeah you have the qualifications.' And that's my first little struggle" (Keung 2011). The high-profiled Augustine was not the first, nor the last, Black West Indian woman that faced barriers to integration despite possessing the required qualifications. Similar to her Barbadian counterparts profiled in this chapter, such as retired Toronto District School Board (TDSB) principal Cyriline Taylor, the Grenadian-born Augustine came to Canada to further her education; she received both her bachelor's degree and her master's degree at the University of Toronto. Following a career in education, which culminated in her appointment as a principal in the TDSB in the 1980s, she was elected the first Black woman in the House of Commons. What is often overlooked in her immigrant "success story" is the history behind the Domestic Scheme during the 1950s and how gendered racism dictated mid-twentieth century West Indian migrant flows to Canada. Augustine was a pioneer who successfully reached the upper echelons of Canadian politics; however, previously nameless Black female emigrants involved in and outside of the Scheme during the 1950s and 1960s also overcame exclusionary barriers. Black Barbadian and West Indian women changed the face of Canadian immigration policy (Keung 2011).

I will engage with the racialized and discriminatory immigration policy towards Black West Indians using the theoretical framework of race, gendered labour divisions and Black identity. This paradox of hypocrisy is discussed using the case of Barbadian and West Indian Emigrant Ambassadors — most notably, highly educated and upwardly mobile women who came to Canada under the Domestic Scheme initiated in 1955. These women challenged the racist and sexist hegemony of Canadian society — and its immigration policy — to ultimately assist in the deconstruction of the racialized Black West Indian emigrant category. The examination of race is interspersed by the class-based and gendered division of Canadian immigration policy and the Domestic Scheme. Barbadian and West Indian women, codified through a gendered labour lens, contributed to the liberalization of West Indian emigration to Canada. I will continue my discussion of the gendered aspects of the emigration of Black Barbadian women including nurses and educators. These women asserted agency within the patriarchal and racist structure of sexist international migration during the early to mid-twentieth century.

Immigration history must acknowledge female migrant autonomy; they were not passive clients and merely victims of exclusionary racist and sexist immigration policies and ideologies. In addition to race and class, a gendered theoretical framework of immigration history must be applied to understand the barriers faced by female migrants, but specifically Black Barbadian and Black West Indian women; these women were at the forefront of Black West Indian emigration to Canada during the mid-twentieth century as Emigrant Ambassadors. The Emigrant Ambassadors represented themselves, their island nations and their governments as they were selected to confront the institutionalized barriers to liberalize migration for Blacks from Barbados and the West Indies. This trailblazing Emigrant Ambassador sentiment was expressed in a January 30, 1956, letter written by Gloria Walcott, one of the first Barbadian women in Canada selected under the Domestic Scheme, to Negro Citizenship Association (NCA) founder and director, Donald W. Moore: "I think all the girls are happy and are going to live up to all expectations so that other West Indian immigrants will be able to come too" (quoted in Moore 1985: 160). I aim to recognize these women for the sacrifices they made as representatives of Black Pride, Black Power, self-empowerment and self-respect; they normalized their role not as the "exceptional" Black Achiever, but as the rule that all Black West Indian migrants had the potential and capital to achieve greatness in Canada. They manipulated their racialized and gendered bodies — as the ideological "Black woman" only suitable for domestic servitude to White masters — to challenge Canadian society's perceived sense of Black West Indian identity and anti-Black racism. I must first examine the history of Black women in Barbados since slavery to contextualize the role of women in Barbadian society, and to highlight that the perseverance and upward mobility of the Barbadian Emigrant Ambassadors are historical characteristics.

Barbadian Women: A History

Since the mid-eighteenth century, Creole African-Barbadian and African women in Barbados were central to the plantation economy. Black Barbadian women were defined as "survivalist social beings" due to their primary role in slave society. Black Barbadian slave women were the "dominant force behind production and labour reproduction," which fulfilled their role as a "dual economic contribution to the survival of the slave economy" and their slave master's financial well-being (Beckles 1989: 2–3). Barbadian women were in the majority in field gangs as forced manual labour; they acted as domestic workers, artisans, provided leisure services in the urban sector, and were sexually exploited through physical and psychological domination and as a means to generate profit for plantation owners. I contend that the survivalist characteristics of these women — the survivalist social beings — paralleled those of the Emigrant Ambassadors. Like the Emigrant Ambassadors of the twentieth century, these slave women were "restless, ambitious, shrewd, and always prepared to seek freedom" (Beckles 1989: 2). Black Barbadian women persevered despite what bell hooks (quoted in Beckles 1989: 27) contended was their "mass brutalization and terrorization" first aboard slave ships and throughout the institution of slavery. The pursuit of freedom and social mobility, albeit defined within the draconian structures of slavery, gender inequalities and colonial domination, were characteristics of women in Barbadian history.

As is true with the Emigrant Ambassadors of the twentieth century, one must qualify the autonomy and freedom of women during the eighteenth and nineteenth century within the structures of the institution of slavery and patriarchal colonial domination. Black Barbadian women experienced the "tripartite structure of race, class, and gender oppression [that] located most black women in positions of greatest material deprivation and social vulnerability" during slavery, but one may argue that this intersectionality of oppression continued well into the twentieth century (Beckles 1989: 3). Slave women in Barbados did find agency within the tyranny of slave society, including their dominance in petty trade as hucksters, leaders in Black and slave revolts on the Island, and in the struggle to maintain family units and cultural institutions. The "moral authority" of elderly Black Barbadian women was also crucial to maintain order and cohesion in slave communities. Black women had both personal and communal objectives in their "social authority" over fellow slaves; it was a form of limited autonomy and limited mobility in a structured slave system (Beckles 1989: 5). These traits were not unique to simply Barbadian women during slavery in the British West Indies; however, Barbados' slave demographics and female to male sex ratios set the island apart from its West Indian neighbours. Barbadian women played a crucial role in the history of Barbados as labourers and reproducers. This was most apparent as women were in the majority of Barbados' slave population from the early eighteenth century (Beckles 1989: 7).

The female majority in Barbados — both Black and White — distinguished Barbados from other slave societies in the Caribbean. In the seventeenth century, men and women worked together in the field gangs and there was no gendered differentiation in terms of manual labour. Richard Ligon, the first person to write a history of Barbados, commented in 1647 that women were present in plantation field gangs and were "perceived as important to the labour policies of the embryonic slavocracy" (quoted in Beckles 1989: 7). Black female slaves during the eighteenth and early nineteenth century "performed, and [were] expected to perform the same work as men" (Beckles 1989: 25). Female slaves were cheaper than males and better suited for agricultural labour; in West African societies, agricultural labour was "women's work" (Beckles 1999: 6). It was possible that Barbados' gender ratio favoured women since the Island was the "first-stop" purchaser in the Slave Trade, which possibly depleted the cheaper female stock of slaves for other islands in the Caribbean (Beckles 1989: 8). It was also "socially rational" for Barbadian planters to buy females slaves to satisfy a socio-ideological need for Black male slaves on plantations. The socio-ideological need was physical and emotional companionship (Beckles 1989: 9). Nevertheless, Barbadian planters' promotion and effective execution of natural reproduction contributed to its large female population. This distinguished Barbados from other West Indian islands and their focus on the importation of a disproportionate number of male slaves for physical labour.

Since the late seventeenth century, Barbados privileged Black women "as part of a revised strategic plan to promote the natural reproduction of the labour force," which did not come into effect throughout the rest of the Caribbean until well after the 1750s (Beckles 1999: 3). Between 1780 and 1806, Barbados had more Creole slaves than any other island in the West Indies. By 1800, natural reproduction became the dominant means of maintaining slave populations, which resulted in Barbados being the only island in the British West Indies that welcomed the end of the Slave Trade in 1807 (Beckles 1989: 20). Figures representing the gendered slave structure between 1801 and 1832 highlighted Barbados' female majority.

A focus on natural reproduction valued a large female slave population in Barbados. Female slaves were much more valuable than males primarily due to the enslavement and control of their physical production and their reproduction; female slaves worked and gave birth to more slaves who also worked. By the mid-eighteenth century until the end of the institution of slavery in 1834, Barbadian planters "intervened in the sexual relations of female slaves as policy in order to encourage reproduction" (Beckles 1989: 15). A "woman's policy" and "slave breeding" programs emerged, which were facilitated by a belief that fertile female slaves had to be treated with "greater humanity and consideration" in order to increase fertility (Beckles 1989: 92, 97). Due to the matrilineal reproduction of slave status, "womanhood, as a gendered formulation, was therefore legally constituted as a reproduction device that offered the slave system continuity and functionality" (Beckles 1999: 8). However, controlling fertility and resisting forced maternity were "placed at the core" of Black female slave resistance (Beckles 1989: 153). Infanticide and abortions were common acts of resistance (Beckles 1989: 159).

A culture of resistance defined the place of women in Barbadian history. Female slave perseverance, determination and resistance were "crucial to the survival of

Table 5-1 Barbadian Slave Population by Sex, 1801–1832[1]

Year	Male No.	Male percent	Female No.	Female percent
1801	29,872	46.5	34,324	53.5
1817	35,354	45.6	42,139	54.4
1823	36,159	45.9	42,657	54.1
1829	37,691	46.0	44,211	54.0
1832	37,762	46.3	43,738	53.7

her family, her community, her culture and her own personal integrity and human dignity" (Bush 1990: 10). There was a significant role that the individual woman and her agency, however limited, played in resisting the draconian structures of the institution of slavery: "In strongly resisting slavery in a multitude of ways, refusing to succumb to the pressures inherent in slave society, the individual slave woman *herself* (author's emphasis) was refusing to conform to the image white society had created for her" (Bush 1990: 22). Black Barbadian female resistance was noted during the 1816 Bussa Rebellion. The Bussa Rebellion of Easter 1816 in Barbados was caused by the "rumour" of emancipation on January 1, 1816. The "whole was strengthened by the information, imported by some free People of Colour," and by slaves "who had gained an ascendancy over their fellows by being enabled to read and write."[2] The slave revolt began "by many of the leading Slaves (directed and encouraged by a few Free People of Colour)," as the "nearer approximation which existed between the Free People of Colour and Slaves, arising frequently from original connection or previous acquaintance," facilitated the exchange of revolutionary ideas.[3] King Wiltshire, a slave belonging to the Bayley's Plantation in Barbados, drew attention to the role the image of the Black woman played in the rebellion. Wiltshire testified:

> The negroes were to be freed, and that their freedom was to be given [to] them through a black woman who was a Queen, for whom Wilberforce acted in England: that some free coloured man, namely, Cain Davis, Roach, and Sarjeant, had told him this."[4]

Nanny Grigg, a Black woman at the forefront of the Bussa Rebellion, was characterized as a "revolutionary ideologue." The Barbados Assembly's official 1816 report described Grigg as a "literate, knowledgeable woman who believed and propagated the view that in order to secure freedom it was possible to replicate the Haitian Revolution" (Beckles 1998: 46). Doll, a Black female slave owned by Elizabeth Newton (owner of Newton and Seawell Plantations in Barbados), negotiated her and her daughters' "semi-free" status upon her master's return to England. Black Barbadian female anti-slavery mentalities "preceded the plantation," and a culture of resistance began in West Africa and continued through the horrors of the Middle Passage (Beckles 1998: 46).

> [Black women were a] fundamental and indispensable part of the black historical process which enabled Africans to survive enslavement with dignity and create a vigorous culture and society. Thus, from Africa, through the slave experience, in the modern Caribbean and Britain itself, black women had and will have a crucial role to play in their own societies. (Bush 1990: 167)

Barbadian women continued to display these characteristics of resistance and perseverance, along with the pursuit of agency and social mobility, well into the late nineteenth and early twentieth century. Between Emancipation and the 1960s, there was a significant decrease in the female labour participation rate as Barbadian women "detached themselves — or were separated by technological developments — from the agricultural labour market" (Coppin 1995: 104). There was a significant amount of rural to urban migration by women seeking employment during this period. Black women sought jobs as domestics and in retailing since Barbados' limited geography could not support an independent agricultural peasantry following Emancipation (Coppin 1995: 104). Cyriline Taylor recalled that her grandmother — "Ma" — who was born in Barbados in 1898, said that there were few job opportunities available for young women in the early twentieth century. In addition to work on plantations as agricultural labour, domestics and in retail services, young Black women also sold fruit and vegetables in Bridgetown and "on the roadside," worked as bartenders, "hawkers," seamstresses, and engaged in prostitution in the "Red Light" district near the capital where they retained sailors as their main clientele.[5] In his memoir, Austin Clarke underlined Barbados' patriarchal society, its discrimination towards girls, and gendered divisions of labour. Clarke (2005: 79) wrote:

> Boys got the best food and attention, and the least floggings, if they were high school boys. Girls were expected to be dressmakers, sugar and silent, spice and stupid, and wash the boys' clothes. So my hero's sister would have helped her mother with the needlework which sustained the family.

Clarke also stated that it was his mother who was the "rock" of his support system. He went into great detail to emphasize the strength and perseverance of his mother and all Barbadian women in the first half of the twentieth century. Clarke (2005: 201) wrote: "She worked hard. All women in those days worked hard."

Black women in Barbados during the early to mid-twentieth century did their best to navigate the oppressive structures of the intersections of race, class and gender. Sex-selective migration policies disproportionately favoured Barbadian male sojourners; however, some Barbadian women did emigrate prior to the 1950s as they sought socio-economic advancement and mobility abroad. Ma emigrated to British Guiana in her twenties as there were job opportunities for women in the British colony and the relatively short travel by ship was affordable. Ma's case is an example of the early emigration of Barbadian women for socio-economic mobility; it is evidence of the autonomy of early Emigrant Ambassadors. Taylor's grandmother also supported her family back in Barbados through remittances and sending foodstuffs including walnuts and the Barbadian dietary staple, rice.[6]

Nevertheless, during the early twentieth century, a large surplus of Barbadian women remained on the Island. At the turn of the twentieth century and the onset of the mass exodus of male sojourners to the Isthmus of Panama, women filled the agricultural labour needs of plantation owners. Early twentieth century emigration left twice as many women on the Island due to sex-selective emigration prior to 1921. Due in part to male emigration, women continued to dominate Barbadian population sex ratios established during slavery. Moreover, in the immediate post-Second World War period up to the late 1950s, women lived longer than men and Barbadian women had the longest life spans in the West Indies. In 1956, for every 1,000 women there were only 853 Barbadian men — the second lowest sex ratio in the West Indies behind only Grenada. Barbadian women thus sought employment to support female-headed households caused in part by circuitous Barbadian male economic transnationalism. Women also gained employment because of the socio-economic racialized marginalization of Black male breadwinners in a White dominated society and the fact that the Barbadian population was dominated by a female majority (Coppin 1995: 104; Lowenthal 1957: 456).

Several Barbadian Government social assistance initiatives improved the lives of women and their families in Barbados during the postwar period. The *Moyne Commission Report* of 1945 stated that there was an "immensity" of social problems in the West Indies, which required a large expansion of both governmental and voluntary social services (Edmonds and Girvan 1973: 229). The Barbadian Government first implemented a National Insurance Scheme, which covered a maternity benefit for women in 1945 (Edmonds and Girvan 1973: 230). In 1950, through the Moyne Commissioner's suggestion, Barbados created the position of a Social Welfare Office (Edmonds and Girvan 1973: 230). This was followed by a childcare program of "day nurseries" under the Housing Authority and the Barbadian Government's support for the Barbados Family Planning Association in 1955 (Edmonds and Girvan 1973: 230). Many of these initiatives improved the welfare of Barbadian women, but were primarily implemented to address the historical issue of population density. Barbados' high birth rate and declining death rate forced Barbadian officials to focus their attention on family planning. In the early 1960s, the pill and other forms of inter-uterine devices for birth control were introduced in Barbados (Edmonds and Girvan 1973: 232). Barbados was the first country in the Western Hemisphere where birth control was sanctioned and supported by government (Lowenthal 1957: 495). One may argue that this was the government's attempt at controlling female bodies; however, the postwar environment focused on social services designed to increase "the self-respect of the individual" rather than a continued dependence on multi-functional institutions and Poor Relief (Edmonds and Girvan 1973: 245). The Barbadian Government gradually addressed gender inequality with these initiatives as women on the Island in the 1950s and 1960s slowly began to achieve higher status in the public sphere.

Declining fertility rates due to the government's active family planning program and the increased access to secondary education for girls in Barbados in the 1950s led to higher Black Barbadian female participation in the labour force in the 1960s. It must be noted that girls and young women did experience sex-stereotyping during the postwar period in schools as clerical skills were emphasized in the all-girls' secondary school curriculum (Coppin 1995: 107, 111). However, early and mid-twentieth century social initiatives allowed many young women to procure the skills and training needed to further their careers and futures abroad. They may have had the skills and education; however, gender discrimination on the Island proved to impede the social mobility of some young women. A young female Barbadian emigrant in London who did not attend an "elite" academic secondary school expressed the gender inequality in the education system. She stated that her education trained her "to be a seamstress, and to do typing. It was more like a finishing school for young ladies; they weren't training you to do a *job!* (author's emphasis)" (quoted in Western 1992: 88). Nevertheless, emigration proved to be an outlet for Barbadian female social mobility. In 1955 and 1956, 2,818 women left Barbados, which was 40 percent of the Island's total net emigration (Lowenthal 1957: 487). Many of these women left Barbados and sought socio-economic advancement in the United Kingdom through government-sponsored programs. Beverly Braithwaite — along with other Black Barbadian women —arrived in London in February 1957 after she was recruited for London Transport. Braithwaite challenged gendered labour divisions and Barbadian sex-stereotypes as she worked in station bars, pressed in a laundromat, worked as a seamstress, worked in a food factory, made tires in a rubber factory, cut tin in a steel business and worked as an industrial engraver. The occupations were primarily manual labour; however, Braithwaite did not fit, nor did she choose to confine herself to, gendered stereotypes. Others including Pauline Alleyne, Dotteen Bannister, Ernestine Farley and Amelia Simmons left Barbados and found social mobility through their work in the female-dominated nursing profession (Western 1992: xxi-xxii, 94). No matter the occupation, emigration proved to be a step forward for Black Barbadian women who have been historically defined by their perseverance, mobility and resistance to oppression.

Barbadian Emigration to Canada: The Eve of the Domestic Scheme

During the early 1950s to 1960s, unemployment continued to curtail Barbadian development, and mass migration to Canada became a viable option to alleviate socio-economic strife on the Island. Unemployment "continue[d] to be one of the gravest problems which the island face[d]," and "permanent and temporary emigration continued to provide an important outlet for the surplus labour force."[7] In 1958, 2,930 people left Barbados to seek permanent employment abroad. In 1959, 3,204 people left for employment.[8] However, prior to the implementation of the Domestic Scheme in 1955, Canadian immigration policy provided "only for the admission from Barbados close relatives of legal residents of Canada and persons whose circumstances have exceptional merit" — individuals who were "especially well suited" to settle in Canada.[9] In reality this meant Black Barbadians that the White Canadian population would tolerate due to their overwhelmingly superior and exceptional qualifications, education and skills. If Black applicants were not of "exceptional merit," the Special Inquiry Officer in charge of their application "would not find it hard ... to find an excuse for rejecting him" (Corbett 1957: 54–55). Canadian officials contended that "unless negro immigrants are chosen who can succeed in Canada and add to white Canadians' respect for them as a group, bringing them here might easily add to prejudice, not decrease it" (Corbett 1957: 196).

Exceedingly high expectations of ill-defined "exceptional merit" barred the vast majority of potential emigrants. In a December 14, 1954, letter to the Governor of the Windward Islands, John Whitney (Jack) Pickersgill, Minister of Citizenship and Immigration and senior advisor under Prime Minister Louis St. Laurent, revealed, "I fear it would not be realistic for me to hold out much hope of any fundamental change in the present policy in the near future."[10] However, recorded correspondence from Barbadian and Canadian authorities provided contradictory positions on the question of immigration in the 1950s prior to the implementation of the Domestic Scheme in 1955. While Canadian officials perpetuated the ominous language of anti-Black xenophobic oppression, high-ranking Barbadians stressed the commonalities of Commonwealth kinship. Brigadier Sir Robert Arundell, Governor of Barbados and the Windward Islands (1953–1959), was among those who reiterated the British kinship and Barbadian loyalty to both the metropole and Canada in an effort to promote increased emigration to the former British North American colony.

Arundell underscored Canada's desperate need for immigrants:

> The loyalty of Barbadians to the British Crown is a historical fact and it is felt that Barbadians could settle as workers, either permanently or temporarily, in Canada, a fellow member of the British Commonwealth of Nations, with profit to Canada and to credit to themselves. I therefore request you to be so good as to advise this Government on the possibilities of employment of Barbadians in the fields suggested in this letter (Arundell focused on domestic servants), and in any others in which there is an unsatisfied demand for man-power.[11]

This request by the governor is quite significant as Arundell actively sought employment opportunities in Canada for British subjects. The Government of Barbados pursued avenues for labour migration throughout the late nineteenth and early to mid-twentieth century. International migration diplomacy at its highest levels, as witnessed by statements from Barbadian Governor Arundell and Canadian Prime Minister William Lyon Mackenzie King's infamous statements in 1947, pushed to reform strict Black West Indian immigration exclusion while navigating Canada's economic needs. Restriction and regulation characterized Barbadian emigration to Canada prior to the official de-racialization of Canadian immigration in 1962 and its further liberalization with the Points System of 1967. While White men controlled migrant flows from diplomatic boardrooms and official correspondence between Canada and the Caribbean, women, specifically Black West Indian women, overcame the gendered, racist and class-based barriers, and became the faces that changed the system.

There was, and is, a "general assumption" that all "immigrants are men and that women and children are the dependents of those men" (Gordon 1990: 116). The female migrant was seen as a client of a patriarchal framework at the mercy of the structures of a migration system designed to facilitate the movement of male labour, and "there has been no immigration policy specific to the sex of potential immigrants" (Gordon 1990: 116). Monica Gordon, who articulated this thought, did not specify who or what constituted the "general assumption" or if this theory is expressed explicitly in the scholarly literature; however, her theory is historically plausible in the Canadian context. Canadian Unionists during the late nineteenth and early twentieth century "were so indifferent to the migration of women that readers of labour sources could be forgiven for wondering whether immigrants came in two sexes" (Goutor 2007: 4). The 1970 *Report of the Royal Commission on the Status of Women in Canada* stated that by the 1950s and 1960s, Canadian immigration held the antiquated idea that men were immigrants and women were objects of a male dominated and facilitated system:

> [The] Immigration Service holds the outmoded view that the husband is always the wage-earner and that a wife should be admitted only if her husband is able to establish himself and support her. Actually a wife will sometimes be better qualified than her husband to become successfully established and the couple should have the opportunity to come to Canada on the basis of her qualifications. (Bird et al. 1970: 359).

The 1970 Report called for a gender-neutral immigration selection process and the recognition of female qualifications as equal participants in Canadian society and its economy (Bird et al. 1970: 360).

Prior to the 1970 Report, Barbadian and West Indian women challenged sex- and gender-based selection criteria. They opened the door, broke down misogynist and racist barriers, and facilitated the emigration of an entire generation of Black men, women and children. Their class and gender created opportunities that directed the course of West Indian emigration for future generations. These women worked within a migration paradigm from the Caribbean that was class-based with a "deliberate selection" of male and female migrants to fill gendered and working-class occupations (Thomas-Hope 1992: 4). For example, male West Indian emigrants, or sojourners, held occupations in construction, transportation and agriculture, while women worked as nurses or domestics. Prior to the 1960s, emigration was dominated by men for labour-intensive work, including the Panama Canal project (Marshall 1987: 28). The post-1960s saw young women working in service sector industries (Simmons and Guengant 1992: 99).

Gender-based immigration policies created a "much greater mutual sense of social and economic independence of men and women in the lower classes as compared to the upper classes. This has allowed increased opportunities for individual migration as opposed to migration of the family unit" (Thomas-Hope 1992: 4). Lower-class men, and most notably women, had more autonomy and independence in their desire and opportunity to emigrate. This explanation is telling in terms of gendered emigration from the Caribbean where between 25 percent and 46 percent of households were headed by women. These women, "whether recognized as head of household or not, the lower-class women frequently [assumed] a large share, if not the sole responsibility for the welfare and economic support of the household" (Thomas-Hope 1992: 4). This was a situation where "immigrant women [tended] to see migration as a means to improve their economic and social status" (Gordon 1990: 121). Black West Indian emigration, as argued here, was a means for socio-economic mobility, and Black West Indian women were "forced to emigrate as domestics as part of their strategy for economic survival" (Silvera 1989: vii). Goulda Kosack (1976: 370–79) reiterated this claim of female migration in search of employment and noted that "emigration is an economic necessity ... women do not migrate to escape second class or patriarchal dominance." Kosack's statement that "patriarchal dominance" was not a reason for emigration is troublesome. I argue, especially with the case of the colonial, racist and patriarchal Caribbean society and its misogynist history of slavery, that in order for women to become financially independent and experience socio-economic upward mobility they had to escape the restrictive confines of a male-dominated society.

All classes of West Indian women emigrated as a means for economic independence, to support their families, and to flee the confines of an oppressive and patriarchal society. A lower-class woman in particular migrated in search of employment and upward mobility, and she went abroad "in her own right and not simply as a dependent of the male migrant" (Thomas-Hope 1992: 4). While her work focused on a much more contemporary period — 1970s–1990s — Elizabeth Thomas-Hope's theories on gendered and class migration are applicable for the period studied for this book. Her theoretical framework is advantageous in that it positions women as subjects, rather than objects of the state and of their male partners in the history of emigration from the West Indies. Thomas-Hope's work addressed the agency of women, of Black West Indian women, and the power they held as catalysts and trailblazers for the emigration of all Black West Indians. Women migrated first and subsequently brought other family members to join them (Thomas-Hope 1992: 4; Henry 1987: 216). As Emigrant Ambassadors, Black Barbadian and West Indian women spearheaded migration to Canada. The distinct feature of women in the majority of West Indian emigrants in Canada, and their initial migration and subsequent sponsoring of male spouses and children, displayed the "occupational profile of West Indian women [that] was closer to that of the [Canadian] female labour force as a whole," and Black female autonomy in a gendered and structured international migration system (Richmond 1988: 89). Despite the decreased earning power of West Indian women as a marginalized and racialized group, they did better economically, "when compared with other women, both immigrant and Canadian-born" (Richmond 1988: 89). They challenged the "White Canada" xenophobic barrier and helped in the migration to Canada of citizens of the Island and the region as a whole. They came to Canada under the Domestic Scheme as nurses, educators and skilled independent migrants.

The Domestic Scheme and the Nurses

On February 28, 1955, Canada's Department of Citizenship and Immigration wrote of the Barbadian Government's proposition for a Domestic Scheme partnership similar to the practice in the United Kingdom. The department stated that it was ready to initiate a program following the successful migration and integration of two hundred female domestic workers to the United Kingdom.[12] Through correspondence with the British Colonial Office in London, it was clear that Canada was open to the "controlled" immigration of Barbadians. However, Canada also opposed the settlement of Barbadians to alleviate unemployment on the Island. Frederick Hudd, born in Kent, England, official secretary to the office of the Canadian High Commission, wrote in February 1955:

> I would like to emphasize that the Barbados Government fully realize that other people also have their employment problems and do not wish to suggest anything in the way of a mass migration, or indeed anything that would cause difficulties in Canada. However, they would welcome anything in the way of a controlled scheme, either for domestic workers

or for any other category of emigrant and, naturally, we in the Colonial Office would be happy to see any such scheme inaugurated.[13] (quoted in the *Montreal Gazette* March 12, 1968)

Hudd's response revealed the Barbadian Government's supposed empathy for Canada's "employment problems." One may argue that he manipulated Barbados' diplomatic sentiment for restricted migration, asserting that it was the Island Government's idea and not Canada's unwillingness and legislated xenophobia against opening its doors to Black Barbadians. The Canadian Government's *Proposal for Controlled Emigration from Barbados for Specified Types of Worker* reiterated this sentiment. With respect to controlled emigration and Barbados' diplomatic appeasement to discriminatory Canadian immigration legislation and ideological beliefs, Hudd proposed:

> The Barbados Government fully realise that other countries have their own population problems, including housing and employment. They do not seek in any way to promote a mass emigration which will cause difficulty in the countries to which emigrants go. They do feel, however, that their own problems could be alleviated if schemes could be arranged for the controlled emigration of different classes of persons. While they would not be unwilling for this controlled emigration to be permanent, they would be equally willing for it to be temporary and they would place no restrictions or obstacles in the way of Barbadians wishing to return to their Island after a period of years.[14]

In his proposal Hudd noted, "the vast majority of the [Barbadian] inhabitants are racially negroid but British by three centuries of tradition and culture," and as per domestics and unemployment, "the need for outlets for emigration from Barbados is acute and the Island can produce a force of many hundreds of domestic servants, and a large number of semi-skilled or unskilled workers, as well as a smaller number of other workers with a secondary education."[15] The proposal highlighted Barbadian officials' willingness to compromise with Canadian authorities for the emigration of Barbadian women. The proposal provided a logical example of a desperate Canadian employment market and the domestic service industry. It also used an equally good example of how the Domestic Scheme worked in the United Kingdom for Barbadian female emigrants with the National Institute of House Workers.[16] With respect to the Domestic Scheme in the United Kingdom:

> The Barbados authorities propose to establish a training scheme, in co-operation with the British authorities, with a view to transporting to the United Kingdom a number of female domestic workers who have been

partly trained in household duties in Barbados; the final training would be completed in the United Kingdom under the National Institute of House Workers, and at the completion of this training, they would be considered efficient for placement in British households and institutions, etc. for domestic duties.[17]

Therefore, it was proposed that the Canadian Government give "sympathetic consideration to the above proposals."[18] On September 13, 1955, Pickersgill wrote to Moore informing him of the new Domestic Scheme and the November 3, 1955, arrival of the first group of Barbadian and Jamaican women.[19] Moore stated that the day "will always be a memorable day and year for [the NCA and Blacks] in Canada, and one which I hope will be remembered in the future with delight."[20] In 1955, seventy-five domestic workers emigrated from Jamaica and twenty-five from Barbados, and in both 1956 and 1957, respectively, a total of eighty (forty each year) trained domestics left Barbados. The Domestic Scheme was "implemented under the aegis of the Canadian government."[21] The Scheme was extended to other West Indian countries, including Trinidad, St. Lucia, and St. Vincent, and totaled 280 by 1960, while Barbados' quota was increased to 42 by 1959 and remained at that level until the program ended.[22] The women selected for the Scheme "became eligible for permanent residence in Canada (irrespective of employment as a domestic) after the completion of one year's service [and] were all selected through the Employment Exchange of the Labour Department."[23] As a form of strategic foreign policy, the Barbadian and West Indian governments managed to use the Domestic Scheme, and Black Barbadian and West Indian women as agents, to push for liberalized immigration and circumvent discriminatory and racist ideology. However, through the objectification of their bodies and labour, these women faced several barriers to integration and acceptance and some suffered physical and sexual violence while in Canada (Silvera 1989: 12).

The Domestic Scheme of 1955 "sought to transfer surplus labour from stagnant Caribbean countries to satisfy the need for cheap domestic labour in an expanding Canadian economy," where these women were treated as "cheap, replaceable labour" (Silvera 1989: vi-vii). It must also be noted that Canada only began to admit West Indian women as domestics once it became clear that British and European women could not be recruited to fill the labour demand for this type of work. Despite their vital contributions to the welfare of the Canadian economy, and arguably to Canadian society as a whole, West Indian women faced prejudice, sexism and violence "imbedded within a system which thrives on the labour of women of colour from Third World countries, women who are brought to Canada to work virtually as legal slaves in the homes of both wealthy and middle class Canadian families"; that system remains an injustice (Silvera 1989: 5). The class-based and racialized Canadian socio-economic system capitalized on the prejudiced and discriminatory ideology of Black female worth and human dignity. The Canadian Government supported the middle- and upper-class Canadian views on Black female labour and perpetuated their marginalization and mistreatment in society. The Black West Indian women under the Domestic Scheme, who found the work "unrewarding, the hours long and the salary inadequate," attempted to use the inequitable system to their advantage following the end of their one-year contracts (Silvera 1989: 7). Many left domestic work after their contracts expired and enrolled in the Canadian education system in search of better and more meaningful employment; however, they experienced "downward mobility," and found barriers to their integration into mainstream society due to their colour and racial discrimination (Silvera 1989: 7–8). In addition to colour and racism as reasons for their "*downward* social mobility," many of the women who came under the Scheme were of a "higher social status than is normally associated with domestic service," but it was their only means to emigrate to Canada (Henry 1968: 83). With a racist Canadian immigration policy and ideology, and the difficulty for untrained and unskilled persons to enter the country during the 1950s, "the scheme affords about the only opportunity for such young women (and their families) to enter Canada on a permanent basis" (Henry 1968: 88).

While all classes of West Indian women emigrated throughout the Caribbean basin, the United Kingdom, the United States and Canada during the twentieth century for socio-economic opportunity, the Domestic Scheme was arguably a West Indian middle-class and higher social standing migratory movement. With the added dimension of single educated female migrants, "many unmarried women who were teachers, nurses, secretaries or clerks used this programme as a means of immigration" (Henry 1968: 83, 88). The women approved for the Scheme came from "lower middle" to "middle middle-class" standing in the West Indies, with most women achieving a higher educational standard than what was needed to apply and be accepted for the Scheme. Frances Henry came to this conclusion following her supervision of sixty-one interviews of domestic workers through a 1965 pilot study at McGill University, conducted by a West Indian nurse trained in sociology. The study noted several of the women's reasons to emigrate, including "to better myself, advance, study"; "desire to travel, see another country"; "desire to get away from home conditions"; and the "desire to join relatives, friends" (Henry 1968: 85). It must be noted that according to Henry's study, many of the women chose to migrate for a variety of reasons and not only for upward socio-economic mobility. Their cultural, social and educational capital in the Caribbean allowed them to pursue further avenues for personal growth in Canada. The Emigrant Ambassador is the direct result of the application and selection of educated and opportunist Black Barbadian and West Indian women for the Scheme. Middle-class values, and the capital procured from a middle-class *habitus*, exposed some of the women to the "cosmopolitan values" worldview and the socio-economic opportunities available to educated women in industrialized nations such as Canada (Henry 1968: 83–85). Barbadian Erma Loretta Gadsby's story of emigrating to Canada in the winter of 1967 and working as a domestic for two years is quite telling. Erma Loretta Gadsby's reason for entering into the Scheme and leaving Barbados was because she wanted to "see what the world had to offer" (Gadsby 2006). The female Emigrant Ambassadors and their respective governments used the working-class underpinnings of the Scheme to facilitate the movement of upwardly mobile and educated middle-class women. Through their temporary "de-skilling" or "downward mobility" as working-class domestics in Canada, these Black West Indian women risked their lives and challenged the ideological myths of Black inferiority to prove that they, and their West Indian sisters and brothers, were worthy and equal partners in the betterment of Canadian society (Bobb-Smith 2003: 8). They did this not in a diplomatic boardroom, but in the heart of Canadian households. The women filled a subordinate role, but did not lose sight of who they were and why they chose and were chosen to come to Canada under the Scheme.

Despite the supposed benevolence of the Scheme and the positive opportunities for the West Indies and their people, Black West Indian women struggled to overcome seemingly insurmountable barriers as they faced exclusion and discrimination from a racist and xenophobic Canadian society. The women under the Scheme had high expectations prior to their arrival, but many were met with disappointment as the employment and the people they met in Canada were cold, unforgiving and deceitful. The women were subject to racial, housing and employment discrimination and experienced "outgroup hostility" — the strong distrust and non-acceptance of and by the Canadian population (Henry 1968: 86–87). The women did have much better opportunities in Canada, but "for many the denial of civil rights ... tarnished [their] experiences" (Denis 2006: 43). Black men and women lived and worked under a system of "racism, gendered racism and immigrant/migrant status [that] interacted with class exploitation" (Calliste and Dei 2000: 143, 152). The Black male porter and the Black female domestic servant perpetuated the malicious image of Black servitude created during slavery. The image in Canadian society of the Black man and woman during the twentieth century was a reified ideology of the debasement and negative connotations of Black identity and the historical legacy of slavery. The porter and the domestic servant maintained the structures of binary race- and class-based Black/White relations in Canadian society. Their immigrant status, their racialized phenotype and their objectified gender confined them to a marginalized space in Canadian society; they were unable to remove the shackles of oppression and discrimination despite their desire and qualifications for upward mobility. The Scheme deterred integration into mainstream Canadian society (Henry 1968: 88). Further problematizing the Black woman's marginalization to the Canadian periphery, the way in which the Canadian Government granted landed immigrant status to women under the Scheme "was highly indicative of racist factors that suggested that Caribbean women would most likely remain permanently as domestics" (Bobb-Smith 2003: 8). Interestingly enough, once Caribbean women began to dominate the Domestic Workers Scheme and demanded fairer treatment, the Canadian state removed their guarantee of automatic landed immigrant status to a more temporary and precarious arrangement. The Black woman's place in Canada was defined to be one of subjugation and servitude. Barbadian commentators at the time had difficulty evaluating the Scheme, since it had both positive and negative attributes and outcomes.

The distinguished Barbadian-Canadian writer, Austin Clarke, commented in Barbados' *The Advocate* on the condition of female domestics. In Mitchie Hewitt's article, "Canada Offers Domestics Chance for Improvement," in the May 21, 1967, edition of *The Advocate*, Clarke was quoted as saying, "for Barbadian girls, far removed from the domestic class, this is an outlet and eagerly grasped as when the year's contract is complete there [sic] are free to seek other employment and to reside permanently in Canada." Similar to Britain's Domestic Scheme, Barbadian women and the Government of Barbados understood the restrictive nature of gendered and racist international migration. As Emigrant Ambassadors facilitated by their government, overqualified Barbadian women — those deemed unsuitable and undesirable for traditional immigration policy categories based on an arbitrary construction of "merit" and assimilability due to their skin colour — triumphed above both racialized and gendered structures and used the Scheme as a vehicle for migration. The penalty was one year's service as a domestic servant, but they could then utilize their skills, training and education in Canada as permanent residents. As argued and reiterated by Clarke, the majority of female emigrants were not domestics through training or by profession. Clarke stated, "the Barbadian girls can survive, and be far better off than if they remained at home, and ready to take advantage of the opportunities which exist in Canada" (quoted in Hewitt 1967). He asserted "if our girls go to Canada as domestics, there is nothing in the world to prevent them from qualifying for good positions during their period of working" (quoted in Hewitt 1967). Again, and acknowledging Clarke's patriarchal language, Barbadian women and their government clearly knew how to circumvent Canada's restrictive immigration policy and use it to their advantage. Female domestics and the Government of Barbados knew that they had to devalue themselves as proud and educated women. Canadian immigration called for the perpetuation of Black female gendered and racialized stereotypes; however, Barbadian women knew that following their period of indentureship they were free to become — and became

— contributing members of Canadian society as Canadian citizens. Barbadians were and are socially mobile and transnational opportunists. More importantly, Barbadian women suffered at the hands of an abusive, racist and sexist Canadian society for the good of themselves and their country. Similar to race, gender played an important role in the history of Barbadian emigration to Canada.

Clarke was quick to buffer his overwhelming positivity for Barbadian women in Canada as domestics and admitted, "Let there be no mistake about it. Canada is a tough place for the Coloured West Indian" (quoted in Hewitt 1967). However, he believed "the privations which the Barbadian will be called upon to endure [her] first few months are nothing to compare with the financial and other benefits which will accrue later" (quoted in Hewitt 1967). He also offered some insight to the Canadian class struggles and ideas of Whiteness that many Barbadians may not have experienced on the Island. He stated, "Canada is a white man's country with the whites doing from menial to executive jobs" (quoted in Hewitt 1967). The Clarke interview revealed the need for more involvement by the Government of Barbados during the late 1960s, or continued and sustained involvement, of sponsoring and training emigrants to fit the needs of the Canadian labour market and economy. Hewitt wrote, "Now that Canada is opening her doors to skilled West Indians everything should be done by the Barbadian Government to train them in the skills which are needed" (Hewitt 1967). That being said, Canadian officials argued that the new immigration regulations of 1962 rendered the Domestic Scheme obsolete. They underscored the liberalization of immigration policy and the possibility of the acceptance of domestic workers through the immigrant stream as long as they met the selection criteria. By October 1967, and following the implementation of the Points System, "it was felt that the special movement could no longer be justified as it would run counter to the principle of universality embodied in the Regulations. Consequently, the various governments concerned were informed of [Canada's] decision to [end] the special movement in 1968."[24] Canadian officials repealed the Domestic Scheme but did not address nor ameliorate the gendered divisions of their immigration policy; xenophobia and discrimination towards Black West Indian women and men persisted throughout Canadian society.

Why would Canadian immigration officials and Canadian society as a whole allow Black immigration at all if it was supposedly such a detriment to the morals and beliefs of its citizens and the "White Canada" social fabric? If Black men and women violated the sanctity of Whiteness, why not eliminate the Scheme, the cases of "exceptional merit," and bar the temporary or permanent settlement of all non-Whites? Cheap and racialized immigrant labour built Canada. For example, immigrant Chinese labour was at the forefront of the construction of the railway that connected Canada from "sea-to-sea" in the late nineteenth century, while immigrant Black labour catered to the whims and needs of its White Canadian passengers. Black West Indian women were a product of a capitalist Canadian and Western ideological belief that the "Other" — the groups that build, support and maintain society — should be marginalized, hidden and discarded once their services are no longer needed. Similar to the Chinese labour on the railroad and West Indian Blacks in the coal industry of Sydney, Nova Scotia, the Black West Indian woman's worth was tied to whether her labour was needed and whether society could accept and control her being, her physical presence in Canada and her "otherness" (Castagna and Dei 2000: 32–33). This extended beyond Black women as domestic servants, but also to the many Black nurses admitted in the 1950s and 1960s. The women were allowed entry only if hospital staff and their employers were "aware of their racial origin," and if they earned the ubiquitous moniker of "exceptional merit" by possessing qualifications "that exceeded those of white nurses" (Calliste 1989: 150). Jamaican-born registered nurse Beatrice Adassa Massop was forced to wait fourteen months as she attempted to convince Canadian immigration officials that hers was a case of "exceptional merit" (Flynn 2008: 445). On October 23, 1952, Massop was the first West Indian nurse to seek assistance from Moore and the NCA. After the first letter written from Jamaica in October 1952, it took the efforts of Moore, Massop and the NCA until December 15, 1953, for her to arrive in Toronto. Moore was pleased by the July 4, 1952, House of Commons announcement by Walter Harris, the Minister of Citizenship and Immigration, concerning the changes to West Indian immigration policy and the implementation of cases of "exceptional merit"; however, even though Massop was offered a position at Mount Sinai Hospital in Toronto, her application was rejected by A.D. Adamson, the Immigration Inspector-in-charge in Toronto, and Massop was told that she did "not come within the classes of persons admissible to Canada" (Moore 1985: 139). Following a rejected appeal, Moore wrote directly to the Minister; Massop was deemed "exceptional," and Harris personally granted her entry. Without the cordial and professional relationship established by Moore and the NCA with Harris and the Canadian Government, it is quite plausible that Massop would have succumbed to the arbitrary nature of the new "liberalized" immigrant class of "exceptional merit" (Moore 1985: 141).

Moore and the NCA presented a brief to Prime Minister Louis St. Laurent as a part of a delegation to Ottawa on April 27, 1954. Moore read the brief to Harris that outlined issues with Canadian immigration policy in regards to the unfair and unequal treatment of West Indian applicants, including climate discrimination, differential immigration policy towards Black British subjects, the fallacy that Black West Indians could not assimilate to Canadian society, the lack of sponsorship possibilities by close relatives already in Canada since the state deliberately barred Black immigration throughout its history, and "cases of exceptional merit." Harris acknowledged Moore's position prior to his replacement as Minister of Immigration by J.W. Pickersgill. Upon his appointment, Pickersgill replied to Moore:

> I wish to assure you that we are always prepared to consider any individual
> cases which appear to have outstanding merit ... In considering cases of
> exceptional merit, we give consideration to humanitarian and compas-
> sionate grounds, and to any special qualifications which an applicant may
> have. (Moore 1985: 120)

Moore also had a good relationship with W.R. Baskerville, the District
Superintendent of Immigration in the Department of Citizenship & Immigration
in 1952. After numerous correspondences with Baskerville and a meeting in May
1952, Moore (1985: 96) recalled that "meeting with Mr. Baskerville forever broke
the barrier of formality and prejudicial coverup [sic] which were always prominent
in refusing applications." Moore and the NCA had set the professional, authoritative,
yet respectable tone with the Canadian Government to seek equity and justice.
Moore (1985: 99) wrote:

> I had established such a rapport with the Immigration Department that
> I was able to phone [Baskerville] in Ottawa to explain any case which
> had created a problem in Toronto. Furthermore, I could phone the Hon.
> J.W. Pickersgill, Minister of Citizenship and Immigration on any urgent
> matter, and be treated with the same courtesy.

Despite the triumph of Massop, nurses from the West Indies continued to face
restrictions and delays in their applications. Gloria Ramsay, the first Black Barbadian
nurse in Canada, followed a similar seven-month struggle that began in May 1954
and ended with her arrival on December 29, 1954, as the second West Indian nurse
to work at Mount Sinai. Pearl Thompson, another Barbadian nurse, experienced
a year-long wait. In his memoir, Moore (1985: 144) recalled, "I was aware that
despite the 'exceptional merit' clause under which the nurses were admitted, future
applicants would still encounter problems." Gloria Baylis, a Barbadian registered
nurse trained in England, experienced arguably one of the most publicized incidents
of overt racial discrimination (Baylis 2003: 145). Baylis submitted an application
to the Queen Elizabeth Hotel in Montreal operated by Hilton Canada Ltd. in
1964 for one of the two vacant positions for graduate nurses. She was told that
the positions had been filled, but upon further investigation the information she
was given was deemed to be false; she was denied the job because she was Black.
With the help of the NCA, and after a thirteen-year battle, the Appeal Court ruled
against Hilton stating that it violated its "general policy of non-discrimination"
(*Montreal Star* January 25, 1977). The arbitrary nature of "exceptional" status did
not guarantee a fair or equitable review of Black West Indian applications, and

the NCA worked feverishly to assist as many nursing applicants as they could. The NCA assisted over fifty applicants with the same effort as they did with Massop, Ramsay and Thompson (Moore 1985: 150). Moore and the NCA's assistance was entirely voluntary; the Canadian organization only expected the nurses to act as ambassadors and follow the NCA's official motto of its dedication to the making "of a better Canadian citizen" (Moore 1985: 89, 146). Nevertheless, racialized institutional structures in Canada remained barriers to the successful and equal integration of Black Barbadian and West Indian nurses.

This "differential" immigration policy "reinforced black nurses' subordination within a racialized and gendered nursing labour force" (Calliste 1993: 85). Black West Indian nurses and nursing students wanting to migrate to Canada between 1950 and 1962 faced racial, gendered and class discrimination as opposed to the permanent settlement of White emigrant nurses. While the Canadian Nurses Association publicly denounced any forms of discrimination for enrollment in nursing schools, "some nursing directors were complicit in supporting the exclusionary policies" of the Canadian state (Flynn 2008: 447). This practice follows Laura Madokoro's (in Webster et al. 2012: 18) position of the relationship between personal and institutionalized racism. In this case the nursing directors circumvented the open declaration of non-discriminatory practices in their field and displayed their own personal anti-Black sentiments. Canadian nursing school directors painstakingly tried to find ways to prove that Black West Indian nurses were poor workers and not "exceptional" in order to bar further applicants on supposedly non-racist grounds (Flynn 2008: 448). Directors and immigration officials openly discriminated against both Black Canadian and Black West Indian immigrant nurses and potential nursing candidates. Black Canadian female applicants were "encouraged" to apply to train in the United States (Flynn 2008: 447). Nursing was one of the few occupations of prestige for Black women in the mid-twentieth century and these women fought to become "agents of their own destinies" (Flynn 2008: 444, 449). Nevertheless, due to their colour — not their qualifications — Black nurses in Canada occupied a subordinate position in the Canadian workforce. Racism dictated their socio-economic marginalization.

When one eliminates the illogical fallacy of race and primordial attachment, Black West Indian women and their male counterparts were the best suited emigrants from the Economic South, or "Third World," to assimilate to Canadian society. Education in their native English language gave them the advantage and knowledge of one of Canada's official languages (Denis 2006: 44). This was most apparent following the introduction of the Points System in 1967; however, the legacy of slavery and colonialism created inseparable political, ideological and imperial links between the Barbadian, West Indian and Canadian people. Many women and men who entered to study in Canada during the 1960s integrated quite well to Canadian society and Canadian values and remained in the country as landed immigrants and permanent residents after the completion of their academic studies. Emigrants from the West Indies were "atypical" since they did not fit the norm of the "inassimilable" immigrant category. They were also atypical because women were in the majority among "independent immigrants" due to the emigration of nurses and domestic workers (Denis 2006: 44).

This assessment is quite interesting when compared to Franca Iacovetta's (2008: 250–63) work on the "typical" working-class peasant female Italian immigrant in Canada during the 1950s in "From Contadina to Woman Worker." As a mere handful (only 25 Black Barbadian women out of a total of 100 Black West Indians — Jamaicans — were accepted under the Domestic Scheme in 1955) of Black West Indian women fought for admission to Canada through the Domestic Scheme and cases of "exceptional merit" during the 1950s, more than 81,000 adult Italian women emigrated to Canada during this same period, which accounted for 30 percent of all Italian migrants. The Canadian or Italian governments did not provide settlement or employment services for the women as they were expected to remain the charges of their husbands and "had obtained low levels of formal education and possessed few marketable skills for an industrial economy" (Iacovetta 2008: 251). In addition to the foreign language barrier stated by Barbados' Prime Minister Errol Barrow, Canada deemed that the English-speaking, educated, skilled and middle-class "atypical" Black West Indian was the immigrant class that had to show their "exceptionalities" for acceptance as compared to the peasant-class of Italian migrants. Furthermore, the independent nature of the Autonomous Bajan's decision to emigrate and settle in Canada without the support of her husband or family was juxtaposed to the Italian story during the 1950s where "women were generally denied a formal voice in the decision of the family to emigrate" (Iacovetta 2008: 255). Black West Indian female migrants challenged the structures of a gendered immigration system and a racist Canadian society during the 1950s, while the dependent condition of Italian immigrant women in Canada reaffirmed preconceived stereotypes and prejudices. Both Italian and Black West Indian women were employed in domestic service and confined to gendered forms of labour; however, the latter did not fall victim to a paternalistic family sphere where "paid employment [was] an empowering experience for immigrant women who might otherwise have been isolated in their homes" (Iacovetta 2008: 261). This is a good comparison in terms of categories of labour since manufacturing and domestic service were the two largest employers of European immigrant women in Canada in 1961, and most Black West Indian women in Canada came under the Domestic Scheme or as nurses of "exceptional merit." Of the 28 percent of European immigrants employed in service work, approximately 75 percent were domestic servants (Iacovetta 2008: 259). Many Black West Indian women were the heads of their households and sponsored their husbands. Black female self-empowerment characterized her "atypical" immigrant condition, and this study argues that Black West Indian women and men were the prototypical immigrant that Canadian society needed and should have desired. It was the nefarious and illogically destructive concept of race and negrophobia that circumvented sound socio-economic reasoning for the settlement of more Black West Indians as opposed to the typical "inassimilable" White, anti-democratic, non-Protestant, non-English-speaking migrant that Canada preferred during the early to mid-twentieth century.

This paradox of hypocrisy defined the geographical and ideological space that Black West Indian women navigated. They defined their agency through the structure of White male patriarchy and "had to endure what has been referred to as the triple oppression of race, sex, and class: West Indian women *as a group* have, in other words, had to resist racism, sexism and class domination" (Dodgson 1984: 63). It was the women who faced the day-to-day discrimination and exclusion, and it was the individual that stood up for her rights and advocated for fairness and equality. As one female West Indian emigrant in the United Kingdom stated:

> I think most of the women who came over are really strong. Most of them came on their own, some came before husbands or fiancés came to join them. I think they were really wonderful. They came here, they coped and they are still coping. (quoted in Dodgson 1984: 65)

The previous excerpt is a testament to the strong will and perseverance of Emigrant Ambassadors. The female migrant was the trailblazer for West Indian emigration and challenged the added barrier of colour-blind sexism and gender inequality in Western industrialized nations. The women understood the confines of their race, but most notably their gender, and challenged the hegemony of male power. One West Indian woman reclaimed the power of her sex while staying true to her West Indian identity and stated:

> I think in every race it's always the woman who holds things together. The woman does everything. She plans, she decides when they should buy a house, she decides the school the kids should go to, and she has retained all her West Indianness. (quoted in Dodgson 1984: 65)

Black West Indian women stood firm and attempted to wield their agentic power in the face of atrocious racial and sexual discrimination in the United Kingdom and Canada. However, their collected voices were muted, and in regards to domestic workers in Canada, "their silence is a result of a society which uses power and powerlessness as weapons to exclude non-white and poor people from any real decision making" (Silvera 1989: 12). The marginalization and objectification of

Black West Indian women in Canadian society challenged their civil and human rights; they were confined to a space where their labour and their bodies were exploited, violated and disposed. According to Makeda Silvera (1989: 12),

> [the] West Indian women talk about their lives as domestic workers in Canada, the bitter-sweet memories of family back home, the frustration of never having enough money and the humiliation of being a legal slave. They tell of working overtime for no pay, of sharing their rooms usually with a baby or the family pet, of shaking off the sexual advances of their male employer, and in the case of Hyacinth (a domestic worker), of being raped. They talk about the experience of being manipulated and degraded by female employers. Although their cries are usually ones of despair at their isolation, they also talk about their lives as mothers and daughters and about continued visions of hope for the future.

As Silvera notes, the domestic worker was a "legal slave"; a woman bound by the racist and sexist confines of Canadian immigration and the impunity of their male and female employers — her safety and immigrant status perched precariously on her acquiescence, silence and acceptance of unbridled power and physical and emotional violence. Hyacinth's rape, and her treatment following the assault, was a telling example of the nefarious power relations involved in domestic work. Hyacinth's story, along with the stories of other victims of harassment and assault, is one of difficulty and pain, but her perseverance is telling of the struggles Black West Indian women faced upon their arrival in Canada. Hyacinth described her first unexpected encounter with sexual harassment by her male employer in Canada: "The first week I walked into the house the man start to bother me and want sex. I was frighten like a mouse, I didn't really expect that" (quoted in Silvera 1989: 55). The male adulterer manipulated her position as a domestic and used his power, as the one responsible for her wages and subsequent financial stability in Canada, to coerce her into sex. Hyacinth stated, "I remember him telling me that if I had sex with him he would raise my pay. I tell him that I couldn't do that because he was married and his wife was upstairs" (quoted in Silvera 1989: 56). She was physically powerless to his advances. He understood his power and impunity in the face of her silenced subaltern position status as a Black immigrant woman bound by the insecurity of her place in Canada. The marginalized and vulnerable position of the domestic worker — not protected by laws and enforced legislation, but by the private and arbitrary authoritarian rule of individual employers — allowed for some of the most heinous violations of human and civil rights. Faced with no place to run, Hyacinth had no other choice but to accept her pending fate.

The more I fight the more he seem to enjoy it, so after a while I just lie down quiet and let him finish. After he finish he jump off me, spit on the floor and tell me if I tell his wife or anybody he would see that they send me back to St. Lucia or that I go to jail. I was really frightened. I really believe that I could get locked up. For what I don't know. It happened again seven or eight other times. I was just scared to say anything to anybody, further I didn't know where to turn to. I didn't know anybody here. (Silvera 1989: 56)

Hyacinth later told immigration officials about her harassment, assaults and rapes. The officials contacted the family, and the wife reacted by blaming her for the entire ordeal. Hyacinth remembered what the wife said: "[She was] telling me that is me bring sex argument to her husband, and that we 'nigger girls' are good for nothing else" (quoted in Silvera 1989: 57). The rapist's wife stood by his side, claiming the sexually deviant "nigger girl," whom they hired to care for their children, was at fault for her own brutalization. Postwar Black West Indian women were stereotyped as "sexually promiscuous single mothers," and eroticized in a "racist, class-based, and heterosexist paradigm" in Canadian society (Iacovetta 2000: 12). The sexual objectification of Black immigrant women in Canada is not surprising. Blacks were deemed undesirable immigrants "because they were 'savages', that is, people who could not control their sexual desires and were thus unlikely to lead orderly and civilized lives" (Valverde 2008: 175). Controlling sexual desire was supposedly a British-Canadian trait that supported early twentieth-century Canadian nation-building and the state's immigration policy (Valverde 2008: 175). It was a civilizing characteristic absent from Hyacinth's rapist, but it justified his innocence and her guilt. Canadian society changed immensely between the early to mid-twentieth century; however, preconceived and misguided negative stereotypes of Black female identity and sexuality made it much easier for the White employers to blame Hyacinth. Whether it was 1905 or 1965, Hyacinth was still treated as a sexual deviant. This Black West Indian woman could not escape her racialized and sexually objectified identity despite the fact that she was the victim and the husband was clearly at fault. Her race, gender, class and immigrant status in Canada facilitated her victimization.

Hyacinth's abuse was not an isolated incident. There are many stories of abuse, including Irma and the attempted rape and constant sexual harassment by her employer's brother. Her employer knew of the sexual harassment, but did nothing about it. Irma described the attempted rape:

One day nobody was home and he come to the house. He try to push me down on the sofa but I manage to push him off me. I was shouting at

him, but he only laugh and say that if is the last thing he get is to sex me.
(Silvera 1989: 85)

Irma also revealed the racial discrimination she faced from her employer and their
children. The children would call her "Blackie"; her employer expected Irma to
use a ladder on her first day as a domestic worker because she assumed that Irma
climbed trees back home in Jamaica. It was this paradox of seemingly unwanted
but solicited help that created a toxic and confusing environment for Black West
Indian women working as domestics in Canadian households. Some men chose
to treat the workers as sexual slaves — objects of their sexually perverted devi-
ance. The female employers believed that the very presence of Black women
molested the sanctity of their household, marriage and their White gendered
identity. Meanwhile, the Canadian Government prided itself on its altruistic and
"humanitarian" venture of opening its doors to West Indian immigration to alleviate
the region's socio-economic ills. Primrose, a West Indian–born domestic worker
featured in Silvera's book, summarized the domestic worker's Canadian dilemma
and unwanted want, succinctly:

> Canadians have the feeling that we are coming here to rob them, to take
> away their jobs, yet we are the ones who clean up all their mess, pick up
> after them. We take the jobs that they wouldn't take, and yet they hate us
> so much. (quoted in Silvera 1989: 88)

The fear of the unknown and the destructive nature of race, class, male and White
privilege created a difficult environment that the women under the Scheme were
forced to work and live. The Black West Indian women overcame the insurmountable; the Emigrant Ambassadors continued their pursuit of upward mobility in
Canadian society. Canada placed many barriers for advancement, but the opportunities outweighed the disadvantages. This was most apparent in the Black West
Indian woman's quest for higher education.

Education in the West Indies "was seen by the majority in the Caribbean as a
way of increasing the chances of migrating, while for others migration was viewed
as a means of improving the opportunities for education," and "both education and
migration were acknowledged by most people as a means of facilitating upward
social mobility" (Thomas-Hope 1992: 120). Education was the key to social mobility and the "primary strategy of resistance" for agency that shaped the identities of
West Indian women within the structures of sexism and racism. The importance
of education in the lives of West Indian women relayed how education supported
and facilitated upward mobility (Bobb-Smith 2003: 45, 132). D'Arcy Holder, a
mid-twentieth-century Barbadian emigrant in London, England, recalled that her
primary school education was a "*solid* base" (quoted in Western 1992: 28). She

stated, "I was surprised when I got here (London) to find my education was better than some of the English people I worked with! I had thought all English people must be wonderfully educated" (quoted in Western 1992: 28).

Through "gender ideology" and the legacy of slavery and colonialism, "older Caribbean women had internalized the importance of education and accepted it as an identifying force in their quest for independence" (Bobb-Smith 2003: 132–133). Education was more than a means for socio-economic mobility; it was a tool for the emancipation of female subordination and dependence in a West Indian and, subsequently, Canadian patriarchal society. Education, and the pursuit of education, galvanized Black West Indian women politically, socially and economically for a better future; "they coveted education as a means of increasing the value of their development and activism" (Bobb-Smith 2003: 134). Black West Indian women strove for self-improvement in the face of many obstacles and barriers in the Caribbean and Canada. The West Indian woman's "historical experience of gender subordination and the struggle to secure educational provisions have become a political legacy that these Caribbean-Canadian women learned at home" (Bobb-Smith 2003: 134). Education was a liberating means of resistance that challenged hegemonic structures in society (Bobb-Smith 2003: 135). The significance of the right to an education for West Indian women, specifically for Barbadian girls, must not be understated; educational capital was the means to self-empowerment, self-reliance and most notably a means to leave their socio-economic circumstances and the region behind.

Education was accessible to all classes of Barbadian girls and boys. It gave all Barbadians the opportunity to remove themselves from generations of destitute poverty. Yaa, a West Indian woman and interviewee in Canada, revealed the importance of education in her family's life as the foundation for upward mobility in the West Indies. She stated:

> We were dirt poor! This whole emphasis on education, they (grandmother, mother and aunts) felt that I could use that as a means to break out of the poverty trap. It was really interesting; I won a scholarship through sitting the 11-plus exam. (Interview 10, June 15, 1995 in Bobb-Smith 2003: 40)

Others, including Toni and Aretha, reinforced the relationship between class, upward mobility and the value of an education. Toni contended that "education was tied to class at home. We were taught that education would broaden your mind and lead you to upward mobility" (quoted in Bobb-Smith 2003: 132). Aretha continued this sentiment, stating "education was key, extremely valuable, and more important than to earn money. I know I had to get an education" (quoted in

Bobb-Smith 2003: 132). The brief excerpts from Yaa, Toni and Aretha highlighted the crucial link between West Indian female identity, education, class and upward mobility. These first-generation Canadian residents shared their stories of how the indoctrination and acculturation of the importance of education in West Indian society allowed them to pursue their goals in Canada. Both girls and boys benefitted from Barbadian education initiatives in the early to mid-twentieth century, which resulted in many young adults seeking post-secondary education in Canada and abroad during the 1950s and 1960s. The Barbadian Emigrant Ambassadors were one of the first generations to benefit from the universal access to free primary education in the Island in the late 1920s.

The Barbadian Educator in Canada

Education, and the pursuit of education, was a defining characteristic of Barbadians at home and abroad. Going "abroad" for higher education defined the successful careers of Barbadian professionals. Barbadian-Canadian educator Cyriline Taylor argued that "those who attended McGill University or medical school in Scotland, or other parts of the U.K., seemed to dominate the Barbadian medical field."[25] Through magazine articles and advertisements, Canada attempted to attract the best and brightest West Indians to their universities. *The Canada–West Indies Magazine* was focused on Canadian issues, but enjoyed West Indian readership. The June 1953 issue of the magazine included a short article entitled "Students from West Indies Graduate at McGill University."[26] The article listed several Barbadians, including Charles Richard Grove Watson (Mechanical Engineering); Stanley Howard Watson (Bachelor of Science); Kenrick Herbert Cecil Thorne (Bachelor of Science in Agriculture); and Margaret Evelyn Johnson (Bachelor of Household Economics). The magazine also included several advertisements for Canadian schools and universities.[27] Taylor continued by stating that Barbados had been known to show preference in leadership positions to those

> who have a hint of a "foreign accent" or those who "went away" — much to the chagrin of those who had never left the Island. One of the comments about a successful Barbadian Prime Minister (Sir Errol Walton Barrow) was that he had gone to school with Canadian Prime Minister Pierre Elliott Trudeau (The London School of Economics), so it was easier for him to communicate in the international political arena.[28]

In addition to the socio-economic push factors that facilitated Barbadian emigration, Taylor indicated that the socially mobile and educated elite that "went away" were better qualified and better received as leaders in their respective industries once they returned to the Island. One may attribute this thinking to a collective colonized mentality; however, it is clear that this perception produced a common belief — particularly during the Pan-African independence movements of the 1960s — that one had to leave the Island in order to reach her or his full intellectual potential. Taylor asserted:

> The "Island Mentality" perception was to leave the Island and you would be more successful and upwardly mobile once you came back. Some could say it was a part of our culture, but I saw it, and most Barbadians at the time would say that it was a status symbol — it enhanced your achieved status. You achieved success through academics. Even today, people who go and receive an education overseas appear to do better than those that didn't. They appear to end up in the top echelons of the labour, economic and political strata. They are the Barbadian upper-middle professional class. I was coming from a working-class background, and I believed that upon return to Barbados after being educated in Canada, it would have helped me to gain entry into the upper middle class. Like many of my colleagues, we never returned home.[29]

Class and upward mobility defined the Barbadian emigrant experience. Academic success and the pursuit of higher education gave Barbadians an opportunity to succeed and improve their socio-economic standing. Contrary to the de-skilling of middle-class women involved in the Scheme in the 1950s, Taylor believed that a brief educational sojourn in Canada in the mid- to late 1960s defined positive class mobility. Within two decades, gender, class and race played a significant role in the migration of Barbadian women. Women such as Hyacinth and Irma were objectified and bound by the constraints of their labour in an inherently sexist and racist immigration system in Canada. Students and educators in the late 1950s — and even more so in the 1960s — utilized their Barbadian education as a means to procure the human capital necessary for upward class mobility as they repatriated after a brief academic and professional excursion abroad. The fundamental link between the two cases of female migrants is that Black Barbadian women saw Canada as a land of opportunity for upward mobility through higher education and academic success. It was an extension of a culture of education created and developed in Barbados in the early to mid-twentieth century.

Barbados' primary and secondary education system produced Barbadians capable of succeeding amongst the best and the brightest prior to the liberalization of Canadian immigration policy in 1962; however, the restrictive nature of Canadian policy forced many Black Barbadian women to devalue their class positions and academic achievements in order to fit the gendered and racist immigration system of the Domestic Scheme. Several of the women used the Scheme as a platform for further education and some chose to repatriate, while others, including a generation of teachers such as Augustine and Taylor, helped build the Canadian education system. It must be noted that several female and male Barbadians earned scholarships and were accepted to attend Canadian Universities prior to 1962 — yet another example of Barbadian academic prowess as a means to circumvent racist and discriminatory immigration policy. Despite racist and sexist barriers, education became the equalizing force for Black Barbadian women and men in Canada. A number of Barbadian-trained teachers emigrated during the 1960s. They followed similar professional and educational trajectories as Taylor, who started her teaching career in Barbados in 1960 after graduating from sixth form at Queen's College.[30] Taylor taught at St. Paul's Girls' School from 1960 to 1964 prior to attending Barbados' teacher training institute, Erdiston Teachers' Training College, which employed instructors with undergraduate and graduate degrees from England, Canada and the University of the West Indies in Jamaica, respectively. Following their graduation, many of the new graduates applied for teaching positions in Canada while also receiving their immigrant status. Taylor recalled:

> There were pages of job opportunities for teaching in the local newspapers in Toronto. A good friend of mine, who was a recent immigrant from England, sent me a copy of the newspaper and I applied to several school boards. I was fortunate to be accepted by the Toronto Catholic Board as a primary teacher. It's amazing that I had a job offer even before my entry (immigration) papers were finalized. I remember fondly that at that time there was news circulating that in the same year (1967) there were 900 teachers from the United Kingdom headed to Canada to take up teaching positions throughout the country. There was such a desperate need for teachers in Canada that they were willing to give me a conditional offer.[31]

Many of the upwardly mobile students of Taylor's graduating class of 1964–1966 at Erdiston left the Island. The new graduates were aware of the limited opportunities in the education field in Barbados for promotion or attaining further qualifications. Taylor recalled that Canada was a preferred destination during the late 1960s as events leading up to Expo 67 put Canada in the spotlight of the Barbadian public; the "maple leaf" was known and better understood by Barbadians, and Canadian ships in the Bridgetown harbour were featured in the national press. Taylor stated that this was a time where the United States was embroiled in the Civil Rights Movement, and due to the *Commonwealth Immigrants Act* and widespread reported cases of overt racism in England, Barbadians looked towards Canada and its new liberalized immigration policy as a suitable destination for settlement. Social issues in the United States and England thus contributed to the Barbadian interest in Canada. There were no publicized situations of racial tensions in Canada compared to England and the United States. Taylor noted:

> England was dealing with an influx of Visible Minority immigrants from the Commonwealth countries and difficulties with adequate housing, racism, and the emergence of the "Teddy Boys" (the postwar counter-culture movement in the 1950s with its propensity for violence against Blacks and non-Whites in Britain) caused many would-be emigrants to turn away from the U.K. We all on the Island were drawn with interest towards Canada.[32]

Taylor exemplified the autonomy and perseverance of the Barbadian woman in Canada. Women who obtained their primary and secondary education in early to mid-twentieth century Barbados capitalized on the Island's equal access to education for boys and girls. Equality and collective advancement through universal and free education defined the respective Autonomous Bajan emigrant's transnational *habitus*. The Barbadian Government indoctrinated education and academic success as means for socio-economic advancement irrespective of each citizen's sex or gender. The following profile of several female and male Barbadian educators in Canada, some of whom emigrated prior to the de-racialization of Canadian immigration policy in 1962, underscores that "exceptional" Black Barbadians were the rule and not the exception as Black Achievers. The educational reforms in Barbados throughout the early to mid-twentieth century facilitated the cultural and social capital needed to emigrate and promote successful integration in Canadian society. The liberalization of Canadian immigration did not change the character and capital of potential emigrants; it finally recognized that Blacks in Barbados exceeded the qualifications needed for entry prior to the 1960s. Racism and gender discrimination dictated Canadian immigration policy, but through its gradual liberalization in the 1960s, a wave of highly mobile Barbadian women and men were given the opportunity to settle and strive for further success in Canada.

The following section will briefly profile several Barbadian-Canadian educators who came to Canada in the late 1950s and early 1960s, beginning with Mr. Glyn Bancroft. After emigrating from Barbados to Toronto in 1960, Bancroft subsequently taught for thirty-five years and retired as a principal in the city.

Mrs. June Bertley completed a business diploma and B.A. in 1955 and 1959, respectively, at Sir George Williams University (now Concordia University) and taught throughout the Montreal region for a number of years. Along with her husband, Leo Bertley, she co-founded the Garvey Institute in Montreal to "cater to students of African descent in a positive environment" (High Commission for Barbados to Canada 2010: 18). The institute is registered with the Quebec

Ministry of Education and "promotes the ideal Black Excellence by emphasizing the contributions made by Blacks throughout history" (High Commission for Barbados to Canada 2010: 25).

Following his primary and secondary school studies at St. Giles Boys' School and Harrison College in Barbados, Harold Brathwaite completed his Bachelor of Arts from the University of the West Indies and received a diploma in education from the University of Bordeaux, France. Brathwaite earned a Master of Arts in French from McMaster University in 1968 and taught throughout Ontario prior to his promotion to principal in Burlington. He earned the positions of Superintendent for French-language schools and Associate Director for the Toronto Board of Education. In 1994, he was the first Black person appointed director of a major board of education in Canada as head of the Peel District School Board (High Commission for Barbados to Canada 2010: 41).

Lionel Brathwaite left for Canada in 1963 and received both his university degree and teaching certification from the University of Manitoba. Brathwaite held numerous positions in the education systems of Manitoba, Ontario and British Columbia (High Commission for Barbados to Canada 2010: 42).

Oscar Brathwaite came to Canada in 1965 following a six-year sojourn in England. He received his teacher education at the University of Toronto, taught secondary school and served as a department head. Brathwaite wrote numerous scholarly papers "with the view of empowering black students to succeed in the education systems in predominantly white countries" (High Commission for Barbados to Canada 2010: 43).

Dr. Stanley Brooks emigrated from Barbados in 1966 after having taught at Combermere School and Parkinson School, respectively, and having worked in Barbados' Ministry of Education. He earned Canadian teaching qualifications and his post-secondary education from McGill University while he taught courses at various schools and institutions in the Montreal area (High Commission for Barbados to Canada 2010: 45).

Cindy Browne served as a head of physical education and subsequently vice principal and principal in the Toronto area. Her immigration story began in 1958 as she believed "minority students need strong, visible role models" (High Commission for Barbados to Canada 2010: 46).

Eureta Bynoe attended Erdiston Teachers' Training College and became a Canadian immigrant in 1967. She dedicated herself to teaching in the Ontario school system and in 1986 became the first Black female principal in the Toronto Board of Education. Her husband, Gordon Bynoe, emigrated with his wife in 1967 and worked as an instructor in the Adult Basic Education Unit of the Toronto Board of Education (High Commission for Barbados to Canada 2010: 49).

Sylvia Pollyne King Greaves also began her teaching career in Barbados and emigrated from the Island in the 1950s. From Concordia University she earned a bachelor's in Early Childhood Education and a master's in Education (High Commission for Barbados to Canada 2010: 89).

John Lascelles Harewood taught in Barbados at Harrison College before he came to Canada in 1958 and earned a bachelor's degree and a master's degree from the University of Toronto. He subsequently obtained a Master of Education from the University of Ottawa and a Teaching Certificate from an institution in Newfoundland and Labrador (High Commission for Barbados to Canada 2010: 95).

Harrison College was and is one of the top First Grade secondary schools in Barbados. It produced a number of Barbados' greatest achievers in and outside of the Island as well as many teachers and educators. Cedolph Hope, another Harrison College alumnus, emigrated from Barbados in 1958. After serving on the Toronto Junior Board of Trade and advocating with Donald W. Moore in their fight for the Canadian Government's liberalization of its racist immigration laws and legislation, Hope pursued post-secondary education at the University of Toronto and began a 25-year teaching career in 1965 (High Commission for Barbados to Canada 2010: 105).

While Moore was born in 1891 and emigrated to Canada in 1913, a generation earlier than the individuals profiled in this section, as a young boy attending Montgomery Moravian Boys' School in Cave Hill, Barbados, he wanted to become a teacher. He chose tailoring as a trade, which subsequently led to a job once he emigrated to Canada in the early twentieth century; however, his influence and position in the Black community in Canada and mainstream federal political circles facilitated the settlement of all Black Barbadians during the mid-twentieth century to pursue their careers as educators and capitalize on their teaching experience on the Island (Moore 1985: 16).

Harrison College and the University of the West Indies graduate Neilton Seale taught for several years at Combermere School before his emigration in 1965. The University of British Columbia Master of Education graduate taught English as a second language (High Commission for Barbados to Canada 2010: 172).

Similar to Hope, Ira Philips also emigrated in 1958 to further his education. He obtained a Bachelor of Science from Concordia University, a Master of Education from the University of Ottawa and a Teacher Training Certificate from McGill University. He subsequently taught secondary school from 1973–1989 (High Commission for Barbados to Canada 2010: 151).

Another 1958 emigrant and Erdiston Teachers' Training College graduate, Marcus Evelyn Sandiford, taught for several years in Barbados prior to obtaining a Bachelor of Arts and a Master of Education. Sandiford taught secondary school classes until his retirement in 1985 (High Commission for Barbados to Canada 2010: 170).

A Concordia University and State University of New York graduate, Lincoln Springer also taught in Barbados for several years prior to his emigration in 1960.

He acquired several roles in all levels of the school system until his retirement in 1999 (High Commission for Barbados to Canada 2010: 185).

This section on Barbadian teachers and educators supports my argument that a highly educated — female and male — Barbadian population emigrated abroad to further pursue their studies at the post-secondary level and seek greater employment opportunities. Bertram Edward Smith, a "very promising athlete, cricketer, footballer and scholar," emigrated from Barbados in 1959 (High Commission for Barbados to Canada 2010: 184). Smith obtained undergraduate and graduate degrees from the University of Manitoba before acquiring librarian and teacher certificates.

Earla Coralyn Walcott emigrated from Barbados in 1961 to Canada. After completing degrees from the University of Toronto and York University, she taught in Ontario with the Durham Region School Board from 1965 to 1994 (High Commission for Barbados to Canada 2010: 197).

After his emigration in 1966 and work as a draughtsman clerk for the City of Toronto, Silfred Worrell completed the requirements for a Bachelor and Master of Education, respectively, from the University of Toronto. Worrell later received a specialization to teach languages, and he taught French, Spanish and English in the Toronto Board of Education from 1975 to 2001 (High Commission for Barbados to Canada 2010: 211).

These brief biographical excerpts of notable Barbadian-Canadian teachers and educators paralleled Taylor's story and supported the theory that educated Barbadians emigrated to pursue higher learning and upward social mobility. Reginald Eric Taylor, the protagonist of this story, did not have the same educational opportunities in Barbados as the above-mentioned emigrants, since he did not get the opportunity to attend secondary school in Barbados and had to work as an apprentice prior to his migration to Britain. However, his perseverance to attend night school in England while he worked during the day showed his dedication to his personal, professional and academic growth. Taylor chose his path to success; he understood that education was the key to his upward mobility, and his academic pursuits recognized the universal Black Power movement of self-empowerment during the 1960s. Taylor was one of the many Black Barbadian migrants in the United Kingdom in the early 1960s that understood their marginalization as a subaltern labouring class. Similar to the domestic workers in Canada profiled earlier in this book, Taylor and his colleagues capitalized on any and all educational opportunities for advancement outside of their contracted positions. Taylor's training and accreditation in England as an automotive engineer led him to a secondary school teaching position following his double-migration to Canada in 1967. While in Canada he defeated the odds of a child that did not finish secondary school; he earned a bachelor's degree and a master's degree from the University of Toronto and was accepted to the school's Doctoral program. Taylor's journey was one characterized by Barbados' "culture-of-academic success." His family's financial situation denied him the educational opportunities as a child, but Barbados' emigration scheme created means for him to pursue higher learning and upward mobility first in England followed by the life he made for himself in Canada as a teacher.

Barbadian teachers and those that became teachers in Canada emigrated independently, but they shared a similar desire to contribute to Canadian society as educators. Many of the aforementioned individuals would not have had the opportunity to pursue their careers in Barbados, as the Island had limited employment opportunities. Barbados could not support the breadth of teachers and well-educated individuals its highly regarded primary and secondary school system produced prior to Independence in 1966. Their success abroad should be attributed to a culture and government that regarded education as a sanctified and revered institution; it was a means for upward mobility and development. The British and internationally recognized Barbadian education standards thus became a vehicle and a means for emigration — they subsequently provided Barbadian migrants with the intellectual tools and mental fortitude to not only survive, but succeed in a discriminatory and sometimes hostile Canadian environment. Their scholarly credentials fulfilled Canadian immigration requirements; most importantly, as characterized by Reginald Taylor's migrant story, their reverence for education and academics provided the wherewithal to integrate, assimilate and persevere in Canadian society.

One may liken this national and moral obligation to succeed to the rhetoric produced by the Barbadian Government for its citizens selected for the Domestic Scheme to Canada. Their obligation was determined in the emigration information booklet, *Advice to West Indian Women Recruited for Work in Canada as Household Helps*, as Barbadian and West Indian domestics became Emigrant Ambassadors from Barbados and the West Indies as a whole. The pamphlet outlined clearly, "Remember, if you fail you will let down not only yourself but your country. If you make good you will be a credit to your country and contribute toward the continuation of the scheme."[33] It noted the virtues of female chastity and West Indian morality, stating "your general conduct should be such as to earn the respect of the Canadian employer and to uphold the highest standard of West Indian womanhood," and warned that women who became pregnant out of wedlock faced the possibility of deportation.[34] The pamphlet outlined the specificities of one's conduct in Canada and warned against illicit behaviour, which would reflect badly on oneself and on all Barbadians and West Indians. Barbadian and West Indian emigrants effectively became the ad hoc diplomatic representatives of the region, its culture and people. The rhetoric and belief produced a sentiment that emigrants were "going to Canada to improve [themselves]."[35] The Barbadian and West Indian governments wanted the women to "remember the West Indies relies on you to do your part towards the success of this scheme," and I argued that Emigrant

Ambassadors were given the responsibility for the success of further Barbadian and West Indian emigration to Canada. Pressured by the outstanding conduct of large-scale female charter emigrants involved in the Domestic Scheme, the nurses of "exceptional merit," and the upwardly mobile educators from a "culture-of-academic success," Barbadian and West Indian women created an emigration outlet for all Barbadians and West Indians and laid the foundation for the liberalization of Canadian immigration policy.[36] Barbadian emigrants like Cyriline Taylor represented more than just herself; she represented the pride and nationhood of her country and her female ancestors. It was expected that the Barbadian in Canada would uphold the virtues and standards of success — ideals indoctrinated in her culture and upwardly mobile *habitus*. Barbadians were obligated to do well in Canada. Education and the pursuit of knowledge as a Barbadian cultural attribute, as well as the willingness to share that knowledge with Canadians, characterized Barbadian-Canadian teachers and immigrants in Canada. The educators, the nurses and the domestics all had a common goal: the obligation to represent Barbados and be "a better Canadian citizen."

Notes

1　Ibid., 15.

2　Barbados National Archives (BNA), *The Report from A Select Committee of the House of Assembly, Appointed to Inquire into the Origin, Causes, and Progress, of the Late Insurrection*. Barbados/Hume Tracts (1816). Printed By Order of the Legislature by W. Walker, Mercury and Gazette Office, 1816.

3　Ibid., 11.

4　Ibid., 27.

5　Cyriline Taylor (retired principal) in discussion with the author, March 3, 2012.

6　Cyriline Taylor (retired principal) in discussion with the author, March 3, 2012.

7　BNA, *Colonial Office Annual Report on Barbados for the Years 1958 and 1959* (Barbados: Government Printing Office, 1961), 6.

8　Ibid.

9　Library and Archives Canada (LAC), RG 76, vol. 1241, file 5850-3-555, *Immigration from Barbados: Background of Immigration Movement*; LAC RG 76, vol. 830, file 552-1-644, pt. 2, Letter from J.W. Pickersgill, to His Excellency Brigadier Sir Robert Duncan Harris Arundel, K.C.M.G., O.B.E., Governor of the Windward Islands, Government House, Barbados, British West Indies, December 16, 1954.

10　LAC, RG 76, vol. 830, file 552-1-644, pt. 2, Letter from J.W. Pickersgill, to His Excellency Brigadier Sir Robert Duncan Harris Arundel, K.C.M.G., O.B.E., Governor of the Windward Islands, Government House, Barbados, British West Indies, December 16, 1954.

11　LAC, RG 76, vol. 830, file 552-1-644, pt. 2, Letter from the Governor at the Government House Barbados, November, 1954.

12　LAC, RG 76, vol. 830, file 552-1-644, pt. 2, Department of Citizenship and Immigration,

Immigration Branch, Intradepartmental Correspondence; to Chief Operations Division, Ottawa; from A/Director, United Kingdom, February 28, 1955.

13 LAC, RG 76, vol. 830, file 552-1-644, pt. 2, Colonial Office, The Church House, Gt. Smith Street London, S.W.1. Letter from Frederick Hudd, Esq., C.B.E., February 24, 1955.

14 LAC, RG 76, vol. 830, file 552-1-644, pt. 2, *Proposal for Controlled Emigration from Barbados for Specified Types of Worker*, (n.d.).

15 Ibid.

16 LAC, RG 76, vol. 830, file 552-1-644, pt. 2, Department of Citizenship and Immigration, Immigration Branch, Intradepartmental Correspondence; to Chief Operations Division, Ottawa; from A/Director, United Kingdom, February 28, 1955.

17 Ibid.

18 LAC, RG 76, vol. 830, file 552-1-644, pt. 2, *Proposal for Controlled Emigration from Barbados for Specified Types of Worker*, 1955.

19 City of Toronto Archives, Donald Willard Moore Fonds, file 2, item 8, *Director's report on the occasion of welcoming to Canada the first contingent of 100 negro immigrant girls from Barbados and Jamaica, Negro Citizenship Association*, November 3, 1955.

20 Ibid.

21 BNA, *Colonial Office Annual Report on Barbados for the Years 1956 and 1957* (London: His Majesty's Stationery Office, 1959), 12.

22 BNA, *Colonial Office Annual Report on Barbados for the Years 1954 and 1955* (London: His Majesty's Stationery Office, 1957), 26; LAC, RG 76, vol. 1241, file 5850-3-555, Immigration from Barbados, Household Services Workers, 1955.

23 BNA, *Colonial Office Annual Report on Barbados for the Years 1958 and 1959* (Barbados: Government Printing Office, 1961), 18; BNA, *Colonial Office Annual Report on Barbados for the Years 1960 and 1961* (Barbados: Government Printing Office, 1962), 15; BNA, *Colonial Office Annual Report on Barbados for the Years 1962 and 1963* (Barbados: Government Printing Office, 1965), 13.

24 LAC, RG 76, vol. 1241, file 5850-3-555, Immigration from Barbados, Household Services Workers, 1955.

25 The following section is based on a series of interviews with Cyriline Taylor during the month of March 2012. Cyriline Taylor (retired principal) in discussion with the author, March 3, 2012.

26 BNA, *Canada–West Indies Magazine*, June 1953, 8, 13–16, 19.

27 Ibid.

28 Cyriline Taylor (retired principal) in discussion with the author, March 3, 2012.

29 Ibid.

30 Cyriline Taylor (retired principal) in discussion with the author, March 4, 2012.

31 Ibid.

32 Ibid.

33 BNA, *Advice to West Indian Women Recruited for Work in Canada as Household Helps (Information Booklet)* (n.d. most likely 1950s or early 1960s).

34 Ibid.

35 Ibid.

36 Ibid.

Conclusion

WHERE DO WE FLY FROM HERE?

The distinction between a white man and a man of colour was for them fundamental. It was their all. In defence of it they would bring down the whole of their world. (James 1989: 34)

The need to locate cultural or ethnic roots and then to use the idea of being in touch with them as a means to refigure the cartography of dispersal and exile is perhaps best understood as a simple and direct response to the varieties of racism which have denied the historical character of black experience and the integrity of black cultures. (Gilroy 1993: 112)

I am not the slave of the Slavery that dehumanized my ancestors. (Fanon 1967: 230)

The physical, emotional and psychological terrorism of the Transatlantic Slave Trade and the institution of slavery in Barbados dehumanized the African in the Americas. The binary and nihilistic relationship "between a white man and a man of colour" was fundamentally destructive; it created an environment where Black subalterns and White hegemons in the West Indies struggled for ideological and physical survival in a world defined by violence, suffering and greed. The reductionist and essentialist properties of racism denied the character and integrity of the Black existence, Black experience and the Black Self in the West Indies. The Black

Barbadian was created as a means for physical and sexual exploitation by Whites. Individuals created institutions that reified a nefarious ideology and dehumanized human beings. Chattel slavery, the calculated act of government-sponsored terrorism, defined human history throughout the Atlantic World, the Americas and the Caribbean; Whites sowed the deracinated humanity from the African continent in the fertile soil of the coral island on the easternmost edges of the Caribbean Sea. Out of these seeds grew a Diaspora that withstood the confines of the institution of slavery, colonialism and the omnipresent debilitating stench of racism and phenotypic discrimination. Black Barbadian agency and perseverance developed within the structures of oppression, first used as a means of individual and collective survival under the physical and ideological whip of the overseer and the slave master, which subsequently epitomized their determination as migrants and Emigrant Ambassadors. The ideology of Blackness denied their human and civil rights, and racist xenophobia defined the immigration policies of the very same nation-states that profited from and facilitated the Caribbean "culture-of-migration." This book highlighted the paradoxical and hypocritical relationship of race and racism and how Black Barbadians, and Black West Indians, navigated the confines of a discriminatory, racist, gendered and class-based immigration system. The arguments focused on the emigration push factors from the Island and the region and how the Barbadian Government's domestic and foreign initiatives for the socio-economic advancement of its people at home and abroad facilitated the emigration of highly educated and highly skilled Barbadians. The government's education policy produced a generation of Barbadians that challenged Canada's officially racist immigration policy prior to 1962. Race and Blackness dictated the international migration system.

This book examined the symbiotic relationship amongst the various factors and events that influenced Barbadian emigration up to 1967. Theoretically, the narrative conceptualized how race, class and gender influenced the political, social and economic international migration climate. Race was the fundamental organizing principle throughout this book and it is also a fundamental feature of Barbadian history and its relationship with Britain and Canada. Without critical race theory, one falsifies the history of Canadian immigration; Canada's settler society was built on the ideology of White superiority. This is a concept that must be acknowledged throughout the historiography as truth. The history must also acknowledge the relationship between gender and Canadian immigration policy. Women were not simply adjuncts to male-dominated immigration schemes; moreover, the inherent gendered bias of labour and Canadian nation-building marginalized immigrant women as unwanted and non-existent in Canadian historical narratives.

The intersectionality of gender and race operated within an analogous exclusionary paradigm, and Black Barbadian and Black West Indian women faced double discrimination based on their race and their sex. Black women overcame racist, gendered and class-based structures of a patriarchal international migration system. Not only did these Black West Indian female migrants personally rise above institutional and ideological barriers as individuals, they acted as Emigrant Ambassadors and spearheaded the mass migration of Black West Indians in the late 1960s. This wave of female emigrants included several teachers and educators that exemplified Barbados' "culture-of-academic success" and upward social mobility. These women and men understood that the Island gave them the tools necessary to compete on the global stage. As this book argued, education and the pursuit of higher education was an integral push factor for the emigration of Barbadians to Canada and beyond. As one of the most literate countries in the world, education is a defining feature of Barbadian culture; a character trait created and instilled by the Barbadian Government in the early twentieth century. Scholars attribute Barbados' intellectual success to four key areas: "high expectations for all students, strict discipline, substantial education spending and a culture that embraces education as a form of nationalism" (Hannah-Jones 2009: 1–2). To be a proud Barbadian was to be an educated Barbadian. Education acted as means for socio-economic advancement and upward mobility where Barbadian youth could leave the Island with the hope of repatriation to repay the nation that invested in their future. Education was an investment in the individual Barbadian and the nation as a whole.

How then does one reconcile Simmons and Guengant's "culture-of-migration" theory? Can one define emigration — the act of leaving Barbados — as a cultural phenomenon? Simmons and Guengant (1992: 101) argued that cultural forces "are of key importance of understanding international migration," whereby "international population movements are influenced not only by economic considerations but also by cultural values, including the propensity to move and resistance and/ or prejudice against newcomers." The authors' idea that international population movements are facilitated by "cultural values" is based on Dawn Marshall's "Caribbean culture-of-migration" theory that West Indian migration was an innate and unconscious movement due to an inherited *habitus*. Simmons and Guengant (1992: 101) stated that "following the culture-of-migration hypothesis, the first response of Caribbean peoples to subsequent economic hardships is to move away to areas of greater opportunity," and West Indians viewed "migration as integral to socio-economic mobility." This monograph agrees with the latter statement on migration as a means for upward mobility; however, Simmons and Guengant's ill-defined and regionally generalized concept of "culture" remains problematic, specifically for Barbadians. Simmons and Guengant (1992: 103) contended that this "culture" emerged "from the uprooted history of the Caribbean people, first as slaves or indentured labourers from abroad, then as free villagers on marginal lands, dependent on seasonal plantation work and circulatory migration for survival." What is problematic with the previous statement with respect to Barbados is that Simmons and Guengant did not take into account the Barbadian Government-sponsored emigration schemes developed in the Island as early as the late nineteenth century. The monograph also confirmed that Barbados was one of the few islands in the Caribbean where the government took an active role in sponsored emigration; however, not for cultural reasons, but due to overpopulation in the late nineteenth century, and they subsequently challenged the racist and discriminatory international migration system in the early to mid-twentieth century. Furthermore, Ceri Peach argued that the Barbadian Government was the only government in the West Indies that encouraged emigration and the author linked population density to migration to the United Kingdom (Peach 1968: 20).

Can one definitely argue that this "culture-of-migration" was a "historically conditioned response" in Barbados, or was it a population movement that was dictated, regulated and controlled? Nevertheless, one may argue, and rightfully so, that the Barbadian Government created this migration culture in the same way it facilitated a "culture-of-education"; free education was one of the fundamental reasons why Barbadian women and men overcame exclusionary Canadian immigration policy. Simmons and Guengant failed to take into account the divergent histories of migration of individual West Indian and Caribbean islands, specifically the Barbadian Government's direct involvement in the emigration of its colonial citizens. The authors disregarded the agency embedded within transnational migration and the autonomy of upwardly mobile Barbadians; Barbadians defined by a "culture-of-academic success," pride and industry.

Academic success was an innate Barbadian cultural attribute. Overpopulation, limited employment on the Island and academic pursuits abroad forced the migration of the educated population. If migration was an inherent feature of Barbadian culture, would the Barbadian emigrants profiled in this book have left the Island if presented by the same or similar teaching and post-secondary opportunities in Barbados? A "culture-of-migration" implies migration was intrinsic and natural and did not account for social, economic, political and other external and causal factors. Migration defined by culture becomes a rigidified structure, facilitated by a belief and manifested as a symptom of one's membership to a specific national or primordial group. Marshall, as well as Simmons and Guengant, essentialized Barbadian people, negated their autonomy and represented them as marginalized and objectified clients in the world system. The reductionist categorization of a national or cultural group is analogous to the negative codification of Blackness and its racist and discriminatory connotations. "Black" was, and is, a derogatory classification, as is eliminating the individual Black Barbadian's agency in the transnational structure of migration due to an innate and "cultural" explanation. Does one's "culture" encompass dehumanizing and forced identities? Can "culture" be defined as a life destroyed and replaced by a socially constructed subjective identity? The term "culture-of-migration" alludes to elements of altruistic and even benevolent actions, whereas a "culture-of-forced-migration" is a more adequate description.

The authors' theory of a "culture-of-migration" fails to account for the diachronic explanation of the destruction caused by the Transatlantic Slave Trade and British colonialism; it creates an ideology that Barbadians chose to migrate because they were (in)voluntarily migratory creatures. Furthermore, geographically, the Caribbean had — and still has — several of the smallest nation-states in the world; Barbados' land mass is only 166 square miles. Overpopulation was a constant threat on the Island and as a result there were finite possibilities for social, economic and political mobility. As one of the most stable and developed countries in the region in the early and mid-twentieth century, Barbados only needed so many teachers, doctors, engineers, lawyers and other professionals. Moreover, the Caribbean is a series of heterogeneous island states in a tropical region; migration is inevitable. The dehumanizing structure, characterized by a transnational culture, circumvents the agentic individual and autonomous achievements of Barbadians in Barbados and Canada. The "culture-of-migration" theory does not account for the environment that Barbadians chose to leave, nor does it emphasize the North-South institutionalized barriers to immigration, especially in Canada. Migration is reduced to "something that happened" as opposed to "something that (individual people) made happen." The historiography subsequently represents Black Barbadians as clients of the Canadian immigration system. Isolating their emigration as a result of cultural "migration" attributes negates the social, economic and political push factors surrounding their transnational movement and agentic autonomy.

Was Barbadian emigration to Canada during the mid-twentieth century an innate and inherent cultural attribute? How does it differ from Simmons and Guengant's "culture-of-migration" argument? The answers to these questions lie in Chapter Two and the creation of Blackness and Black identity during slavery. Twentieth-century Black Barbadian migration should not be defined by the forced migration of their African ancestors. The subsequent erasure and denial of their Black Self and Black experience is further marginalized by the belief that their twentieth-century transnational movements were historically conditioned. Unfortunately, the Transatlantic Slave Trade, similar to the negative codification of their Black identity throughout the institution of slavery, continues to define subjective Black Barbadian identity. It perpetuates a belief that Blacks are simply clients of White benefactors in the international migration system. Black Barbadian agency, autonomy and achievements are rendered trivial and meaningless. The historicization and contextualization of the "culture-of-migration" theory, applied to the theoretical framework of Blackness and Black identity, problematizes Simmons and Guengant's argument; it negates causal factors including overpopulation and the emigration of a highly educated citizenry. I conclude that there is some validity in Simmons and Guengant's theory once applied to the Barbadian Diaspora in Canada. Barbadians did escape limited socio-economic opportunities for upward mobility abroad; however, they accomplished this feat through the conviction of their own nurtured abilities. Furthermore, even if emigration was a cultural trait, racist xenophobia in the United States, Britain and Canada prevented the settlement of Black Barbadians and West Indians.

Emigration was a deliberate, conscious and individual act supported and facilitated by the Barbadian Government's domestic policies and international diplomacy and it was executed in spite of institutional obstacles. The Barbadian Diaspora in Canada must acknowledge and thank the perseverance and determination of its mid-twentieth-century charter members. The story of Reginald Eric Taylor lives on in the lives of second- and third-generation Barbadian-Canadians. He is a beacon of hope and a role model to young Black Barbadian-Canadians, and young Canadians irrespective of their race, of how far hard work and perseverance can take you in life. His struggles and successes are a true representation of the Barbadian pursuit of excellence and agency despite structural and institutionalized barriers. His parents could not provide him with material wealth, but they — and his country — instilled him with a sense of pride and a drive that overcame nearly insurmountable odds. The life of Reginald Eric Taylor told in these pages is not a simply a Barbadian or Black or migrant story; it is a Canadian story, a story that is the fabric of who we all are as Canadians. His and the stories of other Barbadian-Canadians must be told accurately and comprehensively. They must also focus on the changing views and interpretations of gender, race, class and Canadian identity and society in the new millennium. Why? Because the Flying Fish are here to stay in the Great White North.

Afterword

FLYING FURTHER

The Future of (Hyphenated) Barbadians in Canada

As the first generation of Flying Fish in the Great White North have landed safely and become true Canadians in every sense of the word, what happens next? What happens to their second- and third-generation Barbadian-Canadian children and grandchildren who simultaneously identify as Black, Canadian and Barbadian? Fluid and multiple identities are fundamental Canadian characteristics championed by our *Canadian Charter of Rights and Freedoms* and our *Multiculturalism Act* (1988); to be from "here" and "there" is an accepted and promoted form of Canadianness. We Canadians pride ourselves in our multi-racial and multi-ethnic liberal democratic society. We, in the twenty-first century, believe that race, ethnicity, gender and class should not be barriers to inclusion in the Canadian democratic meritocracy. All citizens have the fundamental right to equality under the law and are guaranteed racial and religious freedoms. Despite the reality of said equality, it is a contested and problematic scenario in Canadian society, specifically for racialized and Indigenous peoples. The Idle No More and Black Lives Matter social justice movements of the 2010s are testaments to the fires that continue to burn amongst marginalized groups. This book has addressed the barriers to the immigration of Black Barbadians and Black West Indians; however, beyond the scope of this study is an examination of life in Canada for these migration pioneers and, most importantly, their children. I have highlighted stories of several Barbadians in Canada, but what about their offspring born and raised in Canada?

These generations of Canadians were not educated in Barbados, nor did they experience the life-changing effects of international migration and settlement in a new and unknown world. These children are not naturalized Canadians like their parents, but *Jus soli* — citizens by birth on Canadian soil. However, in a Canadian society historically stained by racial discrimination, one's phenotype has become the precursor to one's right as a "true" Canadian. Thankfully, 2016 saw the return of Canada's long-form census; it is paramount that marginalized and racialized groups in Canada are recognized.

Barbadian emigrants fought for the right to come to Canada as ambassadors of their homeland and soon adopted a hyphenated Canadian sense of Self, without discarding their island nationality. Nevertheless, immigrant descendants are the true measure of integration and acceptance in Canadian society as they reveal the state's willingness to incorporate difference as an innate Canadian value. Immigrants navigated a new society, a new culture and new institutional barriers, relying on their transnational *habitus*, while their children and grandchildren have the opportunity to procure the necessary cultural and social capital to succeed in Canada as born Canadians. Second- and even third-generation Barbadian-Canadians should, and for the most part do, experience higher levels of acceptance and social gains as compared to their immigrant parents. However, institutionalized barriers, including the incendiary perpetuation of racial discrimination at every level of Canadian society, continue to inhibit the integration and recognition of an influential Black class. Second- and third-generation West Indian- and Barbadian-Canadians are equal partners within the Canadian mosaic; however, due to their skin colour, Canadians of Barbadian descent are forced to accept a hyphenated identity. It is an identity that may have been appropriate for their emigrant parents who battled racism and discrimination just for the opportunity to come to Canada in the mid-twentieth century, but being forced to accept a hyphenated identity — by the general public, supported by Canadian policy and institutions — in the new millennium as the Black Canadian "Other" is problematic and further marginalizes second-generation Barbadian-Canadians. The normalization of hyphenation in Canada has both negative and positive aspects.

Official Canadian multiculturalism facilitated the multiplicity of the Canadian "I"; individuality is characterized by the fluidity of one's transnational or national belonging. Fluidity facilitates the hyphenation of Self, which is a common characteristic of Canadian identity. Many Canadians accept the positive connotations of the hyphen. It is a means for Black Barbadians and all Canadian immigrants to maintain a "back home" culture and identity, and an avenue for positive transnational and diasporic connections. However, the hyphen connects and divides. It does not remove the ambiguity of Canadian national identity, nor the tie that binds immigrants, racialized peoples and the dominant factions in Canadian society.

The hyphen separates and binds Canadians; it renegotiates social interaction and cohesion. Hyphenation and the hyphen create, maintain and perpetuate imagined divisions in Canada's multicultural society within a bicultural framework. The hyphen and hyphenated identity are products of Canadian multicultural ideology and policy and Canada's history of immigration. The hyphen and hyphenation are intrinsic manipulations of Canadian identity. The hyphen acts as a means of power and dominance, and also as a practice for segmented and constructed identities. The hyphen is a simultaneous mark of endearment and marginalization; the picayune and ambiguous marker essentializes Black immigrant and Canadian identity. This process creates a hyphen hierarchy, where Blacks in Canada, specifically Black Barbadians and West Indians, appropriate its dualistic and malleable properties.

Canadian hyphenation is a "play of identities" and hyphenated identity must be situated within Stuart Hall's discussion of the three types of identity: the enlightenment subject, the sociological subject and the postmodern subject (Hall 2006: 249–53). The hyphen operates in all three types of identity, but is most distinct as a Canadian entity through the subjective and objective characteristics of the sociological subject; hyphenated identity is an interactive construction between the identified and identifier. Individual ownership validates its authority and authenticity. The hyphen's ambiguity is represented by the subjectivity of collective and individual identity. This process is not simply a characteristic of Black Barbadians, West Indians or racialized groups; the fluidity of Canadian identity and what it means to be Canadian provides the convoluted framework for hyphenation (Hall 2006: 259). Identity, and Canadian identity, is not static nor is it durable; it is defined by malleability and situational adaptability. Canadians construct their identity in response to how they are treated by the wider society. Racialized and ethnic Canadians are defined by who they think they are, how others see them and, most importantly, how they react to who the dominant society would like them to be.

Hyphenation and the transnationalism that it implies helps us understand the possibility of acceptance and incorporation of Black Barbadians in multicultural Canada. However, the government's rhetorical obfuscation of the ideals of Canadian multiculturalism and its conflation with negative codifiers have created a stratified hierarchy of acceptance for immigrants, Blacks Barbadians and all racialized Canadians. Stratification exists on all levels of society and incorporates socio-economic factors and volume of capital, but class or generational status masks the racist overtones associated with the hierarchy of acceptance in Canadian society. Race is a fundamental organizing principle of Canadian society. In Canada, the political and social construction of Black identity — negative and ignorant in its origins and usage — is a legislated ethnic identifier. According to Statistics Canada, "Black" is a race, an ethnicity and a place of origin.[1] Its official misappropriation by the Canadian state facilitates the hyphenated manipulation by specific Black ethnic groups, including Black Barbadians, eschewing the racialization of their ideological Black racial identifier. Scholar Cecil Foster (2007: 374) contends that Black ethnicity is analogous to nation-state hyphenations such as Italian- and Ukrainian-Canadian. Where one hyphen celebrates difference and mends the fragmenting effects of multiculturalism, the other perpetuates further marginalization. A self-identified hyphenated Canadian enjoys the "freedom of self-determination." However, few Canadian Blacks "have the choice that allows them to be accepted and fully recognized as unchangeable unhyphenated Canadians" (Foster 2007: 388). The hyphen is subjective, imposed and a barrier for acceptance in Canadian society. Presenting "Black" as an ethnicity once again reifies its historical, social and political construction. Black is no longer the denigrated and socially unacceptable racialized marker, but a sanitized ethnic group; its accepted hyphenated qualification on Canadian citizens "deprives social mobility," most notably when "skin colour is the main determinant of their identity and their social and ethical relations with other Canadians and the [Canadian] state" (Foster 2007: 363–364). Canadian Blacks, codified as Black-Canadians, are denied the "existentialism of infinite multiculturalism" (Foster 2007: 364). The Black ethnic group further perpetuates its dehumanized racial history.

Despite its manipulative and incendiary nature, the hyphen can circumvent the negative connotations of hyphenated Black ethnicity. Contrary to Foster's argument, I contend that Blacks embrace hyphenated nation-state identities. Hyphenated nation-state identities shun the ideological inferiority of their racial identification as Black. They embrace the cultural and historical validity of their ancestral home. Good Barbadian-Canadian values — for example, the importance of education — are dialectical oppositions to supposed Black-Canadian apathy and institutional barriers to academic success. Through co-ethnic transnational identity and hyphenation, Black-Canadians manipulate their sense of Self, their "I," and subsequently politicize their identities for incorporation within the dominant Canadian society (Simmons and Plaza 2006: 142–43). Canadian society must redefine its attitudes towards Blacks when confronted with heterogeneous and positive classifications of people with black skin colour. The hyphen creates positive cultural dialogue. Affixing the cultural virtues of nation-states challenges and successfully negates the ideology of "Blackness." The Caribbean or Africa will no longer be classified as homogenous regions of destitute Black people. A Barbadian-Canadian is not simply Black; he may be White, or of East or South Asian descent. An Arab-Canadian is no longer associated with terrorism, but historically rich Lebanese, Algerian or Egyptian culture. Barriers and stereotypes are removed, and the hyphen has the potential to facilitate real cultural understanding. Positive hyphenation is the act of moving beyond tolerance to build an *allophilic* environment in Canadian society. *Allophilia* is "positive intergroup dynamics," which are measured by affection, comfort, kinship, engagement and enthusiasm (Khan February 28, 2013). The essentialization of "racial" origin is challenged by the ownership of hyphenation. The hyphen divides but the divisions create avenues for positive inter-ethnic relations. Through hyphenation, Black Barbadians, immigrants and racialized Canadians are given the chance to redefine themselves within the concept of inter-culturalism — disposing myths and stereotypes and sharing their reality of existence. The hyphen wields power. Those who own its qualifiers decide its meanings and values. Practical outcomes validate the hyphen's negative or positive effects.

Hyphenation redefines identities. Canadians are cognizant of the political implications of using different identities for purposes of social capital, networks and for avenues for social mobility and inclusion (Vertovec 2009: 36). Canada is a nation built on hyphens — a hyphen-nation. Mobilizing Canadian cultural capital is necessary for social cohesion and national identity formation. Hyphenation for racialized groups, specifically functionalist Black Barbadian and West Indians, is a tool for academic and political success, and an anti-racist and anti-discriminatory avenue for agency. Overarching transnational and hyphenated identity acts as a unique form of collective cohesion with the dominant Canadian society. Each segmented identity is a social tool and the value of hyphenation rests in its individual usage.

Second-generation Canadians are the key to understanding the effects of hyphenation and the merits of multiculturalism and Canadian racial inclusivity. Racialized second-generation Canadians — children born in Canada of immigrant and first-generation Canadian parents — become the true litmus test of whether institutional and ideological racism is an inherent and indoctrinated feature of Canadian society. These individuals may grow up in a culturally hyphenated private sphere, but publicly they enjoy the same cultural and social capital as their White Canadian counterparts. They went to the same schools, watched the same television programs, played in the same baseball and hockey tournaments and, most importantly, spent their formative years inundated by Canadian cultural norms. Second-generation Canadians — specifically Black, West Indian and Barbadian hyphens — should enjoy the same equitable social, political and economic treatment as White Canadians. They should, but they do not. Black youth perpetually rank near the bottom of higher educational enrollment figures, have some of the highest secondary school dropout rates, and have disproportionately lower economic earnings than their White Canadian counterparts. While there are several explanations for the generalized discrepancy, most notably a racialized and epistemically violent system, young second-generation Black Canadians continue to fight this perceived — and real — stereotype. Second-generation Barbadian-Canadians are not simply a marginalized and racialized immigrant group fighting for recognition and respect within the vertical silo of multicultural Canada. We are Canadians, raised as Canadians, of Canadian parents. Similar to countless immigrant stories, Barbadian-Canadian parents came to this country to give their children the opportunities and privileges that they themselves were denied as children or fought valiantly to procure. Racism and xenophobia are real barriers to success in Canada, barriers first-generation Barbadian-Canadians struggled to overcome in order for their children to succeed in a multicultural — but unequal — Canadian society. However, while second-generation Barbadian-Canadians manipulate their sense of Self and attempt to purge the ideologically reified, and ever increasingly picayune, derisive societal stereotype of Black and Blackness, racialized institutional structures continue to restrict their mobility and agency. Canadian society continues to negatively codify second-generation Canadians, while Barbadian-Canadians attempt to eschew ideological debasement and demand to be treated as equal partners within the Canadian mosaic.

Barbadian-Canadian youth continue to struggle for equality in society. Along with their Barbadian Diaspora membership, Barbadian-Canadian youth belong to the much larger Black and African Diaspora. They must straddle their parents' national allegiance and soft primordial connection to their West Indian island home, while navigating the structures of a multicultural society as Black Canadians. Regardless of their colour and their predisposed diasporic allegiance, second-generation Barbadian-Canadian youth are Canadians and have the right to identify solely as Canadian citizens. Despite the marginalizing effects of institutional barriers, like their parents of the 1950s and 1960s, this group of citizens has contributed to all levels of Canadian society; from politics, to academe, to professional hockey. This influential group understands that they must lead by example, first and foremost as Canadian industry leaders, but also as members of an increasingly influential Black political class — a politicized Black Diaspora in Canada. The story began with the emigration of Barbadians in search of avenues for personal and professional growth, and through pride and industry they created a sound platform for the future of the Barbadian Diaspora in Canada.

Notes

1 See the 2006 census and those prior that mention "Black" as a choice for Canadians to self-identify. "Ethnic Origins, 2006 Counts, for Canada, Provinces and Territories" <www12.statcan.ca/census-recensement/2006/dp-pd/hlt/97-562/pages/page.cfm ?Lang=E&Geo=PR&Code=01&Data=Count&Table=2&StartRec=1&Sort=3&Di splay=All&CSDFilter=5000> [accessed December 21, 2012].

REFERENCES

Primary Sources

Acland, F.A. 1926. *Report of the Proceedings of the Canada–West Indies Conference, 1925, with the Canada-British West Indies-Bermuda-British Guiana-British Honduras Trade Agreement, 1925*. Ottawa: Printer to the King's Most Excellent Majesty.

Advice to West Indian Women Recruited for Work in Canada as Household Helps (Information Booklet) (n.d. most likely 1950s or early 1960s).

The Advocate. January 1, 1962.

____. January 3, 1962.

____. January 27, 1962.

____. April 9, 1962. "Immigration statistics were false."

____. May 1, 1962a. "Going to England? Emigrants must first qualify."

____. May 1, 1962b. "The British Immigration Bill restricting the entry of West Indians comes into operation June 30th."

____. September 17, 1967. "Editorial."

Annual Report on the Social and Economic Progress of the People of Barbados, 1931–32. London: His Majesty's Stationery Office, 1932.

Archer, C.V.H., and W.K. Ferguson. 1944. *Laws of Barbados: Vol. II: 1894–6 – 1906–5, Barbados*. Barbados: Advocate Company Limited.

____. *Laws of Barbados: Vol. V: 1928–5 – 1942–8, Barbados*. Barbados: Advocate Company Limited, 1944.

Barbados Emigration Commission, Report, 1895.

Barrow, Errol. 1964. "A Role for Canada in the West Indies." *International Journal: Canadian Institute of International Affairs* 19: 172–187.

Bird, Florence, Jacques Henripin, John P. Humphrey, Lola M. Lange, Jeanne Lapointe, Elsie Gregory MacGill, Doris Ogilvie. 1970. *Report of the Royal Commission on the Status of Women in Canada*. Ottawa: Information Canada.

Bristow, Peggy. "We're Rooted Here and They Can't Pull Us Up." *Essays in African Canadian Women's History*. Toronto: University of Toronto Press, 1994.

Burgie, Irving. "The National Anthem of Barbados." <Barbados.org>. Accessed November 27, 2012. <http://www.barbados.org/anthem.htm>.

___. RG 76, vol. 830. "Immigration from the West Indies (& Coloured Immigration General) Policy & Instructions (part 4)".

___. RG 76, vol. 1241. "Selection & Processing – General Series – Immigration from Barbados."

Canada. Department of Citizenship and Immigration Fonds. RG 26, vol. 123. "Jewish Immigration [with pamphlet by the Jewish Immigrant Aid Society]".

___. Department of Foreign Affairs and International Trade Canada. *Documents on Canadian External Relation. (1950).*

___. *House of Commons Debates,* 1 May 1947 (William Lyon Mackenzie King).

___. *House of Commons Debates,* 17 January 1955.

___. *House of Commons Debates,* 2 June 1954.

___. *House of Commons Debates,* 26 June 1954.

___. Immigration Program Sous-Fonds. RG 76, vol. 820. "Immigration from the Caribbean Area".

___. RG 76, vol. 830. "Coloured Immigration: Policy and Instructions (part 1)".

___. RG 76, vol. 830. "Coloured Immigration: Policy and Instructions (part 2)".

___. RG 76, vol. 830. "Immigration from the West Indies (& Coloured Immigration General) Policy & Instructions (part 3)".

___. RG 76, vol. 830. "Immigration from the West Indies (& Coloured Immigration General) Policy & Instructions (part 4)".

___. RG 76, vol. 1241. "Selection & Processing – General Series – Immigration from Barbados".

The Canada–West Indies Magazine. May 1937, June 1937, June 1953, and November 1957.

Central Bank of Barbados. "Daily Exchange Rates." <www.centralbank.org.bb>. Accessed May 28, 2014. <http://www.centralbank.org.bb/>.

Clarke, Lionel. 1968. *Migration Lectures.* A series of lectures and a panel discussion held at the Centre for Multi-Racial Studies in Barbados between October and December, 1968.

Colonial Office Annual Report on Barbados for the Year 1947. London: His Majesty's Stationery Office, 1948.

Colonial Office Annual Report on Barbados for the Year 1949. London: His Majesty's Stationery Office, 1950.

Colonial Office Annual Report on Barbados for the Years 1950 and 1951. London: His Majesty's Stationery Office, 1952.

Colonial Office Annual Report on Barbados for the Years 1952 and 1953. London: His Majesty's Stationery Office, 1954.

Colonial Office Annual Report on Barbados for the Years 1954 and 1955. London: His Majesty's Stationery Office, 1957.

Colonial Office Annual Report on Barbados for the Years 1956 and 1957. London: His Majesty's Stationery Office, 1959);

Colonial Office Annual Report on Barbados for the Years 1958 and 1959. Barbados: Government Printing Office, 1961.

Colonial Office Annual Report on Barbados for the Years 1960 and 1961. Barbados: Government Printing Office, 1962.

Colonial Office Annual Report on Barbados for the Years 1962 and 1963. Barbados: Government Printing Office, 1965.

Colonial Reports – Annual No. 1422; Barbados, Report for 1927–28. London: His Majesty's Stationery Office, 1929.

Colonial Reports – Annual No. 1462; Barbados, Report for 1928–29. London: His Majesty's Stationery Office, 1929.

Colonial Reports – Annual No. 1499; Barbados, Report for 1929–30. London: His Majesty's Stationery Office, 1930.

Colonial Reports – Annual No. 1544; Barbados, Report for 1930–31. London: His Majesty's Stationery Office, 1931.

Colonial Reports – Annual No. 1595; Annual Report on the Social and Economic Progress of the People of Barbados, 1931–32. London: His Majesty's Stationery Office, 1932.

Colonial Reports – Annual No. 1632; Annual Report on the Social and Economic Progress of the People of Barbados, 1932–33. London: His Majesty's Stationery Office, 1933.

Colonial Reports – Annual No. 1725; Barbados, Report for 1934–35. London: His Majesty's Stationery Office, 1935.

Colonial Reports – Annual No. 1861; Barbados, Report for 1937–1938. London: His Majesty's Stationery Office, 1938.

Colonial Reports – Annual No. 1913; Barbados, Report for 1938–1939. London: His Majesty's Stationery Office, 1939.

Cyriline Taylor (retired principal) in discussion with the author, March 3–4 & 7–8, 2012.

Data. n.d. "GDP Per Capita (Current US$)." The World Bank: Working for a World Free of Poverty. Accessed May 28, 2014. <http://data.worldbank.org/indicator/NY.GDP.PCAP.CD/countries/-XR-BB- CA?display=graph>.

Data-Barbados. n.d. "Public expenditure per pupil as percent of GDP per capita." The World Bank: Working for a World Free of Poverty. Accessed May 23, 2014. <http://data.worldbank.org/country/barbados>.

Data-Canada, n.d. "Public expenditure on education as percent of GDP." The World Bank: Working for a World Free of Poverty. Accessed May 23, 2014. <http://data.worldbank.org/country/canada>.

Dickson, William. 1789. *Letters on Slavery.* London: Printed and Sold by J. Philips, George-Yard, Lombard-Street, and sold by J. Johnson, St. Paul's Church-Yard, and Elliot and Kay, Opposite Somerset Place, Strand.

Donald Willard Moore (431) Fonds.

Garvey, Marcus. "Speech Before Negro Citizens of New York" at Madison Square Garden, Sunday, March 16th, 1924, at 4 o'clock. Reprinted by permission of Mrs. A Jacques Garvey, in *Immigration and the American Tradition (The American Heritage Series),* edited by Moses Rischin, 2–11. Indianapolis: The Bobbs-Merrill Company, Inc., 1976.

Headley, Michael. August 27, 2014. "'Free' education a cost to taxpayers," *Nation News Barbados.*

Hewitt, Mitchie. May 21, 1967. "Canada Offers Domestics Chance for Improvement." *The Advocate.*

Information Booklet for Intending Emigrants to Britain. Broad St. Bridgetown, Barbados: Advocate Co., Ltd., 1955.

Information Booklet for Intending Emigrants to Britain. n.d.

Joseph, Tennyson. August 13, 2013. "Education scapegoat," *Nation News Barbados.*

Keung, Nicholas. June 30, 2011. "From Happy Hill to Parliament Hill" *Toronto Star.*

Khan, Sheema. February 28, 2013. "Beyond tolerance lies true respect." *Globe and Mail.*

MG 26 N. Lester B. Pearson Papers – Speeches.

MG 31 H114. Letters from Austin Clarke to John Harewood.

MG 26 J13. William Lyon Mackenzie King Diary.

Migration. A series of lectures and a Panel Discussion held at the Centre for Multi-Racial Studies in Barbados between October and December, 1968.

Montreal Gazette. June 10, 1911. "Canada–West Indies: League Which Proposes to Promote Their Mutual Interests."

____. March 12, 1968.

Montreal Star. January 25, 1977. "Hilton nicked for 1964 race bias."

Mulvey, Thomas. *Report of Proceedings of the Canada–West Indies Conference, 1920.* Ottawa: Printer to the King's Most Excellent Majesty, 1920.

Nation News Barbados. August 13, 2013. "Bajans to pay tuition fees at UWI from 2014."

____. February 23, 2014. "Thinking Day march focuses on education."

Notice to persons wishing to enter the United Kingdom on or after 1st July, 1962. Barbados: Barbados Government Office. n.d. (most likely early 1960s).

"Proceedings of Canada Conference, 1908." *Minutes of a meeting of the Canadian Trade Relations Conference held at the House of Assembly Room, on Wednesday the 15th January 1908, at 10:15am.*

The Report from a Select Committee of the House of Assembly, Appointed to Inquire into the Origin, Causes, and Progress, of the Late Insurrection. Barbados/Hume Tracts (1816). Printed By Order of the Legislature by W. Walker. Mercury and Gazette Office, 1816.

The Report of the Committee Appointed to Draw up a Detailed Scheme for the Settlement of Barbadians at Vieux Fort, St. Lucia, 1937.

The Report of the Delegation Appointed To Visit Dominica to Examine the Possibilities of a Land Settlement Scheme there for Barbadians. Bay Street, Barbados: Government Printing Office, 1960.

"Report on the Working of the Victorian Emigration Society for 1897." *Official Gazette: Documents laid at Meeting of Assembly of 5th July, 1898,* July 21, 1898.

Roberts, G.W. *Population Trends in the West Indies, 1946–1961,* September 11, 1950.

Rules and Regulations, Framed and Passed by the Governor in Council, Under the authority of the Emigration Act, 1873, September 23, 1873.

Science News-Letter – Society for Science & the Public. 1952. "McCarran Act Unwelcome." 62: 406.

Scottish Government. "Scotland and the Slave Trade: 2007 Bicentenary of the Abolition of the Slave Trade Act." Accessed August 20, 2012. <www.scotland.gov.uk/publications/2007/03/23121622/7>.

Statistics Canada. "Canada Year Book Collection." <www.statscan.gc.ca>. Accessed May 14, 2013. <www66.statcan.gc.ca/acyb_000-eng.htm>.

____. "Ethnic Origins, 2006 Counts, for Canada, Provinces and Territories." <www.statcan.gc.ca>. Accessed November 14, 2012. <www12.statcan.ca/census-recensement/2006/dp- pd/hlt/97- 562/pages/page.cfm?Lang=E&Geo=PR&Code=01&Data=Count&Table=2&Start Rec=1&Sort=3&Display=All&CSDFil

ter=5000>.

———. "Immigration and Emigration." <www.statscan.gc.ca>. Accessed May 14, 2013. <www65.statcan.gc.ca/acyb01/acyb01_0009-eng.htm>.

———. "Table W1-9: Summary of total full-time enrolment, by level of study, Canada, selected years, 1951 to 1975." <www.statscan.gc.ca>. Accessed June 6, 2013. <www.statcan.gc.ca/pub/11-516-x/sectionw/W1_9-eng.csv>.

———. "Table W10-20: Summary of total full-time enrolment, by level of study, related to relevant population, Canada, selected years, 1951 to 1975." <www.statscan.gc.ca>. Accessed June 6, 2013. <www.statscan.gc.ca/pub/11-516-x/sectionw/W10_20-eng.csv>.

———. "Undergraduate tuition fees for full time Canadian students, by discipline, by province (Canada)." <www.statscan.gc.ca>. Accessed May 25, 2014. <www.statscan.gc.ca/tables-tableaux/sum-som/l01/cst01/educ50a-eng.htm>.

———. "Undergraduate tuition fees for full time Canadian students, by discipline, by province (Ontario)." <www.statscan.gc.ca>. Accessed May 25, 2014. <www.statscan.gc.ca/tables-tableaux/sum-som/l01/cst01/educ50a-eng.htm>.

Sunday Advocate. January 14, 1962. "Interview with Frank Jeremiah."

———. January 28, 1962. "Migrants will flood in with the Bill."

Taylor, Reginald Eric. 2010. "Education is the Key: My Life, My Story." Unpublished memoir.

Walters, Sherwyn. August 27, 2013. "Free education is obeah." *Nation News Barbados.*

Windsor Daily Star. December 26, 1936. "The West Indies: Optimism of League Formed 25 Years Ago Shown as Well Founded."

Secondary Sources

Alexander, Lincoln A. 2006. *"Go to School, You're a Little Black Boy": The Honourable Lincoln M. Alexander: A Memoir.* Toronto: Dundurn Press.

Allahar, Anton L. 1993. "When Black First Became Worth Less." *International Journal of Comparative Sociology* 34: 39–55.

———. 1993a. "Unity and Diversity in Caribbean Ethnicity and Culture." *Canadian Ethnic Studies* 25: 70–84.

———. 1995. *Sociology and the Periphery: Theories and Issues, second revised edition.* Toronto: Garamond Press.

Allahar, Anton L., and James E. Cote. 1998. *Richer and Poorer: The Structure of Inequality in Canada.* Toronto: James Lorimer & Company.

Anderson, Christopher G. 2013. *Canadian Liberalism and the Politics of Border Control, 1867–1967.* Vancouver: UBC Press.

Avery, Donald. 1995. *Reluctant Host: Canada's Response to Immigrant Workers, 1896–1994.* Toronto: McClelland and Stewart.

Bangarth, Stephanie D. 2002. "William Lyon Mackenzie King and Japanese Canadians." In John English, Kenneth McLaughlin, and P. Whitney Lackenbauer (eds.), *Mackenzie King: Citizenship and Community,* 99–123. Toronto: Robin Brass Studio Press.

———. 2003. "We Are Not Asking You to Open Wide the Gates for Chinese immigration: The Committee for the Repeal of the Chinese Immigration Act and Early Human

Rights Activism in Canada." *Canadian Historical Review* 84: 395–422.

Baylis, Françoise. 2003. "Black As Me: Narrative Identity." *Developing World Bioethics* 3: 142–150.

Beckles, Hilary McD. 1989. *Natural Rebels: A Social History of Enslaved Black Women in Barbados.* London: Zed Books Ltd.

____. 1990. *A History of Barbados: From Amerindian Settlement to Nation-State.* Cambridge: Cambridge University Press.

____. 1998. "Historicizing Slavery in West Indian Feminisms." *Feminist Review* 59: 34–56.

____. 1999. *Centering Woman: Gender Discourses in Caribbean Slave Society.* Kingston, Jamaica: Ian Randle Publishers.

____. 2004. *Great House Rules: Landless Emancipation and Workers' Protest in Barbados, 1838–1938.* Jamaica: Ian Randle Publishers.

Bobb-Smith, Yvonne. 2003. *I Know Who I Am: A Caribbean Woman's Identity in Canada.* Toronto: Women's Press, an imprint of Canadian Scholars' Press Inc.

Bonacich, Edna. 1972. "A Theory of Ethnic Antagonism: The Split Labour Market." *American Sociological Review* 37: 547–559.

Burrowes, Marcia. 2009. "Collecting the Memories: Migrant Voices in the Barbadian-UK Migration Project." In Elizabeth Thomas-Hope (ed.), *Freedom and Constraint in Caribbean Migration and Diaspora:* 137–156. Kingston, Jamaica: Ian Randle Publishers.

Bush, Barbara. 1990. *Slave Women in Caribbean Society.* Kingston: Heinemann Publishers (Caribbean).

Calliste, Agnes. 1989. "Canada's Immigration Policy and Domestics from the Caribbean: The Second Domestic Scheme." In Jesse Vorst (ed.), *Race, Class, Gender: Bonds and Barriers. Socialist Studies: A Canadian Annual,* vol. 5: 133–165. Toronto: Between the Lines,.

____. 1993. "'Women of "Exceptional Merit': Immigration of Caribbean Nurses to Canada." *Canadian Journal of Women and the Law* 6: 85–99.

Calliste, Agnes, and George J. Sefa Dei (with the assistance of Margarida Aguiar). 2000. *Anti-Racist Feminism: Critical Race and Gender Studies.* Halifax, NS: Fernwood Publishing.

Castagna, Maria, and George J. Sefa Dei. 2000. "An Historical Overview of the Application of the Race Concept in Social Practice." In Agnes Calliste and George J. Sefa Dei (with the assistance of Margarida Aguiar) (eds.), *Anti-Racist Feminism: Critical Race and Gender Studies.* Halifax, NS: Fernwood Publishing

Chilton, Lisa. 2007. *Agents of Empire: British Female Migration to Canada and Australia, 1860–1930.* Toronto: University of Toronto Press.

Chodos, Robert. 1977. *The Caribbean Connection: The Double-edged Canadian Presence in the West Indies.* Toronto: James Lorimer & Company.

Clairmont, Donald H., and Dennis William Magill. 1999. *Africville: The Life and Death of A Canadian Black Community.* Toronto: Canadian Scholars Press.

Clarke, Austin. 2005. *Growing Up Stupid Under the Union Jack: A Memoir.* Toronto: Thomas Allen Publishers.

Cooper, Afua. 2006. *The Hanging of Angélique: The Untold Story of Canadian Slavery and the Burning of Old Montreal.* Toronto: HarperCollins.

Coppin, Addington. 1995. "Women, Men and Work in Caribbean Economy: Barbados."

Social and Economic Studies 44: 103–124.

Corbett, David C. 1957. *Canada's Immigration Policy: A Critique*. Toronto: University of Toronto Press.

Davis, David Brion. 2006. *Inhuman Bondage: The Rise and Fall of Slavery in the New World*. Oxford: Oxford University Press.

Davison, R.B. 1966. *Black British: Immigrants to England*. London: Published for the Institute of Race Relations, London: Oxford University Press.

Denis, Ann. 2006. "Developing a Feminist Analysis of Citizenship of Caribbean Immigrant Women in Canada: Key Dimensions and Conceptual Challenges." In Evangelia Tastsoglou and Alexandra Dobrowolsky (eds.), *Women, Migration and Citizenship: Making Local, National and Transnational Connections*, 37–59. Aldershot, England: Ashgate Publishing.

Dodgson, Elyse. 1984. *Motherland: West Indian Women to Britain in the 1950s*. Oxford: Heinemann Educational Books.

Donaghy, Greg. 2012. "John Price. Orienting Canada: Race, Canada, and the Transpacific." *H-Diplo Roundtable Review* 13, 9.

Donaghy, Greg, and Bruce Muirhead. 2008. "'Interests but No Foreign Policy': Canada and the Commonwealth Caribbean, 1941–1966." *American Review of Canadian Studies* 38: 275–294.

Duval, David Timothy. 2005. "Expressions of Migrant Mobilities among Caribbean Migrants in Toronto, Canada." In Robert B. Potter, Dennis Conway, Joan Phillips (eds.), *The Experience of Return Migration: Caribbean Perspectives* 245–261. Aldershot, England: Ashgate Publishing.

Edmonds, Juliet, and Cherita Girvan. 1973. "Child Care and Family Services in Barbados." *Social and Economic Studies* 22: 229–248.

Edmondson, Locksley G.E. 1964. "Canada and the West Indies: Trends and Prospects." *International Journal* 19: 188–201.

Eltis, David, Stephen D. Behrendt, David Richardson, and Herbert S. Klein. 1999. *The Trans-Atlantic Slave Trade: A Database on CD-ROM*. Cambridge: Cambridge University Press.

Fanon, Frantz. 1967. *Black Skin, White Masks*. Translated by Charles Lam Markmann. New York: Grove Press.

Flynn, Karen. 2008. "'I'm Glad That Someone Is Telling the Nursing Story': Writing Black Canadian Women's History," *Journal of Black Studies* 38: 443–460.

Foster, Cecil. 2007. *Blackness and Modernity: The Colour of Humanity and the Quest for Freedom*. Montreal & Kingston: McGill-Queen's University Press.

Freeman, Gary P. 1987. "Caribbean Migration to Britain and France: From Assimilation to Selection." In Barry B. Levine (ed.), *The Caribbean Exodus*, 185–203. New York: Praeger Publishers.

Gadsby, Meredith M. 2006. *Sucking Salt: Caribbean Women Writers, Migration, and Survival*. Columbia, Missouri: University of Missouri Press.

Gilderhus, Mark T. 2006. "The Monroe Doctrine: Meanings and Implications." *Presidential Studies Quarterly* 36: 5–16.

Gilroy, Paul. 1993. *The Black Atlantic: Modernity and Double Consciousness*. Cambridge: MA: Harvard University Press.

____. 2003. "The Black Atlantic as a Counterculture of Modernity." In Jana Evans Braziel and

Anita Mannur (eds.), *Theorizing Diaspora*, 49–79. Malden, MA: Blackwell Publishers.

Gordon, Monica. 1990. "Dependents or Independent Workers? The Status of Caribbean Immigrant Women in the United States." In Ransford W. Palmer (ed.), *In Search of a Better Life: Perspectives on Migration from the Caribbean*, 115–137. New York: Praeger Publishers.

Gorman, Daniel. 2006. *Imperial Citizenship: Empire and the Question of Belonging*. Manchester: Manchester University Press.

Goutor, David. 2007. *Guarding the Gates: The Canadian Labour Movement and Immigration, 1872–1934*. Vancouver: UBC Press.

Gratus, Jack. 1973. *The Great White Lie: Slavery, Emancipation, and Changing Racial Attitudes*. New York: Monthly Review Press.

Grizzle, Stanley G. 1998. *My Name's Not George: The Story of the Brotherhood of Sleeping Car Porters in Canada: Personal Reminiscences of Stanley G. Grizzle*. Toronto: Umbrella Press.

Hall, Stuart. 2006. "The Future of Identity." In Sean P. Hier and B. Singh Bolaria (eds.), *Identity and Belonging: Rethinking Race and Ethnicity in Canadian Society*, 249–269. Toronto: Canadian Scholars' Press.

Handler, Jerome S., and Frederick W. Large (with the assistance of Robert V. Riordan). 1978. *Plantation Slavery in Barbados: An Archaeological and Historical Investigation*. Cambridge, MA: Harvard University Press.

Hannah-Jones, Nikole. 2009. "Excellence in Barbados Starts With Discipline." *Institute for Advanced Journalism Studies*: 1–8.

Hao, Lingxin. 2007. *Color Lines, Country Lines: Race, Immigration, and Wealth Stratification in America*. New York: Russell Sage Foundation.

Hart, Richard. 1985. *Slaves Who Abolished Slavery: Volume II: Blacks in Rebellion*. Jamaica: Institute of Social and Economic Research University of the West Indies, Mona.

Haselden, Kyle. 1964. *The Racial Problem in Christian Perspective*. New York: Harper & Row.

Henry, Blair Peter, and Conrad Miller. 2009. "Macroeconomic Narratives From Africa and the Diaspora: Institutions versus Policies: A Tale of Two Islands." *American Economic Review: Papers and Proceedings* 99: 261–267.

Henry, Frances. 1968. "The West Indian Domestic Scheme in Canada." *Social and Economic Studies* 17: 83–91.

_____. 1987. "Caribbean Migration to Canada: Prejudice and Opportunity." In Barry B. Levine (ed.), *The Caribbean Exodus*, 214–222. New York: Praeger Publishers.

_____. 1994. *The Caribbean Diaspora in Toronto: Learning to Live with Racism*. Toronto: University of Toronto Press.

High Commission for Barbados to Canada. 2010. *Some Barbadian Canadians: A Biographical Dictionary*. Ottawa.

Hill, Lawrence. 2001. *Black Berry, Sweet Juice: on Being Black and White in Canada*. Toronto: HarperFlamingo.

Hoyos, F.A. 1963. *The Rise of West Indian Democracy: The Life & Times of Sir Grantley Adams*. Barbados: Advocate Press.

Hoyos, F.A. 2003. *Barbados Our Island Home*. Oxford: Macmillan Caribbean.

Iacovetta, Franca. 2000. "Recipes for Democracy? Gender, Family, and Making Female Citizens in Cold War Canada." *Canadian Woman Studies* 20: 12–21.

_____. 2008. "From Contadina to Woman Worker." In Barrington Walker (ed.), *The History of Immigration and Racism in Canada: Essential Readings*, 250–263. Toronto: Canadian Scholars' Press Inc., 2008.

James, C.L.R. 1989. *The Black Jacobins: Toussaint L'Ouverture and the San Domingo Revolution*, second ed. New York: Vintage Books,.

Johnson, Michele A. 1999. "The Beginning and the End: The Montego Bay Conference and the Jamaican Referendum on West Indian Federation." *Social and Economic Studies* 48: 117–149.

Jones, Cecily. 2007. *Engendering Whiteness: White Women and Colonialism in Barbados and North Carolina, 1627–1865*. Manchester: Manchester University Press.

Jordan, Winthrop. 1962. "American Chiaroscuro: The Status and Definition of Mulattoes in the British Colonies." *The William and Mary Quarterly* 19: 183–200.

Kennedy, Edward. 1976. "Favoritism Based on Nationality Will Disappear." In Moses Rischin (ed.), *Immigration and the American Tradition (The American Heritage Series)*, 429– 438. Indianapolis: Bobbs-Merrill Company.

Knowles, Valerie. 1997. *Strangers at Our Gates: Canadian Immigration and Immigration Policy, 1540–1997*. Toronto: Dundurn Press.

Kolchin, Peter. 2003. *American Slavery: 1619–1877*. New York: Whill and Wang.

Kosack, Goulda. 1976. "Migrant Women: The Move to Western Europe – A Step Toward Emancipation." *Race and Class* 17: 370–379.

Layne, Anthony. 1979. "Race, Class, and Development in Barbados." *Caribbean Quarterly* 25: 40–51.

Levine, Barry B. 1987. *The Caribbean Exodus*. New York: Praeger Publishers.

Lewis, Gordon K. 1990. "Foreword." In Ransford W. Palmer (ed.), *In Search of a Better Life: Perspectives in Migration from the Caribbean*. New York: Praeger Publishers.

Lowenthal, David. 1957. "The Population of Barbados." *Social and Economic Studies* 6: 445–501.

Macklin, Audrey. 1992. "Foreign Domestic Workers: Surrogate Housewife or Mail Order Servants?" *McGill Law Journal* 37: 681–760.

Marshall, Dawn I. 1982. "The History of Caribbean Migrations: The Case of the West Indies." *Caribbean Review* 11: 6–9 & 52–53.

_____. 1987. "A History of West Indian Migrations: Overseas Opportunities and 'Safety-Valve' Policies." In Barry B. Levine (ed.), *The Caribbean Exodus*, 15– 31. New York: Praeger Publishers.

McKeown, Adam M. 2008. *Melancholy Order: Asian Migration and the Globalization of Borders*. New York: Columbia University Press.

McLellan, David. 1986. *Ideology*. Milton Keynes: Open University Press.

Menard, Russell. 2006. *Sweet Negotiations: Sugar, Slavery, and Plantation Agriculture in Early Barbados*. Charlottesville: University Press of Virginia.

Mills, Nicolaus. 1994. *Arguing Immigration: The Debate Over the Changing Face of America*. New York: Touchstone, Simon & Schuster.

Ministry of Education, Youth Affairs, and Culture. 2000. *Historical Developments of Education in Barbados, 1686–2000*. Prepared by the Planning Research and Development Unit of the Ministry of Education, Youth Affairs, and Culture, November: 1–19.

Mintz, Sidney W. 1985. *Sweetness and Power: The Place of Sugar in Modern History*. New

York: Penguin Books.

Moore, Donald. 1985. *Don Moore: An Autobiography*. Toronto: Williams-Wallace Publishers.

Nelson, Jennifer J. 2008. *Razing Africville: A Geography of Racism*. Toronto: University of Toronto Press.

Palmer, Ransford W. 1990. *In Search of a Better Life: Perspectives on Migration from the Caribbean*. New York: Praeger Publishers.

Pastor, Robert. 1987. "The Impact of U.S. Immigration Policy on Caribbean Emigration: Does it Matter?" In Barry B. Levine (ed.), *The Caribbean Exodus*, 242–259. New York: Praeger Publishers.

Peach, Ceri. 1968. *West Indian Migration to Britain: A Social Geography*. Published for the Institute of Race Relations, London: Oxford University Press.

Pedraza, Silvia, and Rubén G. Rumbant. 1996. *Origins and Destinies: Immigration, Race, and Ethnicity in America*. Belmont, CA: Wadsworth Publishing.

Price, John. 2011. *Orienting Canada: Race, Empire, and the Transpacific*. Vancouver: UBC Press.

Price, Stephen Wheatley. 2001. "The Employment Adjustment of Male Immigrants in England." *Journal of Population Economics* 14: 193–220.

Pryce, Ken, and Surujrattan Rambachan. 1977. *Occasional Papers: The Black Experience in Britain: A Study of the Life-Styles of West Indians in Bristol (Ken Pryce) & Ahilya Goes to London on BWIA Flight 900 (Surujrattan Rambachan)*. St. Augustine, Trinidad: Institute of Social and Economic Research, University of the West Indies, St. Augustine, Trinidad.

Razack, Sherene. 2002. *Race, Space, and the Law: Unmapping a White Settler Society*. Toronto: Between the Lines.

Richmond, Anthony H. 1988. *Immigration and Ethnic Conflict*. Hamdmills, Basingstoke, Hampshire: MacMillan Press.

Rischin, Moses (ed.). 1976. *Immigration and the American Tradition*. Indianapolis: Bobbs-Merrill Company.

Schorsch, Jonathan. 2004. *Jews and Blacks in the Early Modern World*. Cambridge: Cambridge University Press.

Schultz, John. 1982. "White Man's Country: Canada and the West Indian Immigrant, 1900–1965." *American Review of Canadian Studies*: 53–64.

Sheppard, Jill. 1977. *The "Redlegs" of Barbados: Their Origins and History*. Millwood, NY: KTO Press,

Silvera, Makeda. 1989. *Silenced: Talks with Working Class Caribbean Women about their Lives and Struggles as Domestic Workers in Canada, revised edition*. Toronto: Sista Vision: Black Women and Women of Colour Press.

Simmons, Alan B., and Dwaine E. Plaza. 2006. "The Caribbean Community in Canada: Transnational Connections and Transformations." In Lloyd Wong and Vic Satzewich (eds.), *Negotiating Borders and Belonging: Transnational Identities and Practices in Canada*, 130–149. Vancouver: University of British Columbia Press.

Simmons, Alan B., and Jean-Pierre Guengant. 1992. "Caribbean Exodus and the World System." In Mary M. Kritz, Lin Lean Lim, Hania Zlotnik (eds.), *International Migration Systems: A Global Approach*, 94–114. Oxford: Clarendon Press.

Spivak, Gayatri Chakravorty. 1988. "Can the Subaltern Speak?" In Carey Nelson and

Lawrence Grossberg (eds.), *Marxism and the Interpretation of Culture*, 24–28. London: Macmillan.

Stasiulis, Daiva, and Radha Jhappan. 1995. "The Fractious Politics of a Settler Society." In Daiva Stasiulis and Nira Yuval-Davis (ess.), *Unsettling Settler Societies: Articulations of Gender, Race, Ethnicity, and Class*, 95–131. London: Sage.

Taylor, Sheldon. 1994. "Darkening the Complexion of Canadian Society: Black Activism, Policy-Making and Black Immigration from the Caribbean to Canada, 1940s–1960s." Doctoral thesis, University of Toronto.

Thomas-Hope, Elizabeth M. 1992. *Warwick University Caribbean Studies: Explanation in Caribbean Migration: Perception and the Image: Jamaica, Barbados, St. Vincent.* London: MacMillan Press.

Triadafilopoulos, Triadafilos. 2012. *Becoming Multicultural: Immigration and the Politics of Membership in Canada and Germany.* Vancouver: UBC Press.

Valverde, Mariana. 2008. "Racial Purity, Sexual Purity, and Immigration Policy." In Barrington Walker (ed.), *The History of Immigration and Racism in Canada: Essential Readings*, 175–188. Toronto: Canadian Scholars' Press Inc.

Vertovec, Steven. 2009. *Transnationalism.* London: Routledge.

Walker, Barrington. 2009. "Finding Jim Crow in Canada, 1789–1967." In Janet Miron (ed.), *A History of Human Rights in Canada: Essential Issues*, 81–96. Toronto: Canadian Scholars' Press,

____. 2012. *The African Canadian Legal Odyssey: Historical Essays.* Toronto: Osgoode Society for Canadian Legal History.

Walker, James W. St. G. 1980. *A History of Blacks in Canada: A Study Guide for Teachers and Students.* Ottawa: Minister of State, Multiculturalism.

–––. 1984. *The West Indians in Canada.* Ottawa: Canadian Historical Association.

____. 1997. "Allegories and Orientations in African-Canadian Historiography: The Spirit of Africville." *Dalhousie Review* 77: 155–178.

Webster, David, Greg Donaghy, Erika Lee, Laura Madokoro, Henry Yu, and John Price. 2012. "John Price. Orienting Canada: Race, Canada, and the Transpacific." *H-Diplo Roundtable Review* 13: 1–30.

Western, John. 1992. *A Passage to England: Barbadian Londoners Speak of Home.* Minneapolis: University of Minnesota Press.

Winks, Robin W. 1971. *The Blacks in Canada: A History.* Montreal: McGill-Queen's University Press.

APPENDICES

Appendix A

Barbadian Population Demographics, Labour and Migration Statistics, 1927–1963

	Total Pop.	Density	Immi-grants	Emi-grants	Net M. Growth	Birth Rate	Ill.BR percent	Death Rate	Infant Mortality	IM from Syphilis (percent)
1927	N/A	N/A	N/A	N/A	N/A	31.59	66.81	20.21	201	12.70
1928	167,953	N/A	N/A	N/A	N/A	33.76	65.99	30.1	331	668
1929	170,391	N/A	N/A	N/A	N/A	32.04	63.7	23.74	239	556
1930	172,182	N/A	N/A	N/A	N/A	32.67	62.85	23.08	251	540
1931	173,674	N/A	N/A	N/A	1,127	28.06	60.46	25.95	298	545
1932	176,874	1,066	N/A	N/A	1,134	30.76	59.69	18.97	198	385
1933	180,055	1,205	N/A	N/A	3,181	29.79	59.9	20.13	235	413
1934	182,440	1,219	9,570	8,389	N/A	29.44	57.42	23.04	236	340
1936	188,294	1,114	9,661	8,753	908	31.8	59	18.54	198	172
1937	190,939	1,114	9,761	9,275	486	29.92	58.22	18.52	217	214
1938	193,082	1,163	9,753	9,174	579	27.3	59	19.38	221	217
1943	N/A	N/A	N/A	N/A	N/A	29.01	57.2	15.33	164	N/A
1944	N/A	N/A	N/A	N/A	N/A	29.1	56.91	16.41	186	N/A
1945	N/A	N/A	N/A	N/A	N/A	28.47	54.55	14.89	150	N/A
1946	195,348	1,198	N/A	N/A	N/A	31.6	53.74	16.83	157	N/A
1947	199,012	N/I	15,217	14,774	443	32.28	52.6 (est.)	16.09	163	N/A

Notes

Total Pop.: Total Population of Barbados as of December 31 of the year in question. The reader must be aware that some of the figures are said to be estimations within the Colonial Reports and may not be completely accurate.

Density: Population density — number of persons per square mile.

Immigrants: Number of persons entering the Island.

Emigrants: Number of persons leaving the Island.

Net M. Growth: Net Migration Growth — the population increase through immigration in excess of emigration.

Birthrate: Rate per one thousand people.

Ill. BR percent: Illegitimate Birthrate percentage — the number of births out of wedlock.

Death rate: Rate per one thousand people.

Infant Mortality: Deaths per one thousand live births.

IM from Syphilis: Infant Mortality caused by syphilis — the overall number of deaths (or percentage as stated in 1927) caused by syphilis — one of the leading causes of death for children under the age of five.

Year	Total Pop.	Density	Immi-grants	Emi-grants	Net M. Growth	Birth Rate	Ill. BR percent	Death Rate	Infant Mortality	IM from Syphilis (percent)
1948	202,669	1,220	16,017	15,846	171	32.68	53	15.48	149	N/A
1949	N/A	1,250	16,870	15,847	1,023	31.06	56.54	14.56	133	N/A
1950	211,641	1,288	20,734	21,040	-306	30.74	57.38	12.85	125	N/A
1951	N/A	N/A	N/A	N/A	N/A	31.83	N/A	14.06	136	N/A
1952	219,015	N/A	N/A	N/A	N/A	34.16	N/A	14.93	146	N/A
1953	222,942	1,343	N/A	N/A	N/A	34.51	N/A	14.06	139	N/A
1954	227,550	N/A	20,937	21,288	N/A	33.6	N/A	11.3	109	N/A
1955	229,119	1,380	23,696	28,130	N/A	33.3	N/A	12.7	134	N/A
1956	229,579	N/A	25,758	29,944	N/A	30.9	62.3	10.6	97	N/A
1957	232,227	1,399	33,123	35,320	N/A	31.7	62.3	10.7	87	N/A
1958	236,812	N/A	35,635	35,867	N/A	30.3	62.6	9.8	82	N/A
1959	240,799	1,450	43,510	44,549	N/A	29.8	62.6	8.7	71	N/A
1960	242,274	N/A	50,019	54,250	N/A	32.2	63.6	8.8	60	N/A
1961	241,706	1,450	54,134	59,097	N/A	28	62.1	9.9	83	N/A
1962	237,376	N/A	62,477	63,822	N/A	29.3	64	9	54	N/A
1963	240,468	N/A	69,282	70,983	N/A	29.1	64	8.8	61	N/A

Appendix B

Barbadian Primary and Secondary School Enrolment by Gender, 1927–1963

	P.School	P.Enrol	E.Boy	E.Girl	A.Att	A.Boy	A.Girl	S.School	fgs	A.Boy	A.Girl	Edu.Grant
1927	129	22,732	N/A	N/A	14,649	N/A	N/A	4	N/A	N/A	N/A	£46,148
1928	129	23,380	N/A	N/A	15,197	N/A	N/A	11	N/A	N/A	N/A	£56,925
1929	129	23,374	N/A	N/A	15,717	N/A	N/A	N/A	N/A	N/A	N/A	N/A
1930	127	23,281	N/A	N/A	16,330	N/A	N/A	N/A	N/A	N/A	N/A	£50,196
1931	127	N/A	N/A	N/A	N/A	N/A	N/A	N/A	N/A	N/A	N/A	N/A
1932	128	23,944	N/A	N/A	16,621	N/A	N/A	N/A	N/A	N/A	N/A	N/A
1933	128	24,101	N/A	N/A	16,986	N/A	N/A	N/A	N/A	N/A	N/A	N/A
1934	127	24,888	N/A	N/A	18,257	N/A	N/A	N/A	N/A	N/A	N/A	£52,642
1936	126	26,113	N/A	N/A	19,376	N/A	N/A	N/A	N/A	N/A	N/A	£59,706
1937	126	26,397	N/A	N/A	19,582	N/A	N/A	N/A	N/A	N/A	N/A	N/A
1938	126	27,168	N/A	N/A	20,204	N/A	N/A	N/A	N/A	N/A	N/A	£76,725
1947	126	28,880	14,557	14,323	N/A	N/A	N/A	11	N/A	N/A	N/A	N/A
1948	124	28,982	14,783	14,199	N/A	N/A	N/A	11	N/A	N/A	N/A	N/A
1949	124	29,716	15,223	14,493	N/A	N/A	N/A	11	N/A	N/A	N/A	N/A
1951	124	30,080	N/A	N/A	22,127	10,992	11,135	11	N/A	N/A	N/A	N/A
1952	N/A	N/A	N/A	N/A	22,629	11,485	11,144	N/A	N/A	N/A	N/A	N/A
1953	124	32,010	16,301	15,709	23,821	12,173	11,648	10	1,349	967	382	N/A
1954	N/A	N/A	N/A	N/A	26,039	13,155	12,884	N/A	N/A	N/A	N/A	N/A

	P.School	P.Enrol	E.Boy	E.Girl	A.Att	A.Boy	A.Girl	S.School	fgs	A.Boy	A.Girl	Edu.Grant
1955	124	35,977	18,289	17,688	27,793	14,208	13,595	10	1,341	929	412	$1,602,360
1957	116	34,200	17,545	16,655	27,762	14,058	13,704	10	1,368	953	415	$1,632,895
1959	116	36,311	18,609	17,702	28,613	14,644	13,969	N/A	1,484	1,017	467	N/A
1961	116	38,976	19,819	19,157	30,349	15,432	14,917	10	4,135	2,530	1,605	N/A
1963	117	40,732	20,672	20,060	33,299	15,432	16,333	10	4,325	2,580	1,745	N/A

Notes:

P.School: Total primary schools in Barbados.

P.Enrol: Total primary school students enrolled each year. Note: In 1951, approximately 15 percent of Barbados' total population was enrolled in primary school.

E.Boy: Total boys enrolled in primary schools.

E.Girl: Total girls enrolled in primary schools.

A.Att: Total yearly average attendance in primary schools.

A.Boy: Yearly average attendance for boys in primary schools.

A.Girl: Yearly average attendance for girls in primary schools.

S.School: Number of secondary schools.

fgs: Total number of student attendance at First Grade Schools. Note: Up to 1959, the number only includes three First Grade Schools (Harrison College, Lodge School and Queen's College). For 1961 and 1963, the attendance is for all ten secondary schools in Barbados.

A.Boy: Yearly average attendance for boys in secondary schools.

A.Girl: Yearly average attendance for girls in secondary schools.

Edu.Grant: Education Grant given by the Barbados Government.

Appendix C

Barbadian Revenue, Expenditure and Public Debt, 1947–1963

	Revenue	Expenditure	Public Debt
1947 (£)	1,942,778	1,774,535	605,360
1948 (£)	1,940,467	2,051,626	605,360
1949 ($)	9,553,594	10,290,424	2,905,728
1951–52 ($)	13,181,295	11,010,420	1,498,514
1952–53 ($)	13,757,830	11,423,910	1,630,462
1953–54 ($)	14,155,478	12,543,583	N/A
1954–55 ($)	16,272,736	12,668,071	N/A
1955–56 ($)	16,304,071	14,290,244	2,995,548
1956–57 ($)	19,124,815	16,216,542	N/A
1957–58 ($)	20,132,191	19,303,149	7,405,392
1958–59 ($)	23,761,801	20,723,432	N/A
1959–60 ($)	23,157,771	22,253,481	25,013,891
1960–61 ($)	26,035,81	22,683,604	24,502,219
1961–62 ($)	26,209,316	27,157,008	33,398,979
1962–63 ($)	28,324,718	28,398,654	31,038,720

Note: In 1949, Barbados switched from the British Pound to the British West Indies Dollar.

Appendix D

West Indian and Barbadian Farm Workers in the United States, 1956–1963

	1956	1957	1958	1959	1960	1961	1962	1963
Total West Indians in U.S.	7,502	8,640	7,433	8,626	9,681	10,267	10,123	11,548
Total Barbadians in U.S.	1,360	1,564	1,223	1,446	1,540	1,554	1,152	1,959

Note: All data collected for Appendix A, B, C, and D are from the Colonial Reports between 1927 and 1963 located at the Barbadian National Archives, The Lazaretto, St. Michael, Barbados. See bibliography for complete citation.

Appendix E

Barbadian Total Trade and Total Domestic Exports (Sugar and Molasses) to Canada, 1927–1936[17]

	1927	1928	1929	1930	1931	1932	1933	1934	1936
Barbados Total Trade (£)	3,881,774	3,880,424	3,326,901	2,794,702	2,555,695	3,035,882	3,118,866	3,393,831	3,497,819
Domestic Exports to Canada (£)	1,024,297	923,079	799,230	657,343	619,359	707,533	702,916	1,021,123	759,195
Sugar Exports to Canada (£)	951,792	712,977	641,326	436,210	N/A	N/A	N/A	N/A	N/A
Molasses Exports to Canada (£)	N/A	209,939	157,687	220,474	N/A	N/A	N/A	N/A	N/A

Appendix F

Goods Imported from Canada and Their Value in British Pounds (£), 1927–1936[20]

Goods	1927	1928	1929	1930	1931	1932	1933	1934	1936
Boots and Shoes	10,608	9,911	7,726	8,078	2,372	787	731	1,659	3,054
Butter	5,111	5,677	5,063	1,970	1,353	612	526	318	203
Oilmeal (Cattle food)	38,948	40,262	12,071	7,162	20,757	14,462	4,258	444	1
Coal	nil	nil	nil	nil	nil	nil	nil	nil	nil
Cornmeal	3,170	355	nil	nil	242	19	1	165	47
Fish (salted)	24,687	23,387	34,160	21,636	16,036	16,690	12,664	9,219	5,272
Flour	86,561	106,016	85,949	65,833	56,247	35,117	16,240	37,464	46,738
Oats	29,695	35,329	23,754	8,891	25,115	16,834	18,613	17,489	16,776
Manures	12,553	4,800	16,524	37,846	13,002	nil	nil	25,378	13,800
Salt Beef	1,029	960	nil	289	910	1,117	1,811	31	1,043
Salt Pork	13,614	16,894	13,999	12,797	8,221	9,616	13,963	10,576	27,017
Wood (various)	46,917	50,239	40,260	32,620	26,289	84,634	66,566	87,574	76,532

INDEX